D1522192

Vessel Security Officer

Vessel Security Officer

Joseph Ahlstrom

with
David W. Narby and
Joseph Tenaglia
among others

Cornell Maritime Press
Centreville, Maryland

Library of Congress Cataloging-in-Publication Data

Ahlstrom, Joseph, 1960–
    Vessel security officer / Joseph Ahlstrom.—1st ed.
        p. cm.
    ISBN-13: 978-0-87033-570-9
    1. Merchant marine—Security measures. 2. Shipping—Security measures. 3. Terrorism—Prevention. 4. Pirates. 5. Hijacking of ships—Prevention. I. Title.
    VK203.A56 2006
    362.28'7—dc22
                                    2005037253

Manufactured in the United States of America
First edition, 2006

To my wife Carolyn
and my daughter Emma and son Brendan.
Through all our efforts may my
children grow up in a safer world.

Contents

Acknowledgments

I would like to thank the following people for contributing chapters for this book: David Narby—Chapter 1 and Chapter 6; Joseph Tenaglia—Chapter 2 and Chapter 7; Walter Nadolny—Chapter 11; and Douglas Burnett and Dennis Bryant (Esquires), Law Firm of Holland and Knight LLP—Chapter 3.

In addition I would like to thank for their assistance Captain John Helmich of Kings Point; Ms. Angela Bobrowski, Kawika Lucas, Hillary O'Shea, Kelly Curtin, and the staff of GMATS (Kings Point); Mr. Bill Sullivan and Mr. Thomas Sullivan of KSEA Marine; Captain Arthur Sulzer, Captain Steve Werse, Captain Richard Smith, Professor Larry Howard, Mr. Stu Cohen, and Captain Walter Nadolny from SUNY Maritime; the Maritime Team from Tactical Defense Concepts; Bob Farmer, Kyrm Hickman, and Joe Ferdinando from Military Sealift Command; the staff at Training Center East; Ms. Peg Brandon and the Continuing Education Department at Mass Maritime; the Merchant Marine Reserve Program; Admiral Johnson, Kurt Birkhahn, and the staff at MARAD Region West; and Barry Van Vechten and Joyce Matthews from Calhoon MEBA Engineering School.

Most of all I would like to thank the countless students I have come into contact with teaching vessel security from all levels, Cadet through Captains of the Port. It is through their insight and questions that have led to my understanding of what vessel security is all about. Interaction is the key; in that spirit I encourage any and all critique of this text.

I would like to thank my wife Carolyn and our children Emma and Brendan for their patience while I wrote this book. Finally I would like to thank God for keeping the United States and our maritime industry safe since September 11, 2001. With God's help and our vigilance, it will remain so.

Introduction

It was ten years ago when I first started teaching at SUNY Maritime. The buzzword at the time was Standards of Training and Certification of Watchkeeping (STCW). I created a course at the school that covered one of the elements of STCW called GMDSS (Global Maritime Distress and Safety System). I had sailed as a Captain and Radio Officer on a small tanker in the Mediterranean Sea and felt this would be my niche. Like many maritime educators at the time, I believed STCW would be the biggest change for our generation. But as the implementation of STCW approached, February 2002, something happened.

September 11, 2001, was a beautiful day in New York. I remember waking up, having a nice cup of coffee, and admiring the clear late summer day outside my window; it was just before 8 A.M. At that exact same time American Airlines Flight 11 lifted off from Boston bound for Los Angeles. Just prior United Airlines Flight 175 had taken off from the same airport also bound for Los Angeles. As I prepared for my day, hijackers took control of these planes and changed their destination to New York. At 0846 AA Flight 11 crashed into the North Tower of the World Trade Center. The news showed live coverage and everyone wondered how such an accident could occur with such great visibility. At 0903 all speculation was removed as United Airlines Flight 175 crashed into the South Tower. I rushed down to Richmond Terrace so I could see what was happening. It was from that vantage point at 1028 I saw the South Tower collapse. It was like a waterfall as the glass poured out of a building collapsing in its own footprint. On the street I remember the silence as everybody could not believe what they were seeing. As the commuters returned from Manhattan covered in soot, the surrealism of the situation intensified. What occurred that day is the goal of all terrorists—FEAR.

Just like December 7 to a previous generation September 11 will live on in infamy. But just as December 7 galvanized our nation and led to our eventual victory so too shall September 11. The regulations discussed in this book will play a part in that victory. It is the responsibility of every Vessel Security Officer and Company Security Officer to see that his or her crew is made aware, trained, and familiar with their position in the Vessel Security Plan. Use the book as a guideline in fulfilling that task. Refer back to appendix C, 33 CFR Part 104, when necessary. Keep current on all new information in the war against terrorism. I have supplied some sample sources of this information in the appendixes. An important lesson from 9-11 is that it is essential to communicate information early and keep current on any new information. The creation of the Department of Homeland Security was an effort to streamline that process at the national level. We must do our part at the company and vessel level to gather and pass on as much information as possible. The proper performance of drills and exercises coupled with honest and inclusive debriefs will make your vessel more secure and give confidence and experience to your crew. Your Vessel Security Plan is not cast in stone but can be improved with amendments to correct deficiencies or strengthen your security. Do not make changes simply for appearance sake but after a thorough evaluation at the vessel and company level. Discuss any questions with the Coast Guard, Area Advisory Committees, and other operators. Remember that sharing of information is beneficial to all.

It is a common ailment that as time goes by and nothing happens, we can be lulled into a false feeling of security. I remember my little girl Emma was coming up on her first birthday on 9-11; today she is five. New regulations on ballast water transfer are upon us and due to a united effort there have been no terrorist attacks in the United States since 9-11. In this atmosphere it is easy to slip into a stance of complacency. One need only remember that over eight years passed between the first and second attacks on the World Trade Center. The patience of our enemy is renowned; they have the luxury to sit and wait until the time is right. When that time comes, will the next attack be worse than 9-11? We must always keep this in our minds if we want to never experience such an occurrence. It is not due to fear that we keep up our vigilance but a clear understanding of what can occur. As Vessel and Company Security Officers, the standards and tone of awareness we set aboard the ship will keep that day from ever occurring.

In the maritime industry we have been subject to maritime crimes prior to 9-11. The problems with piracy, smuggling, stowaways, and theft are nothing new. The bonus of a well-written and practiced Security Plan will help eliminate these existing problems. As the Vessel Security Officers we should remember this and pass it on to the crew. It is also important for Company Officers to be aware of this when the compliance with the regulations may encompass valuable time and limited financial resources. A well-trained crew and an aware vessel will actually save time and money when incidents of stowaways, smuggling, and theft are eliminated, not to mention crew lives in the event of piracy or terrorism. Keeping the ships safe and secure does not occur by chance but after the investment of time and effort by both the Vessel Security Officer and crew.

It is important at this point to emphasize that no one individual can carry out the Vessel Security Plan. It must be a unified effort by all crew. In addition the support of the Captain and company is needed to provide information and guidance. Each of your crew has a part in the Security Plan and must be familiar with vessel procedures, MARSEC levels, and who to contact and when. The plan is only as strong as its weakest link. The criminal will monitor your vessel and select the optimum time to attack. Whoever is on watch or at the gangway at that time must be ready and capable to prevent the crime from occurring. False alarms are not uncommon. It is important that any crewmember is supported for his or her efforts regardless of the outcome. Derogatory remarks at this point will only ensure that future incidents will be ignored. Empowering your crew at this critical juncture will ensure no potential criminal activity will go unreported. Empowering the crew will make the job of the Vessel Security Officer much easier. In addition the vessel that practices and supports awareness will continue that policy as the years roll by and nothing occurs.

I hope that this book can be used by maritime educators in teaching the Company and Vessel Security Officer course. I have included elements of the IMO Model Course in appendix A. The book can be used in conjunction with other training tools such as handouts, PowerPoint presentations, and videos. I have been teaching the course at SUNY Maritime for the past three years, at GMATS (Kings Point) in their Continuing Education Department, and with Tactical Defense Concepts in Europe and the United States. The classes have been a great source of information as ships officers and government officials provide insight to problems and various solutions. I have found running scenarios in table top exercises or performing assessments and preparing plans to be very informative. In spirit with STCW it is important for students to perform tasks in addition to listening to how they are to be performed. Reviewing the written test and Security Plan is also good for additional discussion and education. I welcome any comments from educators on this book and how to improve it.

I also feel the book will be useful to already certified Vessel and Company Security Officers. If for no other reason I have included 33 CFR Part 104 as appendix C. I am aware of how fast those yellow books can fly out of Coast Guard Stations. I have provided insight and guidance to you for upcoming drills, exercises, and audits. It is important to be honest with your lessons learned segment. Do not paint a rosy picture if one doesn't exist. On the other hand don't make up deficiencies to fill out forms. As you go through your plan, when sections appear in order and the crew are comfortable with that area, move on to something new. Do not repeat the same drill because it has good results; as the Vessel Security Officer use the three months between drills to identify areas you feel may need work. Then run the drill in that area for that section. As for educators, I encourage Vessel and Company Security Officers to provide insight on areas you feel should be covered or covered in more detail.

I would like to thank Cornell Maritime Press for their patience with me in writing this book. As the threat of terrorism changed, I modified the book. I felt a section on Weapons of Mass Destruction was essential. I tried to follow the MSC course that the Maritime Administration has mandated all academies to teach. In this area especially, new and modern technology for detection is becoming available. If you are involved in this area, it is imperative to stay current.

I feel the cruise industry is a potential target so with the assistance of Walter Nadolny I included a chapter on Security Challenges for the Cruise Industry. Attorneys Dennis Bryant and Douglas Burnett from Holland and Knight LLP provided a chapter on Maritime Security Law. Dave Narby and Joe Tenaglia from Tactical Defense Concepts and Military Sealift Command have been invaluable with their help in writing this book and also for keeping me abreast of new security risks, conferences, and regulations. This book like security itself is not a one-man show. It is important to continue to interact with educators and company and government officials to keep current on what is best for maintaining security and complying with federal and local regulations.

To all who read this book it is important to understand the threat is real. Attacks in Madrid and London are clear indication that the enemy is still probing for soft targets.

As defenses in aviation and public transportation increase, it is only logical that the focus will shift to the maritime industry. The existing regulations are adequate and your approved Vessel Security Plan is a good basis for vessel security. The application and practice of that plan is essential for your safety and security. By making your vessel a hard target all will benefit. It has been four years now since I stood on Richmond Terrace on Staten Island and watched the Twin Towers collapse. Due to the concerted effort of a lot of good people, no other atrocity has occurred in the United States through 2005. The Vessel Security Officer with his crew are some of those people. It is important that we remain aware.

Enjoy the book!

Captain Joseph Ahlstrom
Associate Professor SUNY Maritime
Master USMM
Captain USNR

ONE

ISPS Code—Maritime Security Rules and Responsibilities

Beginning on July 1, 2004, the international maritime industry entered a new era. The rules and regulations that govern maritime security are now mandated by the International Ship and Port Facility Security (ISPS) Code. The international maritime community will share the burden and responsibility of protecting this vital transportation industry from the threat of terrorism. Ships, facilities, and governments will all have a share in this effort. No longer will a certain level of pilferage, crime, and a certain number of stowaway incidents be acceptable. Each and every such occurrence from this day forward shall be deemed a security incident. A security incident onboard your vessel will indicate a flaw in the vessel security posture and demonstrates vulnerabilities. These are vulnerabilities that could be exploited by terrorist in the future. As a Company Security Officer (CSO) or Site Security Officer (SSO), your immediate goal will be to protect your vessel from costly delays and fines that may be incurred if your vessel is identified as being in noncompliant status. Such an occurrence could lead to unwanted scrutiny by port state control officials as well as fines and in the most severe instance criminal prosecution. When considering the number of vessels plying the world's oceans, it should be understood that overall, being the victim of a maritime crime, is a low probability. However, the cost of not protecting the most important mode of transportation to the global economy is unfathomable.

In the aftermath of September 11, 2001, the International Maritime Organization (IMO), an agency of the United Nations whose primary purpose is to facilitate cooperation among governments in the field of regulation and practices relating to technical matters that affect shipping, adopted the ISPS Code at the SOLAS convention in London in December 2002. These regulations are broad in scope and mandate ships, companies, port facilities, and contracting governments to take actions to harden the maritime industry. Because after 9-11, the cost of complacency cannot be measured and could be far too great not to take prudent, reasonable, and necessary steps to protect the industry and the world community from the global threat of terrorism. The ISPS Code is mandated for U.S. flag vessels by the Maritime Transportation Security Act (MTSA) of 2002 and final rules are outlined in 33 CFR parts 101–106. The regulations defined the general structure in new terms and shared responsibilities that a military organization may refer to as a "layered defense," a concept that will be discussed in later chapters of this text. It is important for every SSO and CSO to have knowledge of the regulations to completely understand their role in the program. ISPS Code Part B Section 13.1 (Training) states that, "The company security officer (CSO) and appropriate shore-based Company personnel, and the ship security officer (SSO), should have knowledge of, and receive training, in some or all of the following, as appropriate:

1. Security administration
2. Relevant international conventions, codes, and recommendations
3. Relevant government legislation and regulations
4. Responsibilities and functions of other security organizations

And more."

The equivalent in the Code of Federal Regulations (CFR) reference is found in 33 CFR parts 104.210 and 215. Awareness of the threat and through knowledge and understanding of the rules and regulations are a requirement of both the ISPS Code and MTSA. Therefore, a full reading and complete understanding of the regulation is the duty of each CSO and SSO. To maintain current threat awareness, the CSO and SSO must become a student of current events as they pertain to the terrorist threat to the maritime industry. The term "knowledge and understanding" is used throughout the CFRs and ISPS Code. This is important to understand because although the Code does not specifically mandate training, the responsibility lies directly with the CSO and SSO. However, the Code does not specify how this knowledge and understanding is achieved. Eventually you will see the certification of Maritime Security courses and Maritime Security professionals. Until that time, the amount of training and knowledge that is required will vary depending on the inspecting official and the willingness of the operating concerns to provide "adequate" training and support.

This chapter will not attempt to educate you on every fine point and requirement of international maritime security but instead will define the roles and responsibilities of the CSO and SSO against the backdrop of the worldwide maritime security strategy.

To be an effective SSO or CSO, an individual must endeavor to be a perpetual student of the subject of terrorism both at sea and on land by reading everything available from any source, whenever possible. Keep in mind that your job as a CSO/SSO revolves around one concept: *keep your ships safe!* To do this, you must provide your ships and crews with accurate, useful, and up-to-date information. This important responsibility lies mostly on the CSO due to his increased availability to information. Then, a constant sharing of information between the CSO and SSO will complete the circle of information and domain awareness.

For the purposes of this text, ISPS Code and the U.S. CFR for U.S. flag vessels are the same. While there are some subtle differences, the implementation remains basically the same. The most obvious difference is the use of the term "vessel" in the MTSA regulations and the term "ship" in the ISPS Code. In this text, the terms are used similarly. So, Ship Security Officer is the same as Vessel Security Officer, or SSO is the same as VSO.

A GLOBAL MARITIME STRATEGY

The ISPS Code encompasses a global maritime strategy for anti-terrorism that shares cost and responsibility along a broad spectrum of government and private institutions.

Layered security measures are designed to provide continuous protection throughout the supply chain, starting with the origination point overseas, while in transit, and at the final destination. The ISPS Code and U.S. MTSA of 2002 make security of our ports everyone's responsibility, from local governments and private citizens to the international community.

In *America the Vulnerable,* Dr. Steven Flynn comments, "Five 60% solutions equal 99% effectiveness." A CSO or SSO must realize that 100% security is an unattainable goal. Rather several partial measures linked together will give us cost-effective security and decrease our vulnerability. The overall goal is to increase the odds of detecting and deterring risk to our ships from both criminal and terrorist activities. Remember terrorist behavior is criminal behavior. The old "hard target" concept still applies and is woven into every effective maritime security strategy giving us a layered defense. The common conception concerning criminal behavior is that a criminal will always choose the most vulnerable or "softest" target. He will choose the ship to attack that presents him with the greatest probability of success. Therefore, if you maintain a strong security posture, you become a hard target and less likely to be attacked.

In any good security strategy, security starts as far away from the area you are trying to protect as possible. For U.S. commerce that means security starts overseas. Several initiatives are in place today to allow time to assess any possible threats. Having determined a threat to exist, you can hopefully prevent that threat from reaching our shores.

24-hour Advance Manifests
Effective December 2, 2002, carriers and/or automated Nonvessel Operating Common Carriers (NVOCCs) must submit a cargo declaration 24 hours before cargo is laden aboard the vessel at a foreign port. This allows intelligence to access and identify the most likely shipments that may pose a risk to national security, therefore allowing time to track and inspect inbound cargoes as necessary.

Customs-Trade Partnership Against Terrorism
C-TPAT is a joint government-business initiative to build cooperative relationships that strengthen overall supply chain and border security. C-TPAT recognizes that Customs can provide the highest level of security only through close cooperation with the ultimate owners of the supply chain, importers, carriers, brokers, warehouse operators, and manufacturers. Through this initiative, Customs is asking businesses to ensure the integrity of their security practices and communicate their security guidelines to their business partners within the supply chain.

International Port Security Program
The U.S. Coast Guard, through its International Port Security Program (IPSP), encourages bilateral or multilateral discussions with nations around the world in an effort to exchange information and share best practices that align implementation and enforcement requirements of the MTSA with the ISPS Code and other international maritime security standards. As lead agency for maritime security in the U.S., the Coast Guard works closely with its international trading partners to promote reasonable and consistent implementation and enforcement of the ISPS Code for enhanced maritime security in countries (and ports) that participate in global trade. To conduct the information exchange, USCG International Port Security Liaison Officers (IPSLO) are assigned to three regions (Asia-Pacific, Europe/Africa/Middle East, and Central/South America) for worldwide coverage in order to assist other nations in facilitating bilateral exchanges. In addition an IPSP team has been established in Washington, D.C., to conduct country/port visits, discuss security measures implemented, and develop best practices between countries.

This site http://www.uscg.mil/hq/g-m/mp/ipsp.shtml includes MTSA-ISPS regulations and policy information, forms, frequently asked questions, (FAQ/best practices), presentations, training modules, and public affairs guidance to assist in CG education initiatives with maritime transportation system stakeholders.

Container Security Initiative

Announced in January 2002, CSI allows Customs to screen for high-risk, U.S.-bound containers at key foreign ports, a task previously carried out only at U.S. seaports. To do this, Customs negotiates and enters into bilateral arrangements with foreign governments. These arrangements contain common language that specifies on a pilot basis the placement of Customs officials at foreign ports and the exchange of information between U.S. Customs and foreign customs administrations. Customs first targeted for CSI the 20 foreign ports that shipped the highest volume of ocean containers to the United States. These top 20 ports are located in 14 nations and shipped a total of 66 percent of all containers that arrived in U.S. seaports in 2001. Customs also plans to expand CSI to an additional 20 to 25 strategic ports that ship a significant volume of containers to the United States and are considered to be strategic locations. According to Customs, these strategic ports must meet minimum requirements such as having nonintrusive inspection equipment and having customs officials capable of conducting inspections to support the CSI program.

INTERNATIONAL SHIP AND PORT SECURITY CODE (ISPS CODE)

A new comprehensive security regime for international shipping was set into force by the IMO on July 1, 2004. The code represents the culmination of a year's intense work by the IMO's Maritime Safety Committee and its intercessional working group on maritime security. The conference adopted a number of amendments to the 1974 Safety of Life at Sea (SOLAS) agreements. The code contains detailed security-related requirements for:

- Governments
- Port Authorities
- Shipping Companies

The objectives of this Code are:

- To establish an international framework involving cooperation between contracting governments, government agencies, local administrations, and the shipping and port industries to detect security threats and take preventive measures against security incidents affecting ships or port facilities used in international trade;

- To establish the respective roles and responsibilities of the contracting governments, government agencies, local administrations, and the shipping and port industries at the national and international level for ensuring maritime security;
- To ensure the early and efficient collection and exchange of security-related information;
- To provide a methodology for security assessments so as to have in place plans and procedures to react to changing security levels; and
- To ensure confidence that adequate and proportionate maritime security measures are in place.

Operational elements of the ISPS Code that are of most importance to the CSO/SSO will be discussed later in this chapter.

Operation Safe Commerce

Operation Safe Commerce is a pilot program that brings together private business, ports, local, state, and federal representatives to analyze current security procedures for cargo entering the country. The program will function like a venture capital fund to use existing technology to monitor the movement and integrity of containers through the supply chain.

The Transportation Security Administration (TSA) is the primary grant coordinator of the Operation Safe Commerce program. TSA grant officers and program officers in the TSA's Office of Maritime and Land will monitor recipients' projects to ensure they stay within budgetary and operational guidelines. Grant recipients who do not meet these strict standards may be denied reimbursement.

Smart Box Initiative

While ships are at sea, assessments are made as to the risk a vessel or cargo may present to its port of call. To aid in this calculation, there are several programs at work. The Smart Box couples an internationally approved mechanical seal affixed to an alternate location on the container door with an electronic container security device designed to deter and detect tampering of the container door. If someone attempts to open the cargo door after it has been sealed, the Smart Box device on the door would reflect that there had been an attempted intrusion into the container. Robert C. Bonner described the

Smart Box at the Third Annual U.S. Marine Security Conference and Expo in New York:

> The Smart Box involves more than an appropriately placed ISO standard mechanical security seal, although that would be a good first step. It involves securing cargo containers with an electronic Container Security Device. This is a device that, at a minimum, will allow us to reliably detect tampering with a container en route, and that have a very low rate of false positives.

Automated Targeting System

The Automated Targeting System (ATS) is an aggressive, sophisticated targeting tool that enhances Customs' ability to perform narcotics enforcement operations. The system standardizes bill-of-lading, entry, and entry summary data received from the Automated Commercial System (ACS) and creates integrated records called "shipments." These shipments are then evaluated and scored by ATS through the use of over 300 weighted rules derived from targeting methods used by experienced Customs personnel. The higher the score, the more the shipment warrants attention. Future plans include the installation of ATSs at all major seaports, airports, and land border ports of entry. It may also be expanded to outbound operations to target export cargo for antiterrorism, currency smuggling, and other export violations.

Ship Security Alert System (SSAS)

Regulation 6 of the ISPS Code requires SSAS for all applicable ships constructed on or after July 1, 2004 but not later than the first survey of the radio installation after July 1, 2004. When activated it will transmit a ship-to-shore security alert to a competent authority, identifying the ship and location and indicating security threat. The system will not send the alert to any other ship nor raise an alarm onboard. It will continue the alert until deactivated and/or reset. The alert system shall be capable of activation from the bridge and at least one other location and conform to IMO performance standards. An administration shall notify the state(s) in the vicinity of an alert. When a contract government receives an alert from another flag's ship, the contract government will notify the flag state.

The Ship Security Alert System (SSAS) is similar to the silent alarm commonly used at a bank. Although in some cases instead of calling the local police, it will alert authorities on the other side of the world or the RSO of the vessel's flag state. The vessel's flag state would then be required to contact the closest possible government to render assistance. This time delay could be crucial. The activation of the SSAS by no means discourages the vessel's crew from activating any other alarm or alerting system deemed necessary.

96-Hour Advanced Notice of Arrival

The U.S. Coast Guard requires persons responsible for ships scheduled to make port calls in the United States to make Advance Notice of Arrival (ANOA). The ANOA must be submitted to the USCG National Vessel Movement Center (NVMC) at least 96 hours prior to the scheduled arrival. The ANOA must be complete and accurate. Incomplete, inaccurate, or late submittals may result in denial of entry, delayed entry, issuance of a letter of warning, issuance of a notice of violation, assessment of a civil penalty of up to $32,500, or a combination of these enforcement options. ANOA's may be submitted electronically at E-NOA. Electronic submittal is fast and easy to use. It also provides the submitter with an electronic receipt. The Internet site for USCG NOA is http://www.nvmc.uscg.gov/download. aspx.

Upon arriving in the coastal waters of your destination, a more invasive set of security protocols go into effect. Terms will differ from country to country, but for a U.S. port the following assets and initiatives are in effect:

NATIONAL TARGETING CENTER

The Customs and Border Protection (CBP) National Targeting Center (NTC) came into existence in October 2001 in the immediate aftermath of the events of 9-11. From its beginnings as the Office of Border Security, the NTC has grown swiftly, providing nationally directed targeting technology, targeting methodology, subject matter expertise, and training that encompasses the enforcement and regulatory missions of CBPs predecessor agencies.

In January 2003 the NTC staff moved to a state-of-the-art facility in Northern Virginia, and CBP personnel assigned there represent subject matter areas in agriculture, customs, and immigration. Other CBP offices providing staff to this effort include the Border Patrol, Office of Intelligence, and Office of Information and Technology. Additionally, the NTC supports the enforcement and regulatory missions of various agencies through a network of liaisons, which includes the Transportation Security Administration, the U.S. Coast Guard, the Department of Energy, and U.S. Immigration and Customs Enforcement. Contact is maintained with members of the intelligence community to include the Federal Bureau of Investigation, the Central Intelligence Agency, and other intelligence services. CBP's commitment to collaborative targeting efforts is also demonstrated by the Food and Drug Administration Prior Notice Center located at the NTC and operational since December 11, 2003. There,

CBP and FDA personnel conduct joint targeting on a round-the-clock basis in support of the Bio-Terrorism Act.

SECURITY BOARDINGS

Based on information from the National Targeting Center, U.S. Coast Guard personnel will board vessels deemed to pose the greatest risk to national security. The information that may be considered when ranking vessels as "high interest" includes cargo, size, voyage history, crew makeup, ownership or charterer, and intelligence. When identified for boarding, Coast Guard personnel will board the vessel offshore by small boat or by repelling from a helicopter to ensure potential security concerns are addressed before the vessel enters port. Vessels are also boarded on a random basis to foster unpredictability and to add an element of deterrence.

AUTOMATIC IDENTIFICATION SYSTEMS (AIS)

The Maritime Transportation Security Act of 2002 requires that all self-propelled commercial vessels falling into a certain category (e.g., over 65 feet in length or passenger vessels certified to carry more than 149 passengers) install and use AIS in all U.S. Vessel Traffic Services (VTS) areas by December 31, 2004. The AIS is a transponder that works on VHF frequencies. The AIS increases security by increasing maritime domain awareness, especially regarding vessels operating in U.S. ports. AIS allow identification and tracking of vessels not available through voice radio communication or radar as the AIS transponder communicates vessel's static ship data (including name, vessel type and length), dynamic ship data (including position and navigational status), and their dynamic voyage data (including type of cargo and destination). Future plans for AIS include working with NOAA (National Oceanographic Atmospheric Administration) to add AIS transponders to existing offshore weather buoys to increase the range of AIS and increase domain awareness of U.S. borders in excess of 100 nautical miles from U.S. shores.

Still there are proponents of the AIS that feel that this gives more of an advantage to the pirates and terrorists than coastal authorities. They feel that the AIS can be used by the opposition as targeting data rather than for its intended use to identify nonthreats in the coastal regions. It should also be kept in mind that the information put out by the AIS is subject to what is programmed in by the user. This means the operator can purport to be anyone he wants. This may be both an advantage and disadvantage to the legitimate maritime community.

SECURITY COMMITTEES

Adding yet another layer to our security strategy are Area Maritime Transportation Security Plans that will detail the response and preventative security policies. In addition, port security committees have already been informally established around the country and the new regulations establish Area Maritime Security (AMS) committees that will address the complex and diverse security needs of each of our 361 ports.

The AMS committee brings together appropriately experienced representatives from a variety of sources in the port to continually assess security risks to the port, determine appropriate risk mitigation strategies, and develop, revise, and implement the AMS plan. The AMS committee may also be the mechanism by which security threats and changes in Maritime Security (MARSEC) levels are communicated to port stakeholders. AMS committee members may include: USCG, federal, state, and local law enforcement, emergency response, port managers, etc. The AMS committees will be composed of not less than seven members. At least seven of the total number of members must each have five years or more experience related to maritime or port security operations. The USCG added labor to the list of stakeholders that should be included on the AMS.

PORT SECURITY GRANTS

U.S. Secretary of Homeland Security Tom Ridge (2001–2005), during an event at Port Elizabeth, New Jersey, highlighting the department's efforts to secure our nation's ports, announced new port security initiatives and investments to provide increased international cooperation, greater use of technology, and additional funds for port security facility enhancements. He stated:

> The port security measures we are putting in place—both here at home and abroad—are about building on our capabilities and strengthening each layer of defense. Through information sharing with our international partners; several different levels of inspection; review of intelligence information on the crew, cargo, and vessel long before they reach our shores; state-of-the-art technology; and, of course, vigilance at every turn, we are able to screen and board 100 percent of high-risk vessels coming into our ports.

OPERATION DRY DOCK

In a U.S. Coast Guard initiative to validate seaman's credentials to identify all persons that may have obtained valid seamen's documents and may be a threat to security, the 14-month investigation by the U.S. Coast Guard and FBI has uncovered nine merchant mariners with possible terrorist links, raising renewed concerns that U.S. ships and ports are vulnerable to attack. Coast Guard spokeswoman Jolie Shifflet said that Operation Drydock, prompted by national security concerns after the 9-11 attacks, had also led to the arrest of about a dozen others whose active arrest warrants for crimes from minor misdemeanors to attempted murder had long gone unnoticed. The Coast Guard said it investigated the records of more than 200,000 people who hold U.S. merchant mariner credentials. It also revoked or suspended the licenses of roughly 200 other commercial seamen for a range of offenses, Shifflet said. None of those arrested, dismissed, or suspended had been linked to terrorism.

Concerned about possible national security threats from fraudulent merchant mariner documents, the Coast Guard said it had strengthened its background checking process for commercial seamen and began issuing more tamper-resistant credentials in February 2003.

"Through extensive and detailed investigative efforts, we have reduced vulnerabilities to terrorism by preventing the fraudulent use of credentials by those who seek to harm our nation and its citizens," said Admiral Thomas H. Collins, Commandant of the Coast Guard (2004). "This is a great example of interagency cooperation in the war on terror. Using our combined resources and expertise, we will continue to make America safer and more secure."

Merchant mariner credentials certify that an individual is qualified to work aboard a ship and are required for all people who work aboard most commercial ships, including passenger vessels, and are often used as an identification document that allows mariners to come and go from the ship while it is docked in a foreign port.

The Coast Guard, working with the Federal Bureau of Investigation and other interagency partners, examined the records of over 200,000 individuals who hold a U.S. merchant mariner credential to identify potential terrorist links and detect document fraud.

AMERICA'S WATERWAY WATCH

This national awareness program asks those who work, live, or recreate on or near the water to be aware of suspicious activity that might indicate threats to our country's homeland security. These are exactly the right people to enlist. Members of small and even large waterway communities know the common behavior patterns in the area and, therefore, are uniquely suited to identify anomalies that may indicate terrorist precursors to an attack.

Americans are urged to adopt a heightened sensitivity toward unusual events or individuals they may encounter in or around ports, docks, marinas, riversides, beaches, or communities.

One example of such an incident happened to a U.S. government-owned cargo vessel moored in the New York area shortly after 9-11. Members of the crew sighted three men in a white fiberglass boat with a blue stripe and an outboard motor, seemingly fishing near their ship. Normally this would not have been of concern. However, this boat had been there for several days and had consistently drawn closer to the ship. At one point it even came in contact with this National Defense asset. Nothing was reported. One crewmember noted that the type of fishing that the suspect boat was doing was not consistent with the time of year. It was also noted that the three apparently "Middle Eastern" men were holding their fishing poles incorrectly. How, you ask? They were holding their poles with the reels . . . outboard! None of this was reported until weeks after the incident and local authorities then commenced a search for the white fiberglass boat with a blue stripe and outboard motor in the New York area. The search was successful . . . . They found thousands!

If this incident were reported immediately, the individuals could have been apprehended and questioned to determine whether they were just really bad fishermen or had other nefarious deeds in mind. This incident is consistent with a probe that tests the vessel's security and response. If the men had been apprehended, little or no legal action could be taken against them because they were just "fishing."

INTELLIGENCE FUSION CENTERS

The difficulty of detecting terrorist activity once it has entered the maritime system may point to the value of intelligence. There is simply too much cargo to physically inspect each shipment thoroughly. To uncover terrorist activity, you will need actionable intelligence that will target the exact shipment or ship. Intelligence fusion centers are located in Norfolk, Va., and Alameda, Calif. These centers will gather information from federal, state, and local authorities relevant to maritime security. The information and analysis is then forwarded to security across the country actively involved in securing our port and waterways. Critics of the customs and border patrol security measures will say that it is unacceptable to inspect only 2% to 5% of inbound container shipments. Intelligence Fusion Centers give us the ability to inspect the right 2% to 5%. Everyone would like to inspect a higher percentage of inbound cargos. However, there is great financial ramification to slowing down the global transportation industry even for a short period of time. This was demonstrated by the Stevedore labor union strike on the West Coast of the United States in fall of 2002. A 10-day shutdown at West Coast ports could strip $19.4 billion from the U.S. economy. After 20 days, the price jumps to $48.6 billion. (Monday, June 10, 2002, *Seattle Post-Intelligencer Reporter*)

No matter if the shipments are containerized or not, reliance on the fusion centers as well as other national intelligence assets is crucial to keep inspection capabilities focused on the right shipments.

OPERATION PORT SHIELD

Operation Port Shield focuses on the implementation and enforcement of the new security measures implemented under the international requirements or MTSA. Under this verification program, the Coast Guard will be boarding every vessel, at sea or at the dock, on its first visit to a U.S. port to ensure that the vessel is compliant with U.S. security standards. As part of Operation Port Shield, the U.S. Coast Guard will be checking the compliance of U.S. vessels and facilities and of foreign vessels calling on U.S. ports. The Coast Guard understands and is making every effort to find the appropriate balance between security and the free flow of commerce. "All of our personnel will be out in force to ensure that all vessels and facilities subject to MTSA security requirements are in compliance and have fully implemented security measures in accordance with their approved plans," said Lt. Cmdr. Rogers Henderson, Commanding Officer of Marine Safety Unit, Houma, La., (2003).

Securing our ports and waterways is a team effort—everyone, from maritime industry to local governments and private citizens, to the international community, plays an important role in ensuring that our waterways remain open for business," said Henderson. These program officers will also visit foreign countries to evaluate antiterrorism measures in place at ports abroad.

The MTSA allows for civil penalties of up to $25,000 per violation. In addition, the Coast Guard may require facility or vessel operators to implement additional security measures, limit the operations of the vessel or facility, or shut down the operations entirely.

MARINE TRANSPORTATION SECURITY ACT OF 2002 (MTSA)

The MTSA is the U.S. law that mandates the ISPS Code for applicable vessels of the U.S. flag. Nearly identical to the ISPS Code, the U.S. regulations meet or exceed the requirements of ISPS. In general terms, the MSTA combines both parts A and B of the ISPS Code. The most obvious difference is the use of the term "vessel" vs. "ship," i.e., Vessel Security Plan (VSP) vs. Ship Security Plan (SSP). While this subtle change may seem insignificant, it is necessary to align security regulations with the U.S. Code of Federal Regulations and Rules of the Road. Rule Three of the COLREGS states: The word "vessel" includes every description of water craft, including nondisplacement craft and sea plane, used or capable of being used as a means of transportation on water.

The MTSA mandates vulnerability assessments by USCG for ports and vessels. Vessel assessments are limited to identification of vessel types that pose a high risk of being involved in a transportation security incident. Security plans are required for ports, facilities, and vessels to conform to the ISPS Code. The similarities between MSTA and ISPS are no accident. The ISPS Code is widely seen as a U.S.-led requirement on the international maritime community, and the MTSA was written specifically to enact the international regulation for the United States.

REQUIREMENTS OF MTSA

For the CSO/SSO, the Vessel Security Plan (VSP) approved by Coast Guard G-MSC for domestic vessels will outline the requirements for Maritime Security Compliance. Administrations for foreign vessels, if vessel has other independent operators, each operator is required to submit a VSP unless the owner submits a plan that encompasses the operations of each operator OR completed plan under approved Alternate Security Program (ASP). All vessels must conduct Vessel Security Assessment and designated Company Security Officer and Vessel Security Officers. Security training will be required for all vessel personnel along with drills and exercises. Drills will be conducted quarterly while exercises will be required every year and will not be more than 18 months apart. Vessel records must be kept for two years to include:

- Training
- Drills and exercises
- Incidents and breaches of security
- Changes in MARSEC levels
- Maintenance, calibration, and testing of equipment
- Security threats
- Declarations of Security (DoS)

The following measures will be implemented to improve vessel security for:

- Access control
- Restricted areas
- Handling cargo
- Delivery of vessel stores and bunkers
- Monitoring

All of the above measures must be met before a vessel or facility is granted an International Ship Security Certificate (ISSC) and, therefore, be allowed to operate. Achieving the original certificate may seem to be an arduous task; maintaining a vessel security program on a daily basis will be the challenge of every CSO and SSO.

PORT SECURITY ASSESSMENT PROGRAM

The Coast Guard is in the process of closely examining the key infrastructure in the nation's 55 most economically and strategically important ports. Preliminary assessments have been completed. Comprehensive assessments are currently being conducted that will provide local threat profiles and evaluate all aspects of security surrounding each port. This program is aimed at increasing the information and best practices available to port officials across the country to help them make decisions about how to reduce the vulnerability of their ports. In addition to these assessments, the Coast Guard is creating a system to display key port information in an electronic geospatially referenced format to serve as a database that can be easily searched for national, regional, and local information.

NONINTRUSIVE INSPECTION (NII) TECHNOLOGY

In an attempt to meet the demands of this increased traffic, Customs developed a five-year Nonintrusive Inspection (NII) technology plan. The plan was developed to address the narcotics smuggling threat of increasingly sophisticated techniques of deep concealment in commercial cargo and conveyances.

NII systems, in many cases, give Customs inspectors the capability to perform thorough examinations of cargo without having to resort to the costly, time-consuming process of unloading cargo for manual searches, or intrusive examinations of conveyances by methods such as drilling and dismantling. One of the most common forms of NII technology that is seen in the ports today is the VACIS. The Mobile VACIS® unit consists of a truck-mounted, nonintrusive gamma ray imaging system that produces radiographic images used in the evaluation of the contents of trucks, containers, cargo, and passenger vehicles to determine the possible presence of many types of contraband.

MARITIME SAFETY AND SECURITY TEAMS

Maritime Safety and Security Teams are a Coast Guard rapid response force capable of nationwide deployment via air, ground, or sea transportation to meet emerging threats and were created in direct response to the terrorist attacks on 9-11. These are two separate organizations run by the U.S. Coast Guard. Maritime Safety Teams are concerned with security compliance with the maritime security regulations and may board your vessel for verification. Maritime

Security Teams are the armed contingent and may board your vessel to assess any risk that may be posed by your vessel. This program was formerly referred to as the "Sea Marshall" program.

TRANSPORTATION SECURITY CARDS

The Transportation Security Administration is working on developing the Transportation Worker Identification Credential (TWIC). Over time, the TWIC will be used as a credential for transportation workers from all modes who have undergone, and passed, required background checks. TWIC will introduce a common credential, one that positively ties the person—to the credential—to the background check that can be used in conjunction with access control to critical components of the nation's transportation infrastructure.

SOLAS (SAFETY OF LIFE AT SEA)

The SOLAS amendments are the tools used to bring the international community into alignment. The programs and regulations mentioned above are part of an overall global maritime antiterrorism strategy. As a CSO or SSO, you are mostly concerned with your ship and its operations. From this point on, those regulations that are a requirement of implementing the code will be discussed. It is the CSO/SSO responsibility to understand the specific regulations that affect their vessel/vessels.

Amendments

Amendments to chapters V and XI of SOLAS became mandatory on July 1, 2004.

The existing SOLAS chapter XI was re-identified as XI-1 and XI-2; the new chapter was adopted on special measures to enhance maritime security. The objective of the codes are to establish an international framework involving cooperation between contracting governments, agencies, local administrations, and the shipping and port industries to detect and assess security threats and take preventive measures against security incidents affecting ships and port facilities used in international trade.

SOLAS, Chapter XI:
Special Measures to Enhance Maritime Safety

Maritime security was not invented after 9-11. The IMO identified the need for increased security and took action with the original drafting of a new chapter that was adopted in May 1994 and entered into force on January 1, 1996. The chapter clarifies requirements relating to authorization of recognized organizations (responsible for carrying out surveys and inspections on Administration's behalf), enhanced surveys, ship identification number scheme, and port state control on operational requirements.

SOLAS, Chapter XI-2:
Special Measures to Enhance Maritime Security

No matter how well your Ship Security Plan is written or how many new requirements are levied on ships, there is an inherent vulnerability of every merchant vessel in the inability to defend itself against a determined and well-armed aggressor. The current most effective and most widely used countermeasures against maritime threats are an alert and aware lookout, effective use of lights, and the use of the common fire hose. Today these measures have been mostly effective against common criminals and pirates but will not be effective against a motivated and prepared terrorist attack.

Where the responsibility to defend against these types of attacks lies is left to the armed navies and coastal patrols of the international maritime community. Shipowners and operators are left with copious amounts of regulations that cannot defend them against an armed assault at sea or in port. The attacks on the USS *Cole* and M/V *Limburg,* as well as the attack plans for maritime terrorism outlined in Al Qaeda's book of Naval Jihad, illustrate the impotence of the current legislations without government-backed naval assets to protect the life line of maritime trade on the high seas.

For the Ship Security Officer or Company Security Officer, a well-written Vessel/Ship Security Plan (VSP/SSP) is the simplest way to ensure maritime security compliance in accordance with the vessel's flag state regulations. Whether the vessel is U.S. flag and follows the MTSA guidance or other flag that follows the ISPS Code, the applicable regulations come from the international convention know as SOLAS (Safety of Life at Sea).

Chapter XI-2 requires the following measures to enhance maritime security:

(Note to the reader. The text below in italics comes directly from the relevant code/regulation or references the location where it may be found in SOLAS, ISPS, or CFR.)

SHIP IDENTIFICATION NUMBERS

Regulation 3 requires that owner affix the ship identification numbers to the vessel. These will be permanent markings that are plainly visible on the stern or on either side of the hull and on the transverse bulkhead of the machinery space. This regulation attempts to minimize the existence of "ghost ships" that have been hijacked and their markings and documentation changed in order to sell the cargo and or the ship for profit. Normally in these cases the ship is taken and the legitimate crew is never heard from again.

Exterior numbers must be 200 mm in height, plainly visible on the stern or port and starboard side of the vessel. Raised numbers, cutting in or center punching must permanently affix the hull number. This must be completed by the ship's first dry-docking after July 1, 2004. The required number is the vessel's IMO number.

Requirements for the interior numbers are similar but only need to be 100 mm in height.

SOLAS, Ch XI Reg 3

CONTINUOUS SYNOPSIS RECORD (CSR)

The CRS will be a historical document that tracks the vessel's owners thoughout its service life and will contain the following information:

- Ship's flag, registry data, and ID number
- Name of ship and port of registry
- Registered owner, charterer, and company
- Country or recognized organization issuing Safety Management & International Security

The record remains with ship, even if flag, registry, or ownership changes. This record also will be available for inspection onboard the ship if requested by proper authorities.

The CSR will be maintained in English, French, or Spanish and the official language of the flag state. Every ship under the new code will have a continuous synopsis record that is intended to provide an onboard record of the history of the ship with respect to the information recorded. The CSR shall be issued by the flag state or RSO (recognized security organization) of the ship. All changes to the information required by regulation 5 must be added to the CSR. Consult SOLAS chapter XI for a complete listing of required entries.

SOLAS, Ch 11 Reg 5

OBLIGATIONS OF CONTRACTING GOVERNMENTS

Administrations shall set security levels and ensure provision of information to ships and set security levels and ensure provision of information to port facilities and ships entering those facilities.

SOLAS Ch XI-2, Reg 3/ISPS Part A.4-B.4/33CFR101.200

The specifics of how contacting governments will disseminate this information are still undecided. The international code uses the term Security Level, the highest threat level being 3 and lowest being 1. In the U.S. regulations, the term MARSEC (Maritime Security) level is used. In the U.S., Flash fax has become the most common means used by the individual Captains of the Port. Currently the MARSEC level is loosely associated with the DHS (Department of Homeland Security) threat advisory system that uses a 5-color-coded system ranging from green (low) to red (severe) describing the probability of a terrorist attack. Generally speaking, the first three tiers in the DHS system are associated with MARSEC level 1 as set by the local USCG COTP (Captain of the Port). The fourth level orange (high) is associated with MARSEC level 2. The highest level red (severe) is associated with the highest MARSEC level 3. The regulations call for increased security when there is an increased threat.

To have an effective security program, you must have more information pertaining to the threat than just the threat level. To tailor your security posture to the specific threat, you must obtain detailed information about the existence, presence, capability, and intent of any threat that may be present in your area of operation. Currently the most common form of information provided to ships are the IMO piracy report and threats to worldwide shipping as promulgated by the Office of U.S. Naval intelligence and U.S. Coast Guard Marine Safety Offices. Other flag state/port state threat information is available.

In his 2002 book *Leadership,* Rudolph W. Giuliani writes "Leaders may possess brilliance, extraordinary vision, fate, even luck. Those help; but no one, no matter how gifted, can perform without preparation, thoughtful experiment, and determined follow through . . . I realized that preparation . . . was the single most important key to success, no matter what the field." As a CSO/SSO, the "preparation" Mr. Giuliani is speaking of should be considered the gathering, assessment, and dissemination of terrorist threat information.

REQUIREMENTS OF COMPANIES & SHIPS

Companies and Ships shall comply with relevant requirements of this chapter & ISPS Code Part A, taking ISPS Code Part B into account. Contracting governments will set the security level and inform the ship prior to entering port. When the security level of the administration for the ship and the contacting government of the port differ, the higher security level will be maintained by the ship. When a ship is not in compliance, the ship will notify the proper authorities prior to conducting any operation and before entry into the port.
SOLAS, Ch XI-2 Reg 4/ISPS Part A.6, B.6/33CFR104.105

Company and vessel personnel will share equally in the responsibility and liability that are inherent in the various maritime security requirements. While a flag state may require all vessels flying their flag to maintain a certain level of security, a port may require a higher security level. In these cases the vessel must always comply with the higher security level.

If a vessel for any reason is out of compliance, such as not meeting any requirement set forth in the Vessel Security Plan, this must be transmitted to port state control as well as the Company Security Officer before entering port or conducting any operations.

SPECIFIC RESPONSIBILITIES OF COMPANIES

Company shall ensure master has information regarding: who is authorized to be on board the ship in any capacity, who is responsible for deciding the employment of the ship and if the ship is chartered, who are the parties of the charter.

SOLAS Ch XI-2, Reg 5/ISPS Part B6.1/33CFR104.200

Due to multiple charter parties or change in ownership, the Master of a vessel may be unsure of who exactly is making decisions that affect his vessel. Regulation 5 mandates that these facts be clear to the Master. Today as vessels operate around the globe, assessments are made to determine the possible risk that a vessel may pose. Part of the criteria that affect the prioritization of vessels is the ownership, flag state, crewmembers, and route a vessel travels including previous ports. Since 9-11 there has been a lot written about the possibility of the Al Qaeda Navy. While there are reports that terrorists along with weapons and equipment have been transported by sea, and through seaports, none fly the flag of "Osama bin Laden." The vessels referred to are those vessels that meet some or all of the criteria mentioned above that may be sympathetic to or be supporting of the terrorist networks. Therefore, information pertaining to the legitimate operation of any vessel must be readily available to proper authorities. Also, companies must transmit to the Master of the vessel all persons who are authorized to be on the vessel. This includes crewmembers, contractors, visitors, and stevedores.

THREATS TO SHIPS

Governments will set security levels and ensure security information is provided to ships in their territorial sea and those vessels that intend to enter their territorial seas. Contracting governments will:

- *Set security levels*
- *Ensure provision of security level information*
- *Provide point of contact for advice & assistance*

When a risk of attack is identified, the Contracting Government concerned shall advise the concerned ships & their administration:

- *Current security level*
- *Any security measure to be put in place*

- *Security measures that the coastal State has put in place*
SOLAS Ch XI-2, Reg 7/ISPS Part B6.1/33CFR101.200

This regulation identifies who is responsible for setting the security level. This responsibility remains with the contracting government. Companies and vessels do not have the authority to raise the security level. This does not restrict the Master or company from taking whatever measures are necessary to protect their vessels. A prudent Master will assess the threat and take whatever countermeasures are necessary to reduce the threat. The contracting government will provide the company and ship any information that will assist in awareness of the threat. This notification, if the threat warrants it, will include raising the security level. If the security level is raised, the contracting government will alert the company and ship as to what is the heightened risk. This will allow the ship to better establish adequate countermeasures within the confines of the Ship Security Plan.

MASTER'S DISCRETION FOR SHIP SAFETY AND SECURITY

"The master shall not be constrained by the Company, the charterer or any other person from taking or executing any decision which, in the professional judgment of the master, is necessary to maintain the safety and security of the ship."

In a conflict between safety and security, the master will give effect to those requirements to maintain safety. He may institute temporary security measures and inform the administration and contracting government.
SOLAS Ch XI-2 Reg 8/33CFR104.205

This regulation clearly identifies the Master's responsibility in the security plan. The contracting government will supply any threat information it receives and if needed will raise the security level. However, if the Master identifies a security threat, he will take whatever countermeasures are necessary to protect his vessel, crew, and cargo. It is possible under this scenario that the vessel will at a higher security level than the one required by the flag state or port state control. This can be a double-edged sword. On the one hand it gives the Master authority to take action if needed, but it also holds him responsible to take action.

CONTROL & COMPLIANCE MEASURES

Control of Ships in Port
Every ship to which this regulation applies is subject to control when in a port of another Contracting Government by officers authorized by that government.

With clear grounds, or the absence of a valid Security Certificate, the following controls may be applied:

- *Inspection*
- *Delaying or detaining the ship*
- *Restriction of ship operations & movement*
- *Expulsion from the port*

SOLAS Ch XI-2, Reg 9/ISPS Part B4.29-B4.44/33CFR101.410

Regulation 9 is the "teeth" of ISPS. In reality there would not be as much interest in ISPS if Regulation 9 were not included. But make no mistake, port state controls are empowered to take actions against a vessel if they find vessels not complying with their security plans. The overall goal is to protect the ship from criminal and terrorist attack. From the perspective of a single ship, the short-term goal is not to be delayed or detained for noncompliance. As in all regulations the best way to comply is to set and maintain good operating procedures. A port state control inspection team will easily identify certain "nonconformities." No gangway watch or complacent gangway watch is bound to bring scrutiny. The crew having no knowledge of the security plan or security levels is another "red" flag. A proactive approach, along with a good training program, is the best insurance against noncompliance.

Ships Entering Port of Another Contract Government
May be required to provide the following:
- *Valid ship security certificate*
- *Ship's security level*
- *Security level of ship in previous 10 ports of call*

Ship security plans are not subject to inspection by duly authorized officers of Contracting Governments, except with some, limited exceptions

These Exceptions are:
- *Clear grounds to believe the ship is non-compliant*
- *Inspection is the only way to verify or rectify compliance*
- *Limited access to the specific sections of the plan*
- *Consent of the ship's master or Contracting Government*

SOLAS Ch XI-2, Reg 9/ISPS Part B4.37–.39/33CFR104.120

In such cases the Company Security Officer should be contacted before allowing access to the Ship Security Plan. Port state control is not a new concept. Whatever flag your ship flies, whatever country's port you enter, you are always bound by local law. In the case of maritime security the laws are consistent. The common thread is the SOLAS regulations. Be it ISPS Code or CFR (for U.S. flagged vessels only), the rules are generally the same. The only differencs are organization and terms used in the applicable rules.

Security plans include the vessel response measures and vulnerabilities. This is the vessel's playbook for security. You would not want an opposing team to have your playbook. The Vessel Security Plan is security sensitive information and should be handled as such. Guidelines for protection and distribution of your VSP will be included in your vessel plan.

There are cases where it may be reasonable to show parts of your plan to an inspecting official to prove compliance, i.e., your vessel is in a foreign port and the inspecting official has accused you of noncompliance with the ISPS Code by not inspecting personal baggage at the gangway. The security level in the port is 1. In accordance with your approved Ship Security Plan (SSP), you are only required to search 10% of baggage. Your vessel has only eight visitors on the day. As long as you inspect one of the next two visitors, you are still in compliance with your security plan. By showing only that page of your Ship Security Plan and your visitors' logbook you have proven your compliance. It is recommended that prior to showing any part of your SSP, that the Ship Security Officer (SSO) contact the Company Security Officer (CSO) for approval.

Ships entering port of another contract government may be required to provide the following:
- *Any additional or special security measures in those ports*
- *Appropriate security measures used during ship-to-ship activities*
- *Other practical security-related information (not details of the security plan)*

SOLAS Ch XI-2, Reg 9/ISPS Part B4.34.39/33CFR104.120

Special security measures have included security guards, bomb sweeps, picket boats, and underwater hull surveys. Vessel operators are not normally equipped to provide these requirements. It is recommended that CSOs identify means of providing these services throughout the route that their vessels travel. Security procedures covering ship-to-ship activities such as lightering and bunkering will be covered in the SSP.

Requirements for Port Facilities

Port facility will comply with applicable regulations in part A or the ISPS code taking part B into account as guidance.
   Contracting Governments shall ensure the completion of:
- *Port facility security assessments*
- *Port security plans*

SOLAS Ch XI-2, Reg 10/ISPS Part B4.34–.39/33CFR105

Port facilities servicing SOLAS vessels or vessels on international voyages must comply with the ISPS Code to the same extent as ships. The fact that port facilities are complying with the same security measures increase the probability of detecting and deterring criminal or terrorist activity. Working closely with the Port Facility Security Officer (PFSO) can help the CSO/SSO reduce redundancies and increase efficiency. The form that identifies shared security responsibilities is the Declaration of Security (DoS).

Alternative Security Agreements

Contracting governments can agree on rules regarding ships on short, international voyages on fixed routes.

These agreements:

* *Cannot compromise security*
* *Do not cover ship-to-ship activities*

These agreements shall be reviewed periodically taking into account the current threat assessment and particular circumstances.

SOLAS Ch XI-2, Reg 11/ISPS Part B4.26/33CFR104.140

A good example where this regulation could be applied is in the cruise ship industry where vessels make daily runs between the United States and the Bahamas. In this case arrangements can be made between the two countries to wave certain security measures such as the 96-hour notification. This is possible because the vessel is on a fixed route and makes no other voyages. In the United States the following organizations have been approved for alternative security agreements with the USCG. These agreements allow the organizations to operate under an approved plan for all vessels in good standing within their organization but do not relinquish the requirements of the CFR.

* North American Export Grain Association and National Grain and Feed Association
* Greater New Orleans Barge Fleeting Association (GNOBFA)
* Washington State Ferries
* American Gaming Association
* Passenger Vessel Association
* American Waterways Organization
* Lake Carriers Association
* Offshore Marine Services Association
* American Chemistry Council (ACC)

In the U.S. regulations this is referred to an Alternative Security Program (ASP) and also applies to port facilities.

ISPS CODE

The SSO or the CSO of a non-U.S. flag vessel will be most concerned with the International Ship and Port Security (ISPS) Code. In many ways SOLAS XI-2 is similar to the ISPS Code and 33CFR Part 104; however, there are some clear differences. It is, therefore, imperative that CSOs and SSOs review all regulations in this chapter. The code contains a series of rules (Part A) and guidelines (Part B). The ISPS Code enables the detection and deterrence of security threats within an international framework. The ISPS Code:

- Establishes roles and responsibilities
- Enables collection and exchange of security information
- Provides a methodology for assessing security
- Ensures that adequate security measures are in place

It requires ship and port facility staff to:

- Gather and assess information
- Maintain communication protocols
- Restrict access; prevent the introduction of unauthorized weapons, etc.
- Provide the means to raise alarms
- Put in place vessel and port security plans
- Ensure training and drills are conducted.

Declaration of Security (DoS)

Contracting Government shall determine when a DoS is required by assessing the port/ship interface risk. Ships can request completion of a DoS when:
- *Ship operating at higher security level than port or interfacing ship*
- *There is an agreement with contracting government*
- *There has been a security threat or incident involving the ship or port facility*
- *The ship is in a port not required to have a security plan*
- *The ship interfaces with another ship not required to have a security plan*

Declaration of Security shall be completed by the Master or SSO and the FSO or the body responsible for shoreside security. The DoS shall address shared (port & ship) and individual responsibilities.
ISPS Part A5/33CFR104.225

In many cases the DoS is not required until the implementation of Security Level 2. However, interaction with the shoreside authorities and Port Facility Security Officer can only be to the advantage of the

CSO/SSO. A DoS is provided as an example in appendix B. Completing a DoS may result in eliminating redundant security operations by ship and shore personnel and will ensure direct and accurate contact information in case of an emergency situation. Copies of a completed DoS should remain on file for presentation to appropriate authorities.

Ship Security

Each ship is required to act upon security levels set by contracting government.
  Security Level 1: (take into account guidance in Part B)
  * *Ensure performance of all ship security duties*
  * *Access control onboard*
  * *Control embarkation of persons & their effects*
  * *Monitor restricted areas for authorized access*
  * *Monitor deck areas and area surrounding ship*
  * *Supervise handling of cargo & ship's stores*
  * *Ensure security communication is readily available*
  Security Level 2: Additional protective measures, specified in ship's plan.
  * *Take into account guidance in Part B*
  Security Level 3: Risk of imminent danger
  * *Further protective measures. Take into account guidance in Part B.*
  * *Each ship shall acknowledge receipt of instructions for Security Levels 2 & 3*
  ISPS Part A7/33CFR104.240

Security Level or MARSEC level 1 is the baseline security posture for all ship and port facilities. This is the new reality for the maritime industry as a whole. Operations must involve elements of security. Your approved VSP will identify specific measures to be taken at each MARSEC level. The primary goal of the CSO/SSO should be to incorporate security seamlessly into the vessel's standard operating procedure. Although this may be difficult in the beginning, once accepted by the crew together with the constant and unwavering support of the company and ship's officers, the vessel will be able to maintain its security posture with little or no extra effort. Once you have your plan approved, there is little in the regulations that takes extensive time or effort. Secure spaces not in use, maintain a roving patrol, know who is on your ship at all times (access control), inspect bags as per your SSP, have appropriate signage posted, keep crew informed as to the port specific threat (if any), and monitor your vessel and surrounding areas. Almost every industry, including the maritime industry, has cooped with similar regulatory compliance issues in the form of increased safety regulation. It was not long ago the maritime industry had to adjust to a new set of oil spill prevention regulations. When OPA 90 was first implemented we heard much of the same cries we here today over security. Today we comply with OPA 90 without a second thought and realize that in the end we can operate more safely, cheaply, and efficiently. The same will happen with security. If your vessel were to experience one less stowaway incident over a period of time, how much would that save the shipping company? Now consider reduced theft of ships equipage over the life cycle of every ship. This is where the ISPS Code will be an asset to the shipping industry over time, and added defense against global maritime terrorism hasn't even been mentioned. That cost cannot be calculated!

Records

Records shall be kept addressing the following:
- *Training, drills & exercises*
- *Security threats & incidents & breaches of security*
- *Changes in security level*
- *Communications related directly to ship security*
- *Internal audits & reviews*
- *Periodic reviews of security assessment & security plan*
- *Implementation of any amendments to plan*
- *Maintenance, calibration & testing of security equipment*

Records shall be kept in the working language of the ship with a translation into English, Spanish, or French. Records may be kept in electronic format and must be protected from unauthorized deletion, destruction, or amendment. Records shall be protected from unauthorized access or disclosure.
ISPS Part A10/33CFR104.235

Your Ship Security Plan will identify the required records that are to be maintained for at least two years. Besides a well-maintained gangway watch and dynamic and overt security procedure, a well-maintained and thorough record keeping is the best way to prevent port state control from digging too deep into your security program. Since port state control is not permitted to view your SSP, the records you keep are the only way to demonstrate your compliance with the ISPS Code. A security journal or daily occurrence log should be kept by both the SSO and CSO. This log will contain all information relevant to security.

Company Security Officer (CSO)

Each Company shall designate a CSO. More than one CSO can be designated but must clearly identify for which ship each is responsible. Duties include (but not limited to):

1. *Advising the level of threats likely to be encountered by the ship, using appropriate security assessments and other relevant information;*

2. *Ensuring that ship security assessments are carried out;*
3. *Ensuring the development, the submission for approval, and thereafter the implementation and maintenance of the ship security plan;*
4. *Ensuring that the ship security plan is modified, as appropriate, to correct deficiencies and satisfy the security requirements of the individual ship;*
5. *Arranging for internal audits and reviews of security activities;*
6. *Arranging for the initial and subsequent verifications of the ship by the Administration or the recognized security Organization;*
7. *Ensuring that deficiencies and non-conformities identified during internal audits, periodic reviews, security inspections and verifications of compliance are promptly addressed and dealt with;*
8. *Enhancing security awareness and vigilance;*
9. *Ensuring adequate training for personnel responsible for the security of the ship;*
10. *Ensuring effective communication and co-operation between the ship security officer and the relevant port facility security officers;*
11. *Ensuring consistency between security requirements and safety requirement;*
12. *Ensuring that, if sister-ship or fleet security plans are used, the plan for each ship reflects the ship-specific information accurately; and*
13. *Ensuring that any alternative or equivalent arrangements approved for a particular ship or group of ships are implemented and maintained.*

ISPS Part A11/33CFR104.210

A Company Security Officer must be designated in writing by the vessel owners. He may be responsible for various vessels or for vessels in a designated area, i.e., all vessels operated by XYZ company operating in the Atlantic Ocean south of latitude 45 degrees north. He may be responsible for other duties within the company; however, this is not a hands-off position. As a CSO you are an integral part of the security program. Once you have overseen the completion of each vessel security assessment and plan, you must maintain constant contact with the SSO and give "adequate support" to maintain a successful security program. Regular duties of the CSO should include overseeing the vessel's drill and exercise program by directing security drills and training responding to feedback from the ship's crew to make changes to the VSP. The CSO must conduct annual audits of the VSA and VSP. He must provide training materials and ensure the vessel security activities are audited. Arguably, his most important job is to keep the SSO and thereby the crew aware of any potential threats the vessel may encounter. To do this he must maintain contact with intelligence sources at the federal and local level and must pass along information to the ships for which he is responsible. Later chapters on risk assessment and analysis will provide specific guidance on this very important responsibility.

Ship Security Officer (SSO)

A ship security officer shall be designated on each ship. In addition to those specified elsewhere in the Code, the duties and responsibilities of the ship security officer shall include, but are not limited to:

1. *Undertaking regular security inspections*
2. *Maintaining & supervising the implementation of the ship security plan*
3. *Coordinating the security aspects of cargo handling*
4. *Proposing modifications to the ship security plan*
5. *Reporting to the CSO*
6. *Enhancing security awareness*
7. *Ensuring adequate training to shipboard personnel*
8. *Reporting all security incidents*
9. *Coordinate implementation of the security plan with the CSO*
10. *Ensuring that security equip is properly operated, tested, calibrated & maintained*

ISPS Part A12/33CFR104.215

Though not specifically mentioned above, the goal of the SSO is to cultivate and maintain a positive security posture. The tools and assets provided to the SSO by the CSO are critical. This includes training and awareness of the crew, equipment such as lights, radios, procedures, and information regarding the threat. Given the primary duties of the SSO (no matter which officer is selected), time will have to be allocated or freed up using other personnel to allow the SSO to conduct his security responsibilities. The SSO must be a member of the crew. He may assign security duties to other crewmembers; however, he remains responsible for those duties. He must have general knowledge, through training or equivalent job experience in the subject matter as the CSO as well as vessel layout, the VSP and scenario-based response training, crowd control, and operations and testing of security equipment. It can be argued that through the years of experience and testing required to become a chief mate that anyone filling that bill would be inherently qualified. Although that assessment may be correct, the true test becomes one of demonstrated security compliance. Any security incident or perceived lack of security would be cause to scrutinize the SSO's knowledge and ability to maintain vessel security. There are many training programs available.

Until such time as the USCG approves Maritime Security Training, it is recommended that you find a training provider that is highly recognized and provides training that meets all the requirements of the established IMO model courses.

Training, Drills, and Exercises
(Taking into Account Guidance in Part B)

- *CSO's & appropriate shore-based personnel shall have knowledge & receive training*
- *SSO shall have knowledge through training or equivalent job experience*
- *Shipboard personnel with specific security duties & responsibilities shall understand their duties, have sufficient knowledge & ability to perform their duties*
- *Ensure effective implementation of ship security plan & drills are carried out at appropriate intervals.*
- *CSO shall ensure effective coordination of ship security plans by participating in exercises.*

ISPS Part A13/33CFR104.225–.230

The code requires different levels of awareness as you move up in responsibility and allows the operating company to decide how best to meet these requirements. Several things are not up for interpretation. The vessel must conduct at least three drills each year and the drills must be logged and recorded. The vessel must conduct at least one exercise each year. The difference being roles to be taken by outside entities. These may include but are not limited to the CSO, port state control, local law enforcement and emergency responders, and port facility security personnel. Later chapters in this text will give specific guidance on drills and exercises. The approved VSP will give directions to the SSO on drills and exercise procedures.

Issue or Endorsement of Certificate

An International Ship Security Certificate (ISSC) shall be issued after the initial or renewal verification. The ISSC shall be issued by the Administration or an authorized RSO. Ships will have to carry an ISSC indicating that they comply with the requirements of SOLAS chapter XI-2 and part A of the ISPS Code. When a ship is at a port or is proceeding to a port of contracting government, the contracting government has the right, under the provisions of regulation XI-2/9, to exercise various control and compliance measures with respect to that ship. The ship is subject to port state control inspections but such inspections will not normally extend to examination of the ship security plan itself except in specific circumstances. The only RSO in the United States is the

U.S. Coast Guard. The certificate will be good for five years and may be renewed within three months of expiration except in certain circumstances.
ISPS Part A19.2/33CFR104.120

Interim Certification

May be issued by an Administration or RSO after July 1, 2004, for the purpose of: a ship without a certificate, on delivery or prior to entry / re-entry into service transfer of a ship from one flag to another where both are contracting governments transfer of a ship to a contracting government flag from a state which is not a contracting government. An ISSC will only be issued when the company has submitted a VSP for approval and that plan is onboard the ship. The ship has an SSAS if required and there is a CSO and SSO designated for the vessel in writing.
ISPS Part A19.4/33CFR104.225–.230

NVIC 10-02

Security Guidelines for Vessels is a very useful document for anyone involved in maritime security and is available on the World Wide Web at http://www.uscg.mil/hq/g-m/mp/nvic.html as well as other U.S. regulatory information. The Navigation and Vessel Inspection Curricular (NVIC) is specifically applicable to U.S. flag vessels but provides easy to understand guidance for developing Ship Security Plans and reaffirms COTP's existing authority regarding vessel and security. The NVIC established security levels: MARSEC 1–3 as directed by the MTSA. This document is written is plain language and amplifies the requirements of the CFR for the U.S. Merchant Marine using a common sense approach.

USCG CODE OF FEDERAL REGULATIONS (CFRS)

The ISPS Code establishes the SOLAS requirements for security in two parts. Part A is considered mandatory while part B is considered guidance. The CFRs mandate both parts and spread out the regulations throughout 33 CFR parts 101 to part 106 as follows:

- General Provisions, part 101
- Reserved for future use, part 102
- Area Maritime Security, part 103
- Vessel Security, part 104
- Facility Security, part 105
- Outer Continental Shelf Security, part 106

The most important part for CSO and VSO is part 104 of course. 33 CFR Part 104 is provided in the appendix and should be read in its entirety. Implementation remains the same as the aforementioned ISPS Code.

33 CFR Part 104: Maritime Security: Vessels

This part applies to the owner or operator of any:

    (1) Mobile Offshore Drilling Unit (MODU), cargo, or passenger vessel subject to the International Convention for Safety of Life at Sea, 1974, (SOLAS);

    (2) Foreign commercial vessel greater than 100 gross register tons not subject to SOLAS;

    (3) Commercial vessel greater than 100 gross register tons subject to 46 CFR subchapter I, except commercial fishing vessels inspected under 46 CFR part 105;

On or before December 29, 2003, each vessel owner or operator must submit to USCG for each vessel the Vessel Security Plan.

On or before June 30, 2004, each vessel must be operating in compliance with this part.

On or before July 1, 2004, foreign vessels must carry on board a valid International Ship Security Certificate that certifies the verifications required by section 19.1 of part A of the ISPS Code.

Noncompliance - When a vessel is not in compliance with the requirements of this part, the vessel owner or operator must notify the cognizant COTP and request a waiver to continue operations.

SUMMARY

Depending on your specific circumstance, there are multiple regulations that may affect the way you do business. The new regulations call for knowledge of the threat as well as the knowledge of "international conventions, codes, and recommendations, as well as government legislation and regulations." You may have to work with vessels under the ISPS Code or CFR, but they all must meet the requirement of SOLAS. The global maritime strategy requires everyone to take part and do his or her job. As CSOs and SSOs, you will play an integral role. Your efforts and attitudes become crucial because you affect those under you. If you are motivated to maintain a high level of security, so will those who work for you. Unfortunately the same is true if proper motivation is lacking. Keep in mind the entire industry can be affected by an attack of any size. It will not matter if an attack targets the "highest" value or symbolic assets of the industry.

CIA Director George Tenet stated, "As we have increased security around government and military facilities, terrorists are seeking out 'softer' targets that provide opportunities for mass casualties." Only through complete knowledge of the rules and regulations and a detailed knowledge of the potential threats that face the maritime industry today can success in our efforts to defend our ships from terrorism be realized.

A terrorist Hiroshima-sized nuclear bomb (15 kilotons, the equivalent of 15,000 tons of TNT) detonated in a port would destroy buildings out to a mile or two; start fires, especially in a port that handled petroleum and chemicals; spread fallout over many square miles; disrupt commerce; and kill many people. Many ports are in major cities. By one estimate, a 10- to 20-kiloton weapon detonated in a major seaport would kill 50,000 to 1 million people and would result in direct property damage of $50 to $500 billion, losses due to trade disruption of $100 billion to $200 billion, and indirect costs of $300 billion to $1.2 trillion.
—ABT Associates, "The Economic Impact of Nuclear Terrorist Attacks on Freight Transport Systems in an Age of Seaport Vulnerability," executive summary, April 30, 2003

Remember your job is to protect your ships and, therefore, the global maritime economy from terrorism. The threat is real! The attack on the M/V *Limburg* demonstrated the enemy's willingness to attack commercial and civilian targets in order to disrupt the commercial shipping industry. You cannot afford to solely rely on the U.S. or foreign authorities to protect your financial interest.

In order to defeat the terrorists everyone must take responsibility to safeguard our livelihood. Everyone *must* realize the threat, change their way of doing business to *deter* terrorist attacks and be able to *detect* potential threats and then *defend* ourselves as well as our economic interests. Maritime security can be a daunting task. When you feel yourself becoming complacent or distracted by other matters, remember, consider the cost of doing nothing.

TWO

Maritime Terrorism

With the Cold War a chapter in history books, a billion-dollar Aegis destroyer, the USS *Cole,* a symbol of American power, makes its approach to a remote fueling pier in a former Soviet client state Yemen. With an average age of 20, most of the crew are too young to have experienced war in their lifetimes. This is the age of the global economy, where trade barriers have fallen and goods produced in far corners of the globe would arrive at a local Walmart taking advantage of cheap labor in developing countries and regions. Oil is at a historic low of less than $20 a barrel. With few exceptions, the threat of a protracted war anywhere in the world seemed remote. With the arrival alongside of a small husbandry boat its smiling and waving occupants revealed nothing of the coming carnage. Suddenly a horrific explosion, 17 dead, scores injured, and this symbol of American power lay hopelessly injured—a gaping hole in its side. The scourge of 21st-century terrorism that had been mainly confined to shore-based targets had ominously moved to sea.

Meanwhile across the world, a line of tankers moves endlessly through the Straits of Mallacca. A chemical tanker is quietly approached by a small boat piloted by men armed with AK-47 rifles and knives. Making their approach in the darkest area of the vessel's stern, they expertly throw lines with grappling hooks up to the vessel's main deck and gain access to the vessel carefully, avoiding the lone deck watch on patrol on the bow of the tanker. Heading for the ship's bridge, they quickly overpower the unarmed crew and take over the ship. One crewman is shot while the Master is told to hand over all the cash and valuables in the Master's cabin. Satisfied with their bounty, they then gag and bind the Master and lower him over the side to a small boat, never to be seen again.

Months later in a Middle East port, a containership is loaded to near capacity. As the stevedores stop for an afternoon break, a truck loaded with a container marked for Halifax parks to deliver its cargo. The container is routinely loaded onboard; inside an Al Qaeda operative keeps silent awaiting his 10-day transit to the North American continent and his eventual journey to Paterson, New Jersey. He carries with him a vial of anthrax and coded orders to join a terrorist cell poised to attack targets in the United States.

THREATS TO MARITIME SECURITY

The previous scenarios, some real, some imagined, illustrate the vulnerability of military and commercial maritime assets. The events of 9-11 initiated an overall assessment of the nation's vulnerabilities to terrorist acts and other forms of asymmetric warfare. The vast U.S. and global transportation system has been of particular concern because of its historic vulnerability as an effective target rich environment and as a potential means of access for those involved in criminal activities. In recent years worldwide, Al Qaeda and allied terrorist groups have attacked aviation, maritime, rail, and ground transportation targets. Available intelligence and indicators remind us that the threat to our transportation system will remain into the foreseeable future.

Worldwide, 5.8 billion tons of goods were traded by sea in 2001. This accounts for over 80 percent of world trade by volume. With more than 45,000 vessels and over 4,000 ports in the world's maritime transport system, commercial shipping is a critical component of global commerce. Previous to the adoption of the ISPS Code, the MTSA, and cargo security initiatives, much of this system has been open and unsecured, which adds to its vulnerability and the risk of use by terrorist and criminal groups. Perhaps no sector is more dangerously exposed than ports and intermodal freight and passenger transportation systems to which they are connected.

Maritime security in its broadest sense also includes the problems of piracy, violence at sea, cargo theft, drug trafficking, alien smuggling, fraudulent certification of personnel, misdeclaration of cargoes, importation of counterfeit merchandise, and other forms of contraband and organized crime activities. Although each of these is a major problem on its own, they are issues that are directly related to terrorism. It has been reported and established that terrorist organizations frequently finance their activities through criminal use of the transportation, business, and financial systems. Thus the context of maritime security has vital implications for homeland security. In a recent study, a major and coordinated attack on the U.S. maritime infrastructure would cause countless casualties and could cost an estimated $58 billion.

While piracy, crime, wars at sea, and terrorism have plagued mariners from the beginnings that man has used the sea, this chapter will not be a comprehensive history of threats to seafarers but provide an awareness of threats in the 21st century in our age of a global economy and reliance on Middle East oil to fuel our economies.

This chapter will present an overview of the various threats facing mariners and more specifically point out the threats posed by terrorism, piracy, and organized and nonorganized crime including premise that criminal groups can and do cooperate to threaten global trade. The CSO and SSO have a critical role in securing and protecting a ship, its crew and cargo. It is incumbent that personnel in these positions become students of threats to their ships and understand the various methods criminal organizations, pirates, and terrorists use to threaten shipping and the economic well being of target nations.

OVERVIEW OF MARITIME TERRORISM

The threat from organized terrorist groups such as Al Qaeda and its allies is a relatively new and ominous development. Terrorists use maritime attacks to advance their political and economic goals. While there is a wide spectrum of terrorist groups that have a maritime capability, Al Qaeda and its allies are considered to pose the gravest threat to the maritime industry whether against military or commercial vessels plying the world's waterways, ports, and facilities. In their proclamations Al Qaeda has referred to the petroleum industry as the "lifeblood of the crusaders" and a target of particular interest to achieve their agenda. Terrorist groups worldwide have and probably will continue to use the maritime sector to transport operatives, arms, and supplies to intended recipients as well as narcotics and contraband used to finance their operations. Terrorist groups can often be in cooperation with criminal groups and/or state sponsors such as North Korea or Iran to traffic in arms, drugs, humans, and contraband. Vessels and ports may ask a vehicle to transport illicit cargoes including Weapons of Mass Destruction (WMD) or become the weapon itself to threaten the life and economic livelihood of a region or country.

In this context maritime terrorism differs little from attacks against land or aviation targets. The airline industry prior to the initiation of hijackings and hostage taking by Middle Eastern and Palestinian terrorist groups was relatively open and unsecure. Unfortunately those events necessitated enhanced security that over time failed in the 9-11 attacks. The cost of terrorism to the airline industry has been tremendous; the costs to the maritime industry is estimated to be a 600 million dollars per year, which is considerable. But in comparison to the effects of a major successful attack quite reasonable.

TERRORIST OPERATIONS

While recent events have shown that terrorists are imaginative and flexible in their operations, anticipating how terrorists will attempt to exploit vulnerabilities at sea and in port is the key to prevent an incident. Understanding how terrorists think and operate will assist the CSO/SSO develop measures to decrease vulnerabilities. The problem of countering the threat from terrorists is difficult for many reasons. The terrorists can pick the target, time, and method of attack based on their capabilities and the operational environment, while we have to defend against all known or perceived threats. They can use deceptive techniques to hide in normal activities while we have to deter, detect, and identify threats from the normal background noise. No one will argue that the bad guys have a lot of advantages. Preventing terrorism is a formidable challenge but they are not an invinceable enemy. It is important to study terrorist tactics and know that Al Qaeda and other groups have extensively documented and published guidance for its operatives on how to conduct attacks. Many Jihadist have been trained in camps in Afghanistan and elsewhere. This guidance includes such areas as communications, security, deception, surveillance techniques, weapons/bomb-making, and armed assault tactics. They have also published an "Encyclopedia of Naval Jihad," which contains guidance on ship attacks, ship types, and vulnerabilities.

A review of terrorist publications and guidance reveals that their operations are conducted much like a formally trained "special operations" commando mission would be carried out. In the recent past their list of maritime targets as evidenced by actual assaults, thwarted plots, intelligence, or reports of "suspicious surveillance activity" have included warships, tankers, supply ships carrying cargo to support United States and coalition forces in the Middle East, cruise ships, ports facilities, oil terminals, and ferries.

PHASES OF TERRORIST OPERATIONS

A review of past terrorist operations and documents reveals that terrorist operations are divided into distinct but integrated phases. They include research of potential targets, surveillance, preoperational planning of the operation, and execution. Groups such as Al Qaeda are composed of cells that accomplish each phase, pass on the required information to leaders, but remain unknown to each other for security purposes.

Research Phase

Most terrorist groups will generate a list of targets based on the political, economic, military, philosophical, and religious significance of the target based on the group's agenda. In the era of 21st century terrorism, targets are selected that will generate the most "impact."

This includes the media, casualties produced, embarrassment and symbolic value to governments and societies, and the economic impact to a country or a region. The significance of the 9-11 attacks and attacks on U.S. embassies is well understood—maritime assets in many cases fit the terrorist's agenda of providing "trophy targets." The October 2000 suicide attack on the USS *Cole,* and the bombing of the French tanker *Limberg* in the Gulf of Aden in 2002 represent attacks on icons of economic and military power. In a likewise manner, when Egyptian terrorist groups attacked cruise ships on the Nile River on four occasions in the early 90s, tourists steered clear. One can only imagine the "victory" of a terrorist group if they managed to detonate or release a weapon of mass destruction in a port city, sink a congested ferry, or use a ship as a weapon against a bridge, tunnel, or national symbol in a harbor. As the 9-11 commission report pointed out, there was much discussion by the leaders of Al Qaeda in selecting their targets, including the significance, symbology, and vulnerability of those selected. It is a fair assumption that any future potential targets will be analyzed by terrorists in a similar manner.

Surveillance Phase

Surveillance of potential targets can take weeks, months, or years. Generally terrorists will conduct preliminary surveillance seeking information on a target's vulnerabilities, patterns, behaviors, routines, and defenses. Then a more detailed surveillance can be conducted to provide the operational details necessary to conduct an attack. The October 2000 attack on the USS *Cole* in Yemen was preceded by months of operational surveillance from an apartment overlooking Aden Harbor. In certain high threat areas, use of "insiders" with access to restricted port areas, schedules, and local knowledge of security measures have been used, most notably in Saudi Arabia where attacks on the U.S. Embassy and gated housing communities included attackers dressed as local police officers and Saudi National Guard members. The attackers demonstrated an in depth knowledge of the gates, locks, and physical layout of their targets.

For SSOs and crews it is important to be trained to become aware of signs of surveillance and preoperational activity and report suspicious behaviors to local and national authorities. This is the best method to deter possible attack. Surveillance can be conducted by men, women, and children of any description. It can be done in a stationary post like a hotel room, house, or apartment, or from a vehicle. Surveillance can be covert and difficult to spot or very casual and out in the open. Surveillance can be conducted on foot, in vehicles, boats, and aircraft. There have been reports of plots thwarted by crews reporting individuals filming ports, vessels, and facilities with cameras and video recorders. Operatives can be disguised as security guards, vendors, repair men, pilots, or fishermen. The rule to spotting surveillance is "if it does not look or feel right it probably isn't." Crewmembers should be wary of individuals asking too many questions about vessel and port operations and report such incidents to the SSO. Documents recovered from terrorists have shown an incredible amount of detail and information is gathered on potential targets. In the years since 9-11, there have been numerous reports of suspicious surveillance activity in and around ports and vessels; accurate reports by mariners, alert citizens, and security personnel have led to uncovering of operational cells and probable thwarting of attacks.

Preoperational Phase

Once the target has been selected additional surveillance by more highly trained individuals may begin. Terrorist operatives may move to locations close to the target and assimilate into the surrounding environment. False IDs, bogus uniforms, weapons, bombs, vehicles, and funds begin to assemble. In the USS *Cole* case, the attackers rented a house and built a fence around the yard to conceal their construction of a suicide boat. Operatives may case the target area and probe the security forces noting reaction times and the security posture of guard forces. It is important that security forces and crewmembers are aware that such activity occurs, in the event they notice suspicious individuals. Operatives may drive vehicles such as trucks, cars, and boats to the target area to get a feel for the operation. The 9-11 hijackers took the same flights before their assault, and Timothy McVeigh visited the Morrow Building nursery before he destroyed it. Again it has been proven time and again that an alert and well-trained watch on ship or shore can deter would be attackers. Terrorists are taught to conduct surveillance until shortly before the attack is initiated to see if anything has changed. A robust watch and constantly changing security posture can confound and complicate an attackers plans. Routines and complacency are a terrorist's ally; a constantly changing pattern of security is an excellent defense.

Operational Phase

After months if not years of preparation, local terrorists are generally given some leeway in the timing of an attack. Depending on the type of attack, there is much to consider once an attack is in motion. The use of deception, ruses, and decoys cannot be ruled out in a sophisticated attack. In the attack on the *Cole,* the suicide bombers waved and smiled before they rammed the ship and detonated approximately 600 pounds of explosives. The tanker *Limberg* was stopping to pick up the pilot when she was attacked. Use of official looking vehicles and uniforms have been used in the past. Persons who appear anxious or nervous should be viewed with suspicion. Unseasonal clothing may be hiding explosives, an indicator of a suicide bomber. Rapid approach and use of speed and force by vehicles or boats after a diversion have been reported. In other cases like the bombing of Khobar Towers in Saudi Arabia in 1996, a large truck was driven next to the security fence with enough explosives to demolish the building. In Turkey in 2004 a truck bombing of an Israeli cruise ship was averted because the ship did not arrive on schedule. Sometimes luck or lack of it can change history. An alert crew must be aware that an attack can take place from any direction at any time from the pier, water, air, or under the water. The use of feints and lures cannot be discounted. It will take a case of caution and paranoia to do the job correctly. Terrorist groups do not go by the rules of war, do not care about innocent casualties and will use any device or trick to destroy their target. Another factor to consider is the notion of a soft target. As the United States and allied navies aggressively improve their force protection procedures and posture, the merchant fleet becomes a more inviting target.

A ship in port is probably more vulnerable than a ship at sea, but at sea a ship is not invulnerable especially in constricted waters, chokepoints, or near hostile shorelines.

An innocent approach or a false distress call can lead to a disaster. Terrorists are schooled in the use of disguises so a crew must endeavor to act prudently until everything and everybody can be positively identified as friendly. A CSO/SSO should be aware of the threat in the areas in which they operate. Liason with government, port security, law enforcement, other mariners, and local officials is critical in assessing the security situation of a port or region.

AN OVERVIEW OF TERRORIST GROUPS WITH A MARITIME ATTACK AND CRIMINAL LOGISTICS CAPABILITY

A variety of criminal, terrorist groups, and pirates use the sea to commit crimes from petty larceny to murder and possibly mass destruction or disruption. The smuggling of weapons, humans, narcotics, contraband, and acts of piracy are sometimes conducted independently for commercial gain or linked with organized crime and terrorist groups.

Narco-terrorism

Frequently the production, shipment, and sale of narcotics is carried out by terrorist groups to finance their agenda and operations. Conversely terror tactics are against governments and security forces to protect such operations. There are reports of terrorist involvement in drug trafficking across the globe from South America to Asia. Examples include Columbia, Afghanistan, Burma, North Korea, Thailand, and many others. These groups ship narcotics in a myriad of vessels, containers, go-fast boats, hidden compartments both inside and outside the hulls of vessels. Many times drugs are transferred at sea from larger craft to smaller waiting vessels that are easier to come ashore without inspection. The Columbian FARC is the best known narco-terrorist organization. Well funded, the FARC is a formidable foe, one that uses the latest technology in communications, propulsion, and stealth technology to accomplish its mission. In 2000 the Columbian police discovered a partially built submarine in Bogota, ostensibly to be used to smuggle drugs. The FARC has been linked to organized crime groups from Russia, the Far East, Europe, and Asia. They also reportedly have links to the IRA and Middle East terrorist groups. The FARC and other narco groups are in a continuous battle with both the United States and other police and maritime law enforcement agencies. The war will probably not end soon.

The Liberation Tigers of Tamil Ealam (LTTE)

The Tamil Tigers of Sri Lanka are the most highly organized and potent maritime terrorist group in the world. Using high speed boats, innovative tactics, conventional and unconventional weapons, suicide attacks, and a highly trained and organized cadre, they have terrorized the Sri Lankan Navy in their quest for independence. Unfortunately, other terrorist groups have likely studied the tactics and methods of the LTTE and wish to emulate their success in creating economic disruption and insecurity.

Southeast Asian Terrorist Groups

Throughout Southeast Asia there are a variety of terrorist groups, insurgencies, and revolutionaries. Of particular concern to mariners are the radical Islamic groups such as Jemaah Islamiyah (JI), Free Aceh Movement (GAM), in Indonesia, and the Abu Sayyaf Group in the Phillipines. The various groups have varied roots and political agendas, however, the groups' Islamic beliefs serve as a unifying bond. Many leaders of these groups were involved in the Afghan war against the Soviet occupation and then returned to their homelands motivated by Jihad and allied with Al Qaeda. There is evidence that these groups cooperate across national boundaries for logistics, training, and weapons. Southeast Asian terrorists have attacked a variety of land and sea targets including the sinking of the Manila Super Ferry in 2004. The biggest fear is that these groups could easily mask themselves in the piracy rampant in the region and make a statement by destroying a large chemical or oil tanker in the Malacca Strait in an attempt to disrupt this vital waterway.

Middle East Terrorist Groups

Long the focal point for modern terrorism, the Middle East with the volatile Arab-Israeli conflict, radical movements and governments that actively support terrorism such as Iran and Syria make the surrounding waters and vital chokepoints high risk areas. Israel has battled Hizballah and Hamas and other Palestinian groups as they have attempted to smuggle arms and explosives to its operatives in disputed territories and carry out attacks against Israeli maritime and land targets. Past incidents range from the hijacking of the cruise ship *Achille Lauro* in 1985, interception of arms smuggling vessels the *Santorini* and *Karine "A"* in 2001, and infiltration by operatives by false compartments in containers in the Port of Ashdod in 2004.

In the Persian Gulf, the Iranian Revolutionary Guard Navy continually shadows vessels transiting the Strait of Hormuz using swarm tactics of small boats to simulate attack runs on merchant ships. Disruption of oil and gas supplies by covert sea mining of Middle East chokepoints as practiced by Libya in 1983 in the Red Sea and in the Persian Gulf by Iran during the 1980–88 Iran-Iraq War continues to worry naval planners. With no end in sight of the Arab-Israeli conflict, the War on Terrorism, or the Iraq War, the waters of the Middle East including the Mediterranean, Suez, Red Sea, Gulf of Aden, Arabian Sea, and the Persian Gulf will remain high threat areas.

Al Qaeda

Al Qaeda presently remains the most threatening of terrorist groups. With its worldwide presence in over 68 countries, its links with other fundamendalist groups, and its anti-western agenda it is a potent enemy. The group has demonstrated several high visibility maritime attacks including the explosive boat attacks on the USS *Cole* in 2000 in Aden and the 299,364 DWT-ton French tanker *Limburg* off Ash Shihr at Mukalla 353 miles east of Aden killing a crewman, causing a devastating fire, rupturing the hull, and tripling insurance rates in Yemen. The damage could have been greater; Al Qaeda maritime plots have been thwarted in their preoperational stages in Singapore in 2001 and Morocco in 2002. The Singapore plot involved elements of Jemaah Islamiyah to attack U.S. vessels and land targets while the Moroccan plot targeted American and British naval ships in the Straits of Gibralter using zodiac boats loaded with explosives.

In the Persian Gulf and other Middle East waters, Al Qaeda has threatened warships, logistic ships, and tankers with air, surface, and subsurface attack. Numerous surveillance and suspicious small boat approaches have been reported with an unknown number of attacks being foiled. Reports continue to surface concerning an Al Qaeda fleet of vessels capable of transporting arms, operatives, and contraband that are capable of being used as weapons. The United States, NATO, allied Navies, and maritime intelligence agencies are constantly on watch to identify and interdict rogue Al Qaeda vessels engaged in terrorist activities.

Al Qaeda operatives have been reported in the United States and Europe conducting surveillance on ports and vessels, while several operatives have been apprehended attempting to infiltrate the United States and other countries hidden in containers. Most notably was the discovery of an alleged Egyptian Al Qaeda operative in Italy in 2001 in a container equipped with a bed, toilet facilities, and contained airport maps, and security passes. The container was bound for Novia Scotia.

With Al Qaeda's emphasis on the petroleum industry, tankers and the ports with an oil infrastructure are high risk areas. Weapons of mass destruction being introduced into or through ports remains a constant concern. Another maritime area of concern is cruise ships and passenger ferries. Capable of carrying over 5,000 passengers, both types of vessels have been reportedly threatened and surveilled by terrorist operatives in the United States and other countries. In 2004 the U.S. government issued warnings about the possibility of terrorist swimmers and vehicle borne bombs against facilities and vessels. The outbreak of the gastrointestinal Norwalk virus in cruise ships in 2002 reminds us that the potential of biological attack against a densely packed cruise ship is a possibility that could cripple the industry. Links between Al Qaeda and criminal groups such as the Russian mafia are a deadly and worrisome development. In 2005 the Director of the U.S. CIA could not assure the U.S. Congress that former Soviet WMD were secure and not a threat to other nations. Al Qaeda links with Chechnya Islamic groups only adds to the concern that terrorists may have had access to acquire chemical, biological and nuclear weapons and material from the former Soviet arsenal as it collapsed late in the 20th century. Reports to Congress in 2005 by U.S. intelligence and military leaders have emphasized that Al Qaeda continues to press for the ability to attack Western nations with weapons of mass destruction.

Piracy

Maritime piracy continues to plague many sectors of the globe. Considered an international crime, piracy is reported and tracked by the International Maritime Bureau in Kuala Lumpur. Long a scourge to shipping, pirates in the 21st century have become bolder and more violent. According to IMB statistics, there has been an upward trend in the number of ships attacked. In 2003 there were a reported 445 attacks with 21 crewmembers killed, 71 missing, and 359 hostages taken with economic losses in the billions of dollars each year. Piracy terrorizes its victims as it employs violent means to rob, steal, and kidnap crews and ships for monetary gain. Piracy incidents range from a clandestine boarding by thieves to steal objects of value such as mooring lines or life rafts; robbing the ship's crew, safe, and cargo; kidnapping and ransom of crewmembers; to the takeover and disappearance of vessels and crews. Adding to threat of piracy has been a surge in seaborne traffic in response to global economic growth, and the use of minimal crews to operate vessels, and a prevailing industry attitude of giving pirates what they want in hopes they will go away without a violent confrontation. As discussed earlier, the possibility that modern pirates are interrelated with terrorists especially in the strategic chokepoints of Southeast Asia threaten the world's economy. Virtually all ships carrying oil and natural gas for the economies of Asia pass through these pirate prone areas. A successful spectacular attack could severely disrupt the flow of commerce and make shipping insurance astronomical. In the spring of 2004, in one month, four chemical tankers were attacked by pirates in the Malacca Straits, raising the specter of a maritime disaster.

Other piracy prone regions include the other areas of Southeast Asia including the South China Sea, Indonesian and Phillipine waters, India, Bangladesh, the Red Sea, the Horn of Africa, Red Sea, Nigeria, Carribean Sea, and South America ports have reported piracy incidents. The weekly IMB piracy reports should be a regular source of a CSO/SSO's source of threat information.

Piracy tactics are as varied as they are effective. Pirates generally attack a ship under way at night or during the day in areas that are seen as blind or unlit. Attacks can emanate from one or more small boats working together, sometimes creating a diversion. Pirates are generally very good climbers and very effective in the use of lines for boarding. Pirates have often been disguised as local law enforcement or naval authorities. Pirates can board a ship while under way, in port, or at anchor. Once onboard they can be armed or unarmed and will usually seek out the Master and the bridge to rob crews, take hostages, or seize vessels.

Piracy prone areas are usually bordered by weak governments that have neither the will or resources to counter pirates. The international community has increased naval patrols and some states in Southeast Asia have increased anti-piracy measures with a positive effect. However, an aware crew, an effective anti-piracy bill, physical security measures, and training are the best defense against pirate attack.

Cargo Crime and Stowaways

The implementation of the ISPS Code and the MTSA was focused on the threat from terrorism. The security measures, cargo container initiatives, and overall security awareness and cooperation will harden the industry to crime. Drug smuggling, cargo theft, bogus manifests, organized contraband, and human smuggling which has impacted the industry and cost billions to legitimate business interests will find the law enforcement measures implemented by international, national, and local port authorities losing many vulnerabilities that have allowed criminal to operate. Cargo container initiatives, improvements in crewing credentials, increased enforcement and penalties for illegal immigation and stowaways will make the maritime industry a much more difficult conduit for criminals and terrorist. No system is foolproof and safeguards will need to be continuously improved through training and technology to close the gaps.

CONCLUSION

Defending the maritime industry and infrastructure by code, legislature, and necessity is a cooperative effort between commercial and governmental entities. The threat is varied and evolving as terrorist and criminal groups will adapt to security enhancements. But as proven time and time again, it is the crewmember on watch who understands the threat and is trained to report suspicious or unusual activity that thwarts an impending attack or a crime. It is increasingly important that CSOs and SSOs cooperate with government agencies and become a part of the on-going effort to safeguard our vessels, ports, and waterways. This will require an investment in training, technology, human, and physical resources. Unfortunately recognition of the terrorist and criminal threat must become a way of doing business for mariners in the 21st century.

THREE

The Law of Maritime Security

Attacks on ships are broadly divided into two categories. If the primary motivation of the attackers is financial, the attack is defined as piracy.[1] If the primary motivation of the attackers is political, the attack is defined as terrorism.[2]

The first modern act of maritime terrorism occurred on January 22, 1961, when the Portuguese cruise ship *Santa Maria* was taken over by a Portuguese rebel group in the Caribbean Sea off the coast of Venezuela. The goal of rebel leader Henrique Galvao was to protest the brutal dictatorship of Antonio Salazar. The third mate, who was on the bridge, was killed during the initial takeover of the cruise ship. After the *Santa Maria* was surrounded by vessels of the U.S. Navy and the events became headline news around the world, the rebels surrendered on February 2 and were granted political asylum in Brazil.[3]

The next significant act of maritime terrorism also did not end peacefully. Four members of the Palestine Liberation Front (PLF) terrorist group seized control of the Italian cruise ship *Achille Lauro* as it sailed waters of the eastern Mediterranean Sea on October 7, 1985. When their demands that the Israeli government release 50 Palestinian prisoners were not met, they shot Leon Klinghoffer, a 69-year-old disabled American passenger and threw him and his wheelchair overboard. The terrorists surrendered in Egypt and were allowed to board an airplane bound for Tunisia, where the PLF headquarters were located. U.S. Navy fighter planes forced the aircraft to land in Italy, where the terrorists were arrested. Several terrorists, including the leader Mohammed "Abul" Abbas, managed to escape or otherwise avoid justice.[4]

Numerous other acts of maritime terrorism have occurred since. Two recent acts were the October 12, 2000, suicide attack on the U.S. Navy destroyer *Cole* in the port of Aden[5] and the October 6, 2002, suicide attack on the French supertanker *Limberg* off the port of Al Mukalla, Yemen.[6]

INITIAL RESPONSES TO THREAT OF MARITIME TERRORISM

The attack on the *Santa Maria* was considered a one-off incident and provoked no systemic reaction. The attack on the *Achille Lauro* highlighted a vulnerability. On September 26, 1986, the Maritime Safety Committee of the International Maritime Organization (IMO) issued a circular entitled "Measures to prevent unlawful acts against passengers and crew on board ships."[7] The circular included provisions for ship and port facility security plans; appointment of ship, operator, and Port Facility Security Officers; security surveys; security measures and procedures (e.g., restricted areas, lighting, identification of persons); and training. Implementation of the circular, though, was voluntary and its recommendations were largely ignored by governments and ship operators.

A diplomatic conference sponsored by the IMO in 1988 adopted the Convention for the Suppression of Unlawful Acts against the Safety of Maritime Navigation (SUA Convention) and the Protocol for the Suppression of Unlawful Acts against the Safety of Fixed Platforms located on the Continental Shelf.[8] The Convention and Protocol obligate state parties to make it a crime for a person to unlawfully seize control over or destroy or damage a ship or offshore platform outside the territory of a nation.[9] State parties are obligated to accept custody of alleged offenders and either try them for the offenses or extradite them to another nation where they can be tried. Efforts are currently under way to strengthen and broaden the SUA Convention and Protocol.[10]

The U.S. Coast Guard initially dealt with security issues for large passenger vessels embarking passengers in the United States through voluntary arrangements with the vessel operators. In 1996, though, the agency promulgated an interim rule establishing security requirements for large passenger vessels and the terminals from which they embarked and disembarked passengers in the United States.[11] The regulations, which apply to most passenger vessels over 100 gross tons carrying more than 12 passengers for hire on voyages lasting over 24 hours and that transit the high seas, largely incorporate the provisions of MSC Circular 443.[12]

RESPONSES FOLLOWING 9-11 TERRORIST ATTACKS

Following the horrific terrorist attacks in New York, Washington, D.C., and Pennsylvania on 9-11, the response to the threat of maritime terrorism accelerated dramatically.

The IMO Assembly adopted a resolution calling for review and enhancement of measures and procedures to prevent acts of terrorism threatening the security of passengers and crews and the safety of ships.[13] After months of negotiation, state parties to the International Convention on the Safety of Life at Sea (SOLAS Convention) adopted the International Ship and Port Facility Security (ISPS) Code.[14] The ISPS Code and related amendments to the SOLAS Convention mandated the state parties to require security plans and enhanced security measures for covered ships engaged in international commerce and the port facilities servicing the covered ships. The ISPS Code came into effect on July 1, 2004. The vast majority of covered ships had their security plans in place by the time the new requirements came into effect. The port facilities seem to have been somewhat less successful in achieving a high level of compliance, but progress continues.

In addition to requiring ship and port facility security plans, amendments to the SOLAS Convention accelerated installation of the automatic identification system (AIS)[15] and mandated installation of a ship security alert system;[16] maintenance of a continuous synopsis record (CSR),[17] and visibly marking the ship with its identification number.[18]

The AIS was originally conceived and developed as a safety measure and its use as a security tool has met with mixed success. While it provides the name and other relevant information regarding a ship on the receiving radar, that information is only as valid as the transmission. The vast majority of information transmitted by the AIS is input or controlled by the transmitting ship. When AIS was strictly a safety tool, there was no incentive to transmit incorrect data. Now that AIS is being used as a security tool, the ability to intentionally transmit incorrect data becomes a problem. Further, experience indicates that, due to installation problems and lack of training, many AIS transceivers are routinely sending incorrect or outdated information.[19] In the United States, there is a legal dispute regarding ownership of the radio-spectrum frequency used by AIS. The Federal Communications Commission (FCC) some years ago sold the frequency to a private entity that is using it for maritime radio communications. The private entity and the federal government are now in litigation over rights to the frequency.[20]

Following promulgation of the ISPS Code in December 2002, the IMO issued various documents explaining and clarifying the Code and related maritime security issues. A code of practice on security in ports was developed by a tripartite meeting of experts on security, safety, and health in ports, under the sponsorship of the IMO and the International Labor Organization (ILO).[21] Model courses for training the Company Security Officer (CSO), the Ship Security Officer (SSO), and the Port Facility Security Officer (PFSO) were developed and promulgated. Contracting governments were advised what information the IMO required in order to better implement the ISPS Code and other amendments to the SOLAS Convention.[22] A number of circulars were issued on maritime security topics.[23] Overall, implementation of the international maritime security measures was accomplished with less difficulty than many had anticipated.[24] The U.S. Coast Guard Port State Control (PSC) program reports that during the first six months that the ISPS Code was in effect (through December 2004), the agency detained 74 foreign ships for noncompliance, denied entry to six foreign ships, and expelled 14 foreign ships from U.S. ports for noncompliance with the ISPS Code. Other nations have been less exacting in their enforcement of the ISPS Code, with substantially fewer control measures taken against foreign ships.[25]

U.S. MARITIME SECURITY PROVISIONS

The major piece of maritime security legislation enacted subsequent to the terrorist attacks of 9-11 was the Maritime Transportation Security Act of 2002 (MTSA).[26] Congress enacted various other bills relating to homeland security in general that impacted in some degree maritime security.[27]

Following enactment of the MTSA, the U.S. Coast Guard promulgated a series of maritime security regulations, first as interim rules[28] and then as final rules.[29] Under the MTSA and the maritime security regulations, vessels and port facilities had to prepare security plans and submit them to the Coast Guard for review and approval not later than December 31, 2003. The security plans had to be implemented not later than July 1, 2004. Overall, implementation of the new maritime security regime by U.S. ships and port facilities went well, with few instances of noncompliance.[30]

The MTSA also directed the Secretary of Homeland Security to establish a National Maritime Security Advisory Committee.[31] The committee will advise the Secretary and the Coast Guard on matters relating to national maritime security.[32] The National Committee was recently constituted and has held its first meeting.[33] The MTSA also authorized establishment of Area Maritime Security Committees.[34] These area committees have been established in each USCG Captain of the Port (COTP) Zone.

Using its preexisting authority under the Ports and Waterways Safety Act,[35] the Coast Guard promulgated a regulation requiring vessels calling at U.S. ports to submit their advance notice of arrival (ANOA) at least 96 hours prior to arrival.[36] The information to be provided in the ANOA was also made more extensive and detailed.[37] The Coast Guard has adopted a policy of strict enforcement of the

ANOA requirement. Vessels submitting an incomplete or inaccurate ANOA can expect to be denied entry into U.S. waters until 96 hours after the ANOA is correctly submitted. Recently, the electronic ANOA submittal process was modified so that a proper electronic submittal will satisfy requirements of the Coast Guard and basic reporting requirements of Customs and Border Protection (CBP).[38]

The Customs Service (recently reconstituted and renamed U.S. Customs and Border Protection—CBP) tightened its inspection regime for cargoes coming to the United States. It offered a somewhat expedited inspection regime for importers and related parties (including carriers) that voluntarily participate in its Customs-Trade Partnership Against Terrorism (C-TPAT). Under the C-TPAT program, the participant conducts a comprehensive self-assessment of its supply chain security and implements a security program in accordance with C-TPAT guidelines.[39]

In another nonregulatory move, the CBP developed arrangements with its counterpart agencies at a number of foreign ports to identify containerized cargo bound for the United States that should be subjected to additional scrutiny prior to loading on a ship in the foreign port. The Container Security Initiative (CSI) is now operational in more than 35 foreign ports and continues to expand.[40] In an inducement for the foreign nation and individual foreign port to participate in the CSI program, CBP provides cargoes going through the screening with expedited processing upon arrival in the United States.[41]

As a corollary to the CSI program, the CBP promulgated a regulation requiring carriers to present to the agency detailed information regarding cargoes to be carried to the United States. The information has to be provided at least 24 hours prior to loading of the cargo on the ship in the foreign port, hence the program was originally called the "24-hour Rule."[42] A modification of the program required that the information be submitted electronically via the Automated Manifest System (AMS).[43] Further, ships are also required to electronically submit manifests of passengers and crew prior to arrival.[44]

Immediately following the terrorist attacks of 9-11, the Immigration and Naturalization Service (INS)—since reconstituted and renamed Immigration and Customs Enforcement (ICE)—enhanced its enforcement of entry controls into the United States. Nonimmigrant foreign seamen on ships calling in U.S. ports had previously been allowed to go on shore leave by means of a waiver of the U.S. visa requirement.[45] INS headquarters issued a directive to severely restrict such shore leave for nonimmigrant foreign seamen who did not possess both a passport and a U.S. visa.[46] The agency also instituted a program requiring some ships with some foreign crewmembers to hire guard service to provide a visible deterrent against crewmembers who might attempt to go ashore illegally. The U.S. Department of State then revoked its long-standing program of allowing shipowners to obtain a single "crew list visa" for the entire crew and now requires each foreign crewmember to obtain his or her personal visa.[47]

The Coast Guard wrote both its interim regulations and its final regulations so as to be consistent with the international standard established by the ISPS Code and other amendments to the SOLAS Convention. It did this by exempting from the strictures of the Vessel Security Plan requirements foreign ships that are subject to the SOLAS Convention and have onboard a valid International Ship Security Certificate.[48] The Coast Guard has emphatically stated that it will use its port state control program to require full compliance by such ships with all applicable international security requirements.[49] At the same time, the agency has stated that it does not want these foreign ships to submit security plans to it for review.[50] The agency stated in an open letter to the marine industry that owners and operators of foreign vessels subject to SOLAS and ISPS are not required to submit Vessel Security Plans to the U.S. Coast Guard for approval.[51]

DECLARATION OF SECURITY

Ships and port facilities impacted by either the International Ship and Port Facility Security (ISPS) Code or the U.S. Maritime Transportation Security Act (MTSA) or both are becoming intimately familiar with the Declaration of Security. But, like so many other aspects of the new maritime security regime, this process involves a significant learning curve for all involved—the ship, the port facility, and the regulators/enforcers.

Declaration of Security (DoS) is defined by the Safety of Life at Sea (SOLAS) Convention as "an agreement reached between a ship and either a port facility or another ship with which it interfaces, specifying the security measures each will implement."[52] Maritime security regulations promulgated by the U.S. Coast Guard are more specific and provide that Declaration of Security (DoS) means:

> An agreement executed between the responsible Vessel and Facility Security Officer, or between Vessel Security Officers in the case of a vessel-to-vessel activity, that provides a means for ensuring that all shared security concerns are properly addressed and security will remain in place throughout the time a vessel is moored to the facility or for the duration of the vessel-to-vessel activity, respectively.[53]

Review of the form recommended in the ISPS Code for document-ing the Declaration of Security between a ship and a port facility re-veals that, after identifying the ship and port facility involved, it provides for: (1) the period of validity of the DoS; (2) the activities cov-ered by the DoS (i.e., mooring, loading or discharging cargo, bunker-ing, etc.); (3) the security levels of the ship and port facility; and (4) the affixing of the initials of the Ship Security Officer and the Port Facility Security Officer for a variety of specific activities indicating that each agrees that the relevant activity will be done in accordance with the relevant approved security plan.[54] Among the specific activities ad-dressed on the Declaration of Security form are monitoring restricted areas to ensure that only authorized personnel have access; handling of cargo; delivery of ship's stores; handling of unaccompanied baggage; controlling the embarkation of persons and their effects; and ensuring that security communication is readily available between the ship and the port facility. The Declaration of Security should be completed in English, French, or Spanish or in a language common to both the port facility and the ship or the ships, as applicable.[55] U.S. Coast Guard maritime security regulations provide that the Declaration of Secu-rity for U.S. ships and port facilities must include at least the informa-tion provided for in the ISPS Code recommended form.[56]

Use of the Declaration of Security may either be mandated by a contracting government[57] or requested by a ship.[58] Reasons why a ship may request completion of a Declaration of Security include: (a) the ship is operating at a higher security level than the port facility or another ship with which it is interfacing;[59] (b) there has been a se-curity threat or a security incident involving the ship or the port fa-cility; or (c) the ship is at a port facility that is not required to have and implement an approved port facility security plan. A change in security levels by either the ship or the port facility or both may ne-cessitate completion of a new or revised Declaration of Security.[60] Retention periods for completed Declaration of Security forms are to be specified for port facilities by their contracting governments and for ships by their administrations.[61]

There is one potentially significant lacuna with regard to use of the recommended Declaration of Security form. While the Declaration of Security is intended to be used when a ship calls at a port facility that is not required to have and implement an approved port facility security plan and (presumably) when the ship calls at a port facility that does not have an approved port facility security plan even though it is required to under the ISPS Code, there is no obvious place on the DoS form to indicate this situation. In this turn of events, the port fa-cility probably has no security officer and no one at the port facility is likely to be willing to sign or initial the DoS form. There is enough blank space on the form, though, for the Ship Security Officer to fully document the situation, including the additional security measures implemented by the ship to inoculate itself from the lack of documented security at the port facility. It is strongly recommended that the Ship Security Officer clearly document on the Declaration of Security form and in the ship's log the additional security measures implemented by the ship during the call at the noncompliant port facility.

The ISPS Code, in a somewhat backhand approach, states that an example of possible clear grounds for a port state to exercise control measures over a ship subject to the ISPS Code is if the ship embarked persons or loaded stores or goods at a port facility or from another source where the port facility or other source was either not required to comply with the ISPS Code or was in violation of the ISPS Code and the ship had not taken appropriate, special, or additional security measures or had not maintained appropriate security procedures.[62] The implication, which should have been more forcefully stated, is that a ship that calls at a noncompliant port facility can inoculate itself against later difficulties if it institutes appropriate additional security measures (such as going to MARSEC 2) and fully documents its actions. The U.S. Coast Guard maritime security regulations provide: "Control and compliance measures under this section may be imposed on a vessel when it has called on a facility or at a port that does not maintain adequate security measures to ensure that the level of security to be achieved by this subchapter has not been compromised."[63] It appears that the above provision, if read literally, makes no allowance for the ship implementing additional security measures (as allowed under the ISPS Code) to inoculate itself. Efforts by the U.S. Coast Guard to enforce strictly this provision without making such allowance would constitute a clear difference with international approach, as noted above, and would appear to serve no useful purpose. There are indications that the Coast Guard is in the process of either modifying this language or issuing guidance intended to soften the edges of this mandate.

Procedures for interfacing with port facility security activities are to be included in the Ship Security Plan.[64] Likewise, procedures for interfacing with ship security activities are to be included in the port facility security plan.[65] Drills for both shipboard and port facility personnel should be conducted at appropriate intervals taking into account, among other things, for the ships—the port facilities visited by the ships and for the port facilities—the type of ship the port facility is serving.[66]

In the United States, the Coast Guard requires that each vessel and port facility owner or operator ensure procedures are established for requesting a DoS and for handling DoS requests from the interfacing entity.[67] A DoS must be completed with regard to any interface involving a cruise ship or a manned vessel carrying Certain Dangerous Cargoes in bulk.[68] For interfaces involving a cruise ship or a manned vessel carrying Certain Dangerous Cargoes in bulk, the security needs and procedures are to be coordinated and agreed prior to arrival and the DoS is to be signed by both the ship and the port facility or another vessel prior to commencement of passenger embarkation/disembarkation or cargo operations. At Maritime Security (MARSEC) levels 2 or 3, the security needs and procedures are to be coordinated and agreed prior to arrival, and the DoS is to be signed by both the ship and the port facility or another vessel for all interfaces involving a manned vessel and either a port facility or another vessel.[69] The port facility owner or operator must ensure that, in the event of a change in the MARSEC level, any ships moored at the facility and any ships scheduled to arrive within 96 hours are promptly notified of the change and that the Declarations of Security are revised as necessary.[70]

In the United States, a continuing DoS may be used for a ship that frequently interfaces with the same facility. The effective period of a continuing DoS at MARSEC level 1 may not exceed 90 days. The effective period of a continuing DoS at MARSEC level 2 may not exceed 30 days. A continuing DoS may not be used during MARSEC level 3. When the MARSEC level increases beyond that provided for in the continuing DoS, it becomes void and a new DoS must be signed and implemented.[71]

Failure of the ship to complete a Declaration of Security when it has interfaced with a port facility or other ship subject to, but in violation of, the ISPS Code or Chapter XI-2 of the SOLAS Convention constitutes clear grounds for a port state control official of a contracting government to exercise control measures with regard to the ship.[72] Proper use of the Declaration of Security is important, not only as a means of coordinating security arrangements between ships and port facilities, but also as a method of documenting appropriate implementation of the ISPS Code and related maritime security requirements. This becomes crucial when a ship calls at a port facility that is not in full compliance with the ISPS Code and does not have an approved security plan. A ship calling at such a port facility must not only institute additional security measures (as provided for in the ISPS Code and its Ship Security Plan), but it must also be able to demonstrate to port state control officials at subsequent port calls that it took the appropriate steps.[73] The way to demonstrate this full compliance with the ISPS Code is to complete and retain onboard a Declaration of Security fully documenting the ship's security measures while at this noncompliant port facility.[74]

PORT STATE CONTROL MEASURES

Port state control is the process by which a nation exercises limited authority over a foreign vessel in its waters. The purpose of this limited exercise of authority is to determine whether the foreign vessel is in substantial compliance with applicable international requirements. The foreign vessel's certificates are to be accepted unless there are clear grounds for believing that the condition of the vessel or its equipment does not correspond substantially with the particulars of any certificates. If the vessel's certificates are invalid or expired or if the condition of the vessel or its equipment do not substantially correspond with the certificate's particulars, the port state control officer is authorized to exercise control measures with regard to the vessel.[75]

The usual control measures consist of: requiring corrective action prior to returning to that nation; requiring the vessel to proceed elsewhere for repairs; denying entry into port; detaining the vessel; or monitoring the vessel's operations while in port.[76]

The 2002 amendments to the SOLAS Convention include specific control and compliance measures supplementary to the general port state control provisions.[77] For ships in the port of a State Party, control measures are as follows: "inspection of the ship, delaying the ship, detention of the ship, restriction of operations, including movement within the port, or expulsion of the ship from the port."[78] Such control measures may additionally or alternatively include other lesser administrative or corrective measures.[79]

For ships intending to enter the port of a State Party, the State Party may require the ship to provide information (e.g., an advance notice of arrival) to ensure that the ship is in compliance with applicable maritime security requirements.[80] If the State Party has clear grounds for believing that the ship is not in compliance with those requirements, the State Party may: (1) require rectification of the noncompliance; (2) require that the ship proceed to a specified location in the territorial sea or internal waters of the State Party; (3) inspect the ship in waters of the State Party; or (4) deny entry into the port.[81]

In the event that control measures are instituted, the port state control official is to notify the flag administration of the ship, specifying the control measures imposed and the reasons thereof.[82] When entry into port has been denied or the ship has been expelled from port, the State Party should communicate appropriate facts to the port state control officials of the next appropriate ports of call.[83] Denial of entry or expulsion from port should only be imposed when the State Party has clear grounds to believe that the ship poses an immediate threat to the security or safety of persons, or of ships or other property and there are no other appropriate means for removing that threat.[84]

In the first six months that the maritime security regulations have been in effect (July 1–December 31, 2004), the U.S. Coast Guard has taken the following security control actions: 74 detentions; 6 denials of entry; and 14 expulsions from port—for a total of 94 such actions.[85] During this same period, records of the Paris Memorandum of Understanding (MOU) on Port State Control indicate that 77 ships were detained for reasons that included noncompliance with maritime security requirements.[86] Records of the Tokyo MOU are less specific and do not lend themselves to easily determining whether a control measure was undertaken for noncompliance with maritime security requirements as opposed to maritime safety requirements.

One practical problem with the port state control program for maritime security is that, for security reasons, port state control officials (particularly the U.S. Coast Guard) frequently fail to disclose the specific rationale for imposing a control measure. This lack of information sometimes makes it difficult for affected private parties to allocate added costs associated with the control measure. With daily hire rates for modern ships generally exceeding $25,000 per day, cost allocation can be an important issue.

POTENTIAL CIVIL LIABILITY

If anyone thinks that a shipowner or operator will never be held liable for damages ensuing from a terrorist attack, your attention is invited not to the terrorist attack on the French tanker *Limburg* in Yemen on October 6, 2002, but to the bombing of Pan Am flight 103 over Lockerbie, Scotland, on December 21, 1988. In subsequent civil litigation, Pan American Airlines was found liable for the wrongful death of the passengers and was not allowed to limit its liability.[87] The airline, which subsequently went into bankruptcy and ceased operations, was found to have had an inadequate system for examining luggage at designated "extraordinary security" airports.[88] In other words, it failed to meet the regulatory and industry standards prevailing at that time. Massive civil liability and, ultimately, bankruptcy ensued.[89] This result was avoidable then and is avoidable now.

The International Maritime Organization (IMO) and the United States have developed and imposed maritime security requirements at a rapid pace. Shipowners and operators have been required to install new equipment, perform security assessments, assign security personnel, and implement security plans without fully understanding what is expected. Training has been mandated for numerous persons, while few accredited institutions offer the training required.

What happens if something goes wrong? Who will be held responsible if there is a *Limburg* incident or worse in Europe or North America?

Fortunately, the likelihood of such an event is slim. But, it is not outside the realm of possibility. The concern, though, is the potential liability of the owner, operator, and others for damages that might result from what (in the United States) is referred to as a "transportation security incident."

It should be assumed that, unlike oil spills in countries like the United States and the United Kingdom, being the subject of a transportation security incident is not (at least yet) a strict liability situation. Those attempting to recover damages will have to demonstrate some degree of negligence or other culpable conduct. The extent of that showing, though, will vary from jurisdiction to jurisdiction. For instance, under U.S. maritime law, if the injured party can show that the incident was caused in part by violation of a federal safety law or regulation, then the burden shifts to the shipowner or operator to prove that the violation could not have caused the loss.[90] In many other jurisdictions and other situations, a showing of simple negligence is sufficient to establish liability.

Negligence may be established, in part, through a showing that the party has not conformed to the normal standard of care prevailing in the trade. Government regulations and industry guidelines are commonly used to establish the standard of care expected in the trade.

With regard to maritime security, the regulations and guidelines are shifting rapidly. Failure to keep pace could lead to a finding of civil liability in the event of a maritime terrorist attack.

Owners and operators who fail to install all the required and recommended security equipment; develop and implement the required security programs; and provide appropriate security training for their personnel face the possibility of being held liable if there is an incident that "might possibly" have been avoided if the equipment were installed, the programs were in place, and the training had been provided.

Litigation relating to the terrorist attacks of 9-11 is ongoing and is not expected to conclude for some time. Persons injured or damaged by those terrorist attacks, including survivors, decedent representatives, family members, and property owners brought suit against the airlines, airport security companies, airport operators, the airplane manufacturer, and the owners and operators of the World Trade Center, alleging negligence. Defendants moved to dismiss, asserting, among other things, that they owed no duty to these plaintiffs and that they could not reasonably have anticipated that terrorists would hijack airplanes and crash them into buildings. The court ruled that defendants owed duties to the plaintiffs sufficient to withstand motions to dismiss.[91] The defendants were in positions to protect the plaintiffs from harm.[92] The defendants knew that terrorists had engaged in suicide missions and that they had hijacked airplanes in the past. While the defendants may not have been able to anticipate this particular attack, they had an obligation to institute measures to reasonably deter terrorist attacks.[93]

This decision is important because it provides guidance regarding how a future court might deal with liability for terrorism in the maritime sector. Owners and operators of ships and others in the maritime industry, such as facility operators, should carefully review their security situation. There were few legal requirements relating to security for the defendants at the time of the attacks, yet the court found sufficient cause for the claims to go forward. As noted above, terrorists have already made a number of attacks in the maritime arena. The goal of a ship or facility owner or operator is not to be a target—or the subject of a "transportation security incident." In light of these events, two lessons can be learned: (1) compliance with all applicable legal requirements is necessary, but not necessarily sufficient; and (2) virtually anything is now considered foreseeable.

CONCLUSION

The case law teaches us that it is negligence to fail to take reasonable steps to avoid those hazards that can be anticipated. The dangers of a terrorist attack are all too real, as may be seen from the maritime terrorist attacks that have occurred to date, as noted above. Significant, but not total, reliance can be placed on governments to deter terrorism. As proven by the successful attacks on the USS *Cole* and the oil tanker *Limburg,* shipowners and operators and Masters must still exercise caution.[94] Terrorists are capable of lengthy and detailed planning and preparation.[95] Potential threats in the maritime sector, particularly with respect to containerized cargo, are manifest.[96] In order to limit legal exposure and, more importantly, deter a terrorist attack upon your ship or port facility, it is incumbent on ship and port facility owners and operators to learn from history and develop and implement a robust security plan that meets, at a minimum, all applicable legal requirements and industry standards and that anticipates and adopts appropriate measures with regard to all reasonably foreseeable methods of attack.

NOTES

1. Piracy consists of, among other things, "any illegal acts of violence or detention, or any act of depredation, *committed for private ends* by the crew or the passengers of a private ship." 1982 United Nations Convention on the Law of the Sea (UNCLOS Convention), Article 101 (emphasis added).

2. See *Terrorism, the Future, and U.S. Foreign Policy,* Congressional Research Service (June 21, 2002).

3. See Beth Day, *Passage Perilous—The Stormy Saga of the* Santa Maria (G. P. Putnam's Sons, New York, 1962). For a totally different perspective, see the book written by the rebel leader, Henrique Galvao, Santa Maria: *My Crusade for Portugal* (World Publishing Co., Cleveland, 1961). Galvao considered the death of the third mate unfortunate and stated: "In any case it was this officer, who fell nobly in the fulfillment of his duty—opposed as it was to our duty—who provoked the clash. All of us deplored the fate of this brave man who tried to defend his position and his ship and who by his conduct, in contrast to the cowardice of his comrades, was certainly the one who deserved to live." (page 129).

4. See Antonio Cassese, *Terrorism, Politics and Law* (Princeton University Press, Princeton, NJ, 1989).

5. Statement of President Clinton on Middle East Situation and Incident on USS *Cole* in Yemen (October 12, 2000); U.S. Navy Press Release, *USS Cole (DDG 67) returns to the Fleet* (April 19, 2002).

6. "Boat Pieces Found on Damaged Tanker," *Washington Post,* October 11, 2002; "Preliminary Investigation Indicates Oil Tanker Was Attacked," *New York Times,* October 11, 2002; "France says TNT Traces Found on Gutted Yemen Tanker," *Reuters,* October 11, 2002; "France: Punish Those in Tanker Blast," *Associated Press,* October 11, 2002; "Bomb blast fallout starts to hit Yemen," *Lloyd's List,* October 17, 2002; "Al-Qaeda suspect admits role in *Limburg,*" *Lloyd's List,* January 21, 2003.

7. MSC Circ. 443.

8. 1992 United Nations Treaty Series 221. The diplomatic conference was concluded in Rome on March 10, 1988. The Convention and Protocol both entered into force for parties on March 1, 1992, and entered into force for the United States on March 6, 1995.

9. The United States established these offenses as domestic crimes in 1994. Pub.L. 103-322, title VI, § 60019(a), 108 Stat. 1975–77 (September 13, 1994), codified at 18 U.S. Code §§ 2280–2281.

10. See "Provisional Agenda of the 88th Session of the IMO Legal Committee," held in London on April 19–23, 2004, LEG 88/1 (4 November 2003).

11. Interim rule with request for comments—*Security for Passenger Vessels and Passenger Terminals,* 61 Fed. Reg. 37648 (July 18, 1996). The regulations are codified at 33 CFR Part 120.

12. 33 CFR § 120.120(b).

13. Resolution A.924(22), adopted November 20, 2001.

14. The ISPS Code and related maritime security measures were adopted as amendments to the Safety of Life at Sea (SOLAS) Convention at a Diplomatic Conference of Contracting Governments to the SOLAS Convention (London, December 9–13, 2002).

15. SOLAS Regulation V/19, as amended.

16. SOLAS Regulation XI-2/6. See also, MSC Circ. 1072, "Guidance on provision of ship security alert systems" (6/26/03).

17. SOLAS Regulation XI-2/5. See also, IMO Resolution A.959(23), *Format and guidelines for the maintenance of the Continuous Synopsis Record (CSR),* adopted December 5, 2003. The CSR is a continuing document showing ownership, operation, and similar matters related to the ship that is intended to provide port state control officers with a concise picture of the ship's legal situation currently and in the past.

18. SOLAS Regulation XI-2/3, as amended.

19. See generally the following IMO documents: SN Circ. 222, "Guidelines for the on board operational use of shipborne automatic identification systems (AIS)" (9/20/02); SN Circ. 227, "Guidelines for the installation of a shipborne automatic identification system (AIS)" (1/6/03); SN Circ. 244, "Guidance on the use of the UN/LOCODE in the destination field in AIS messages" (12/15/04); SN Circ. 245, "Amendments to the guidelines for the installation of a shipborne automatic identification system (AIS)" (12/15/04).
20. See *MariTEL, Inc. v. Collins,* Memorandum Opinion, Civil Action No. 03-2418 (RMU) (D.D.C., August 3, 2004).
21. MESSHP/2003/14 (Geneva, 2003).
22. "Information required from SOLAS Contracting Governments under the provisions of SOLAS regulation XI-2/13," Circular letter No. 2514 (12/8/03).
23. These Circulars included the following: "Early implementation of the special measures to enhance maritime security," MSC Circ. 1067 (2/28/03); "Guidance on provision of ship security alert systems," MSC Circ. 1072 (6/26/03); "Directives for maritime rescue coordination centers (MRCCs) on acts of violence against ships," MSC Circ. 1073 (6/10/03); "Interim guidelines for the authorization of recognized security organizations acting on behalf of the administration and/or designated authority of a contracting government," MSC Circ. 1074 (6/10/03); "Guidance relating to the implementation of SOLAS Chapter XI-2 and the ISPS Code," MSC Circ. 1097 (6/6/03); "Implementation of SOLAS Chapter XI-2 and the ISPS Code," MSC Circ. 1104 (1/15/04); "Implementation of SOLAS Chapter XI-2 and the ISPS Code to port facilities," MSC Circ. 1106 (3/29/04); "Matters related to SOLAS Regulations XI-2/6 and XI-2/7," MSC Circ. 1110 (6/7/04); "Guidance relating to the implementation of SOLAS Chapter XI-2 and the ISPS Code," MSC Circ. 1111 (6/7/04); "Shore leave and access to ships under the ISPS Code," MSC Circ. 1112 (6/7/04); "Guidance to port state control officers on the non-security related elements of the 2002 SOLAS amendments," MSC Circ. 1113 (6/7/04). The title of MSC Circ. 1113 is misleading in that it actually refers to security-related elements of the 2002 SOLAS amendments that were not included in the ISPS Code, such as the automatic identification system (AIS), the ship's identification number, and the continuous synopsis record (CSR).
24. See IMO Press Release (July 1, 2004), "Secretary-General Mitropoulos pays tribute to the efforts made to implement the ISPS Code"; IMO Press Release (August 6, 2004), "Security compliance shows continued improvement."
25. Control and compliance measures regarding international maritime security are addressed at SOLAS Regulation XI/9. Control measures in general are addressed at SOLAS Regulation I/19.
26. Pub.L. 107-295, 116 Stat. 2064 (November 25, 2002). Significant portions of this legislation are codified at 33 U.S.C. §§ 70101–70117.
27. These additional pieces of legislation include: *Uniting and Strengthening America by Providing Appropriate Tools Required to Intercept and Obstruct Terrorism (USA PATRIOT) Act of 2001,* Pub.L. 107-56, 115 Stat. 272 (October 26, 2001); *Aviation and Transportation Security Act,* Pub.L. 107-71, 115 Stat. 597 (November 19, 2001); *Enhanced Border Security and Visa Entry Reform Act of 2002,* Pub.L. 107-173, 116 Stat. 543 (May 14, 2002); *Public Health Security and Bioterrorism Preparedness and Response Act of 2002,* Pub.L. 107-188, 116 Stat. 594 (June 12, 2002); *Terrorist Bombings Convention Implementation Act of 2002,* Pub.L. 107-197, 116 Stat. 721 (June 25, 2002); *Homeland Security Act of 2002,* Pub.L. 107-296, 116 Stat. 2135 (November 25, 2002); and *Terrorism Risk Insurance Act of 2002,* Pub.L. 107-297, 116 Stat. 2322 (November 26, 2002).

28. *Implementation of National Maritime Security Initiatives,* 68 Fed. Reg. 39240 (July 1, 2003); *Area Maritime Security,* 68 Fed. Reg. 39284 (July 1, 2003); *Vessel Security,* 68 Fed. Reg. 39292 (July 1, 2003); *Facility Security,* 68 Fed. Reg. 39315 (July 1, 2003); *Outer Continental Shelf Facility Security,* 68 Fed. Reg. 39338 (July 1, 2003); *Automatic Identification System Vessel Carriage Requirement,* 68 Fed. Reg. 39353 (July 1, 2003). The Coast Guard conducted a series of public meetings prior to development of its interim regulations. *See Notice of meetings and request for comments, Maritime Security,* 67 Fed. Reg. 79742 (December 30, 2002).

29. *Implementation of National Maritime Security Initiatives,* 68 Fed. Reg. 60448 (October 22, 2003); *Area Maritime Security,* 68 Fed. Reg. 60472 (October 22, 2003); *Vessel Security,* 68 Fed. Reg. 60483 (October 22, 2003); *Facility Security,* 68 Fed. Reg. 60515 (October 22, 2003); *Outer Continental Shelf Facility Security,* 68 Fed. Reg. 60545 (October 22, 2003); *Automatic Identification System Vessel Carriage Requirement,* 68 Fed. Reg. 60559 (October 22, 2003).

30. USCG Press Release, "Coast Guard Concludes First Week Enforcing New Security Requirements" (July 8, 2004). The press release reported that only 33 domestic vessels and 18 domestic port facilities were restricted or suspended from conducting certain operations for failing to comply with the new maritime security requirements.

31. 46 U.S.C. § 70112(a)(1), as promulgated by the MTSA, Pub.L. 107-295, § 102, 116 Stat. 2081 (November 25, 2002).

32. See *Notice of committee establishment and request for applications,* 68 Fed. Reg. 40991 (July 9, 2003).

33. See USCG Press Release, "Department of Homeland Security announces Maritime Security Advisory Committee members" (January 6, 2005).

34. 46 U.S.C. § 70112(a)(2), as promulgated by the MTSA, Pub.L. 107-295, § 102, 116 Stat. 2081 (November 25, 2002).

35. The Secretary "may require the receipt of prearrival messages from any vessel, destined for a port or place subject to the jurisdiction of the United States, in sufficient time to permit advance vessel traffic planning prior to port entry, which shall include any information which is not already a matter of record and which the Secretary determines necessary for the control of the vessel and the safety of the port or the marine environment." 33 U.S.C. § 1223(a)(5).

36. A temporary rule was promulgated soon after the terrorist attack. 66 Fed. Reg. 50565 (October 4, 2001). A final rule was promulgated later. 68 Fed. Reg. 9537 (February 28, 2003). Prior to October 2001, the ANOA was to be submitted 24 hours prior to arrival and was much less extensive.

37. Some of the new information required in the ANOA that was not required previously includes: the last five ports or places visited; the names of the specific receiving facilities the ship will be calling at in each U.S. port; the name and telephone number of a 24-hour point of contact; a general description of the nondangerous cargo; a detailed description of any dangerous cargo; and a complete and detailed listing of all persons onboard. 33 CFR § 160.207.

38. See Department of Homeland Security Press Release, "Homeland Security agencies improve customer service by combining maritime industry data submission requirements" (February 1, 2005).

39. See *C-TPAT Fact Sheet and Frequently Asked Questions* (August 4, 2004).

40. See, for example, CBP Press Release, "U.S. Customs and Border Protection announces that ports of Nagoya and Kobe become latest Container Security Initiative (CSI) ports to go operational" (August 2, 2004).

41. For additional information about this program, see *CSI in Brief,* (August 4, 2004).

42. Final rule, *Presentation of Vessel Cargo Declaration to Customs Before Cargo is Laden Aboard Vessel at Foreign Port for Transport to the United States,* 67 Fed. Reg. 66318 (October 31, 2002).
43. Final rule, *Required Advance Electronic Presentation of Cargo Information,* 68 Fed. Reg. 68140 (December 5, 2003). This rule also requires carriers to post an International Carrier Bond and to use a Standard Carrier Alpha Code, among other things.
44. Final Rule, *Electronic Transmission of Passenger and Crew Manifests for Vessels and Aircraft,* 70 Fed. Reg. 17819 (April 7, 2005).
45. 8 CFR § 252.1(d).
46. Unfortunately, the directive was not widely distributed to the INS field offices. See Department of Justice, Office of the Inspector General Report, *A Review of the Norfolk Ship Jumping Incident* (December 2002).
47. Interim Rule, *Elimination of Crew List Visas,* 69 Fed. Reg. 12797 (March 18, 2004). This interim rule came into effect on June 16, 2004. It was then followed by the Final Rule, *Elimination of Crew List Visas,* 69 Fed. Reg. 43515 (July 21, 2004). Contemporaneously, the State Department instituted a program requiring all applicants (with minor exceptions not applicable here) to undergo a personal interview with a U.S. consular official prior to receiving a U.S. visa. Interim Rule, *Visas; Personal Appearance,* 68 Fed. Reg. 40127 (July 7, 2003). This rule came into effect on August 1, 2003.
48. 33 CFR § 104.105(c), as promulgated at 68 Fed. Reg. 39303 (July 1, 2003). This provision was modified slightly in the final rule promulgated at 68 Fed. Reg. 60512-13 (October 22, 2003).
49. In its discussion of the vessel security regulations, the Coast Guard stated:

> If vessels do not meet our security requirements, we have the power to prevent those vessels from entering the U.S., and we will not hesitate to use that power in appropriate cases. The Port State Control measures will include tracking the performance of all owners, operators, flag administrations, RSOs [recognized security organizations], charterers, and port facilities. Noncompliance will subject the vessel to a range of control and compliance measures, which could include denial of entry into port or significant delay. A vessel's or foreign port facility's history of compliance, or lack thereof, or security incidents involving a vessel or port facility will be important factors in determining what actions are deemed appropriate by the Coast Guard to ensure that maritime security is preserved.

68 Fed. Reg. at 60489 (October 22, 2003).
50. 68 Fed. Reg. at 60487 and 60488 (October 22, 2003).
51. Open letter 5500/MTSA from RADM T. H. Gilmour, Assistant Commandant for Marine Safety, Security, and Environmental Protection (9/30/03).
52. SOLAS Regulation XI-2/1.1.15.33 CFR § 101.105, as promulgated by Interim Rule, 68 Fed. Reg. 39278 (July 1, 2003).
53. 33 CFR § 101.105, as promulgated by Interim Rule, 68 Fed Reg. 39278 (July 1, 2003).
54. ISPS Code, Appendix 1 to Part B. Contracting governments are responsible for establishing the requirements for a Declaration of Security. ISPS Code, Part A, Regulation 4.3.6.
55. ISPS Code, Part B, Regulation 5.5.
56. 33 CFR § 101.505(b).
57. ISPS Code, Part A, Regulation 5.1. For example, U.S. Coast Guard regulations provide that the Captain of the Port (COTP) may require a DoS be completed during

periods of critical port operations or special marine events. 33 CFR § 101.505(d). Additional U.S.-unique requirements related to the Declaration of Security will be discussed below.

58. ISPS Code, Part A, Regulation 5.2.

59. In this regard, see ISPS Code, Part B, Regulation 4.12, which provides that the ship should never operate at a lower security level than the port facility with which it is interfacing.

60. ISPS Code, Part B, Regulation 5.4.2.

61. ISPS Code, Part A, Regulation 5.6 (for port facilities) and Regulation 5.7 (for ships). The U.S. Coast Guard, which for the United States serves as both the contracting government and the administration, requires that the DoS be retained by port facilities for at least 90 days after the end of its effective period [33 CFR § 105.225(b)(7)] and by U.S. ships for at least the last 10 DoSs used and, for continuing DoSs, at least 90 days after the end of its effective period [33 CFR § 104.235(b)(7)].

62. ISPS Code, Part B, Regulation 4.33.6 and Regulation 4.33.7. See also, ISPS Code, Part B, Regulation 9.51.4, stating that the Ship Security Plan should establish details of the procedures and security measures the ship should apply when it interfaces with a port or port facility that is not required to comply with the ISPS Code.

63. 33 CFR § 101.410(d).

64. ISPS Code, Part A, Regulation 9.4.10. Similarly, the U.S. Coast Guard requires that Vessel Security Plans include provisions relating to the Declaration of Security. 33 CFR § 104.405(a)(7).

65. ISPS Code, Part A, Regulation 16.3.7. Similarly, the U.S. Coast Guard requires that port facility plans include provisions relating to the Declaration of Security. 33 CFR § 105.405(a)(7).

66. For ships, ISPS Code, Part A, Regulation 13.4 and 33 CFR § 104.230(b)(2). For port facilities, ISPS Code, Part A, Regulation 18.3 and 33 CFR § 105.2209b)(2).

67. For ships, 33 CFR § 104.255(a). For port facilities, 33 CFR § 105.200(b)(6).

68. 33 CFR § 104.255(b) and § 105.245(b).

69. 33 CFR § 104.255(c) and (d) and § 105.245(d).

70. 33 CFR § 105.230(b)(1).

71. 33 CFR § 104.255(e) and § 105.245(e).

72. ISPS Code, Part B, Regulation 4.33.6.

73. See U.S. Coast Guard Port Security Advisory (2-05), dated May 20, 2005. Vessels that have visited a port in a country determined by the USCG to have not instituted adequate maritime security measures during the last five port calls of the vessel prior to entering the United States must have taken certain actions as a condition of entry into U.S. ports. These actions include implementation of Security level 2 while in that foreign port; guarding of all access points to the vessel while in the port; attempting to execute a Declaration of Security with the port facility; documenting all security measures in the ship's log; and reporting the actions taken to the USCG prior to arrival in the United States.

74. The IMO recently issued guidance stating, in part, that the Declaration of Security is intended to be used in exceptional cases and that ships should not request a Declaration in the absence of a specific security reason. MSC Circ. 1132— "Guidance relating to the implementation of SOLAS Chapter XI-2 and the ISPS Code" (12/14/04). The IMO recommendation should only be followed when port states such as the United States cease requiring that ships prove their continuing maintenance of security through production of Declarations of Security regarding previous port calls.

75. SOLAS Regulation I/19.

76. See *USCG Marine Safety Manual,* II.1.C.7.
77. SOLAS Regulation XI-2/9.
78. SOLAS Regulation XI-2/9.1.3.
79. *Ibid.*
80. SOLAS Regulation XI-2/9.2.1.
81. SOLAS Regulation XI-2/9.2.5. Prior to initiating these steps, the Master should be informed of the intentions of the State Party, allowing the Master to withdraw the intention to enter the port.
82. SOLAS Regulation XI-2/9.3.1. The appropriate recognized security organization (RSO) and the IMO are also to be notified when control measures have been imposed.
83. SOLAS Regulation XI-2/9.3.2.
84. SOLAS Regulation XI-2/9.3.3.
85. See USCG Monthly Summaries of all safety and security-related control actions for the months of July through December 2004.
86. See Paris MOU Lists of Detentions for the months of July through December 2004. See also Paris MOU press release, *Paris MOU Advisory Board announces results of security campaign* (December 12, 2004), reporting that during the first three months that the ISPS Code was in effect, Paris MOU nations conducted 4,681 examinations to verify compliance with the new security requirements and only 72 resulted in the ship's detention on security grounds.
87. See *In re Air Disaster at Lockerbie, Scotland on December 21, 1988,* 811 F.Supp. 84 (E.D.N.Y. 1992).
88. Security regulations then applicable required airlines to engage in the time-consuming and expensive process of directly matching passengers with their luggage prior to loading the luggage on the airplane at Frankfort, Germany. At trial, Pan Am alleged that it had obtained a waiver of this requirement from a senior official of the Federal Aviation Administration (FAA), but was unable to present convincing evidence of this waiver or the validity of the waiver, even if granted. *See* Susan & David Cohen, *Pam Am 103* (Signet Books, New York, NY, 2001, pages 49–50). For a litany of security breaches by Pan Am at its Frankfort facility as revealed by the subsequent FAA investigation, see Steven Emerson & Brian Duffy, *The Fall of Pan Am 103* (G. P. Putnam's Sons, New York, NY, 1990, pages 183–196).
89. See *In re Pan American Corporation,* 950 F.2d 839, 26 Collier Bankr. Cas.2d 20, Bankr. L. Rep. P 74,377 (2nd Cir. 1991).
90. "But when, as in this case, a ship at the time of a collision is in actual violation of a statutory rule intended to prevent collisions, it is no more than a reasonable presumption that the fault, if not the sole cause, was at least a contributory cause of the disaster. In such a case the burden rests upon the ship of showing not merely that her fault might not have been one of the causes, or that it probably was not, but that it could not have been. Such a rule is necessary to enforce obedience to the mandate of the statute." *The Pennsylvania,* 86 U.S. (19 Wall.) 125, 136 (1874).
91. See *In re Air Crash Disaster at Cove Neck,* 885 F. Supp. 434 (E.D.N.Y. 1995); *532 Madison Ave. Gourmet Foods, Inc. v. Finlanda Center, Inc.,* 750 N.E.2d 1097 (N.Y. 2001).
92. In *Stanford v. Kuwait Airways Corp.,* 89 F.3d 117 (2nd Cir., 1996), the court held that the airline had a duty to protect passengers on a connecting flight from the risk that terrorists would board the connecting flight from the airline's flight. In that case, suspicious-looking persons (who turned out to be terrorists) were allowed by defendant airline to board its December 3, 1984 flight from Beirut to Dubai. In Dubai, the terrorists transferred to a connecting flight bound for

Karachi. The terrorists hijacked this connecting flight and diverted the airplane to Tehran. While the airplane sat on the tarmac at the Tehran airport, the terrorists tortured and killed several U.S. passengers, including plaintiff's decedent. Evidence showed that the airline was aware of the terrorist risk and of the minimal security at its facility at the Beirut airport.

93. In this regard, the court stated:

> There have been many efforts by terrorists to hijack airplanes, and too many have been successful. The practice of terrorists to blow themselves up in order to kill as many people as possible has also been prevalent. Although there may have been no incidents before the ones of September 11, 2001 where terrorists combined both an airplane hijacking and a suicidal explosion, I am not able to say that the risk of crashes was not reasonably foreseeable to an airplane manufacturer.

94. After all, if suicide bombers in a speedboat can disable a warship, why shouldn't they be capable of doing significant damage to a merchant vessel?

95. See National Commission on Terrorist Attacks upon the United States, *The 9/11 Commission Report* (W.W. Norton & Co., New York, 2004). This report indicates that planning for the terrorist attacks of September 11, 2001 started as early as 1998.

96. See Stephen Flynn, *America the Vulnerable* (Harper Collins, New York, 2004).

FOUR

Threat Identification, Surveillance, and Response

When is the best time to stop terrorists? Simple answer, before they commit the crime. Given that, would it not follow that the earlier we stop them before they commit their crime, the easier the task would be. When is the earliest we can stop them? The best time to stop them is during their initial surveillance phase. We have come a long way in our society to encourage individuals to report potential surveillance. We have also implemented strict rules in regard to photos and access to what we consider potential targets. Public awareness in this area has increased dramatically since 9-11.

It is up to each of us to see that we continue this vigilance—you see on the sides of New York City buses, "If You See Something Say Something" as an advertisement. What this chapter is trying to convey is that simple.

OBJECTIVES OF TERRORIST SURVEILLANCE

The prime objective of terrorist surveillance is to gather information on a particular target. The type of information sought will depend on what type of operation is planned and who the target is. The operative will generally look for certain criteria. These criteria can be:

- Terrain of the target area
- Routine operations of the target
- General security posture of the target

During this phase of the surveillance, it will be necessary for the operative to physically visit the site, possibly take photos, and even ask questions of people at the site. It is during this phase that we can catch or deter them. Individuals with this type of information should also be detained or arrested. The following is an example of this.

A plot to target U.S. servicemen in Singapore was thwarted when surveillance tapes were found in an Al Qaeda safe house in Afghanistan. The tape contained commentary in English by a 40-year-old Singaporean engineer on ways to attack the U.S. servicemen. The individual and much of his cell (Jemaah Islamiyahl JI Singapore) were later arrested by authorities. The tape also included plans to attack U.S. ships off the coast of Singapore. The potential attack was thwarted in the initial phase of surveillance. Unfortunately, you rarely hear of these catches due to the fact that no terrorist attack occurred. But these catches are being made and lives and property are being protected.

The operative is looking for the availability of cover and concealment when analyzing terrain. They also will observe access points to determine the easiest and safest ingress and egress routes including water routes if needed. They also will note active choke points. An individual photographing a gangway, gate, or fence is cause for concern. In addition, an individual loitering near an access point should be reported. After observation, it is possible the operative himself will try to gain access. Again it is during this phase they need to be deterred. Success in this phase by the operative will label your vessel or facility a soft target and make it a potential target for terrorist and criminal activity. An individual gaining access to your vessel for whatever reason is a breakdown in your security plan. You as a crewmember must confront any unknown individual on your vessel without the appropriate visitor's pass.

The operative will also be observing the routine operations of the target. He will be looking for the normal working hours of operation, peak activity time for people coming onboard or leaving. How are deliveries accepted and checked—this will include mail, ship's stores, and packages such as FedEx, UPS, or messenger delivery. What is the vessel posture on vehicles parked or idling near the vessel? A more recent concern since the USS *Cole* will also be small boats' ability to come close to the offshore side of the vessel. In all these areas a clear policy should be identified in the Vessel Security Plan and the Company Standard Operating Procedures. Whatever that policy, all watch standers must ensure it is strictly enforced.

The operative will also be checking for the general security posture of the target. They will note the behavior of security guards, quarterdeck watches, and general level of awareness of the crew. It is important to note here that a sleeping or transient security guard or gangway watch is actually worse than no security guard or gangway watch. It is exactly this identified weakness in the security posture of the vessel that the operative is looking for. This observed behavior by the operative will guarantee you a position on the "soft target" list. The operative will also be looking for shift changes and procedures during shift change. Coffee or meal breaks when the gangway may be unattended will be noted. Proper relief on the gangway for these evolutions and the needed head call must be accounted for in your watch and work rotation. How does the gangway watch check identification and/or bags coming aboard and leaving the vessel? Any physical security equipment will be noted, which may include barriers, fencing, lighting, CCTV, anti-swimmer or small boat barriers, metal detectors, rat guards, and any access control barriers. Any weakness in the security posture of your vessel will be noted and researched to see how they can take advantage.

HARD VS. SOFT TARGET

A terrorist or criminal is looking for a "soft" target. What exactly is a soft target? A soft target is unaware, accessible, and predictable. If your vessel or crew has any of these traits, they may become a target for a terrorist or criminal. Through surveillance, operatives for a criminal or terrorist organization will seek out this type of target. On the other hand finding a "hard" target will deter the terrorist or criminal. A hard target is inaccessible, aware, and unpredictable. These traits will cause the operative to search elsewhere for a target. Now, what type of target do you want to be? What type of target is your vessel? Hopefully you are currently a "hard" target, and this chapter will show you how to stay that way. If you feel you may be a soft target, it is time to get to work. By changing your security posture to a hard target, you can reduce the risk of being subject to a criminal or terrorist activity.

Being aware is very important. Keeping the crew informed and encouraging them to report suspicious activity or people will make the ship safer. Do not discourage crew from reporting anything they feel out of the ordinary. By encouraging the crew to get involved in the security plan, you can create a ship full of Vessel Security Officers instead of just one. It is more than likely that the Captain or Vessel Security Officer will not be the first individual to observe surveillance. It is the crewmember on the gangway or deck who most likely will be that individual. It is important to empower that individual so he informs you immediately before the operative leaves or labels your ship for criminal activity. Not everything or person that is reported to the VSO will be an actual terrorist. It is exactly in these situations where the awareness will become a reality. If you dismiss the crewmembers or berate them for wasting your time, they will be less likely to report anything in the future. If you support them and investigate their concern, you have created another set of eyes and ears for the vessel. A crew full of eyes and ears confronting strangers on the vessel or reporting people loitering near the ship or taking photos will make your ship a "hard" target. A jaded crew letting people wander around the ship, a gangway watch sleeping, taking frequent breaks without relief or reading a book, allowing people to loiter near the vessel or take excessive photos of particular locations are examples of a "soft" target.

GANGWAY WATCH

How accessible is your vessel to strangers or visitors? Does your gangway watch check ID of everyone who comes aboard? Does your gangway watch know what is acceptable ID and that they must check the picture to the face? All of these items will determine the accessibility of your vessel. It is clear that the single most important position to access control is your gangway watch. Proper training of those individuals is critical. Keeping them informed of who is coming aboard and when will help in their screening process. Let them know that all personnel including police and port state control officials (USCG) must show identification to come aboard. Most security plans call for a visitor's log and visitor badge or sticker policy. The entire crew should be aware of what these badges or stickers look like. Anyone onboard without a badge or sticker who is not part of the crew should be questioned or reported immediately. The gangway should have an access list of people who will be boarding that day and when. If someone arrives not on the access list, the Vessel Security Officer or Captain must be immediately informed. The individual should not be granted access to the vessel until cleared by the VSO or Captain. Each ship will have a policy for searching bags coming aboard; whatever the policy is it must be enforced. Any bag coming aboard should be noted and the person leaving with his bag also noted. If not, the individual should be questioned as to where his bag is. It is not uncommon for an operative to make a dry run and leave a bag on your ship to see what your response will be. Confronting them before they leave the vessel as to where their bag is will leave a clear picture.

In addition to the gangway, the vessel may have other access points. Example of this may be a cargo ramp, an open side port, low freeboard or tide that can allow individuals to step on deck from the dock. All access points must be identified by the VSO and in the security plan. These access points must be guarded or have some form of security in place to protect the vessel. Leaving access points unattended and unobserved will present a "soft" target to the operative. Having an alert gangway watch checking ID and ensuring no access to the ship except through them will present a "hard" target. Another item worth mentioning is stevedores or dock workers. It may be necessary to allow several of these people onboard at once as in the bulk trade. It is important to note how many of these people board and that they leave. Stevedores and dock workers in third-world countries have a habit of being stowaways in some cases. Again, to deter the stowaway it is necessary to issue visitor badges and at the end of a shift see that they are returned. When these people board, it may take some time to issue the badges. You must not change your security plan policy for convenience at any time. This is exactly where your security plan will protect the vessel.

The last item of a hard target may be difficult to adjust. Merchant vessels in general pride themselves on their routine. Breakfast, lunch, and coffee are milestones for the mariner on a day-to-day basis. Being at sea is not the most social lifestyle so these events are important. In addition the continuity ensures that all crew relieve each other on time and consistently. It is actually an undesirable trait of a mariner to become unpredictable. However, it is up to the security officer to vary the schedule in such a way as to prevent the operative from gaining any advantage. The unpredictability may lie in the method of security rounds or where the crew tour. It also may have to do with which bags are checked or how ship's stores are checked. Every now and then a package or box is opened on the dock just to ensure the contents on the shipping paper are accurate. It may have to do with when the Vessel Security Officer or mate on watch visits the gangway or makes a round on deck. Whatever the situation, the VSO must ensure that any advantage the operative can take on predictability is eliminated. The gangway watch occasionally asking questions of the individual with a legitimate ID is a good example of a "hard" target. The chief mate opening a box of brooms and scrapers on the dock just to verify its contents is another example of a hard target.

PHASES OF SURVEILLANCE

The two phases of surveillance are:

1. Target Selection and Assessment Phase
2. Operational and Attack Phase

It is easier to succeed against the operative during the initial phase. Preventing a crime during the later phase may be difficult. In addition even if you are successful, you may have collateral or mitigating damage or casualties. It is clear that during the initial phase is when the Vessel Security Officer should prevent the incident. This is also the earliest and weakest phase of the operation. The criminal knows little or nothing about your vessel and is in the process of gaining as much information as possible. In addition this phase tends to use newer and less experienced members of the organization. Generally they are given a shopping list and are simply on a "fishing" trip. Due to the fact they are new to the organization, they may not have criminal records or be on any "watch" list. Therefore, their gaining access to vessels or facilities is extremely possible. Even if they are confronted, an ID check would come back with no history. The good news is that due to their inexperience, they are more likely to make obvious mistakes or just come across nervous. It is in these operatives that you see the "bozo" behavior. It is easy for an alert crew to pick up or rattle these operatives so that they can be caught or give up. That is exactly what you want. Let them do their surveillance elsewhere; your vessel is a "hard" target.

The second stage of surveillance is the operational and attack phase. At this point the surveillance will become more difficult to detect. These operatives are the more experienced members of the organization. They may even do a dry run to see how successful or far in the operation they can get. This phase will also include taking additional photos and videos for a more detailed analysis of your vessel. At this point detecting surveillance will be harder as these operatives are good at blending in or not being seen. They also will be well-prepared with identification, plausible stories for being there, and a calm "matter of fact" manner. That doesn't mean they can't be caught and the gangway watch, officer on duty, or crewmember must be encouraged to inform the Vessel Security Officer or Captain even at the slightest feeling of unease with an individual onboard or near the vessel.

The attack phase is when the operation is actually carried out. It is clear that with proper awareness, your vessel should never reach this phase. However, if it does, there is still a chance for the vessel to stop or mitigate the attack. We see through recent history several successful attacks that were foiled by alert individuals: the aircraft brought down in Pennsylvania by the actions of the passengers; the airline stewardess catching the shoe bomber on an under way commercial jet; and also the Khobar Towers in Saudia Arabia where the action of the Air Force sentry on the roof of the Khobar Towers saved hundreds of lives. This individual sounded the alarm after seeing something wrong with a vehicle left unattended along the perimeter gate. The subsequent evacuation of people from the building resulted in minimum casualties despite the building itself being ripped in half. Therefore, it is important that you act quickly and efficiently on all suspected sightings or reports. The quick response may save lives.

FORMS OF SURVEILLANCE

Terrorists use many types of surveillance. Your best way to foil terrorist operations is being familiar with the methods they use. Keep in mind that a terrorist is only limited by his imagination and ingenuity. The type of surveillance most commonly used is:

- One-person foot surveillance
- Two-person foot surveillance
- Foot surveillance with three or more persons
- Vehicle surveillance
- Stationary surveillance

In the merchant industry the one-person foot surveillance would be most common. The individual will appear as an interested individual or passerby in the initial surveillance. During the operational or attack phase, he may come aboard as a contractor or stevedore. On the shore side, he may be a truck driver or in some ports the casual fisherman. It is important in order to detect surveillance that your crew is familiar with what is "normal."

It takes time and familiarity with an area to determine what is "normal." Some easy signs of not "normal" include excessive clothing in hot months; individuals fishing in areas where fish are rarely caught; fisherman rarely attending their lines, but spending an unusual amount of time watching your vessel; contractors wandering around in areas they do not work in—a good example of this is boiler technician on the bridge or radar repairman wandering around the engine room. Over time your crew can become very adept at identifying unusual behavior. This should be reported and shared with the rest of the crew. A few examples are listed here as an initial brief for your crew:

- Unidentified persons asking technical questions about the ship
- Persons photographing the ship or areas of the ship
- Individuals sitting or waiting near the gangway or vessel
- Drivers who leave a vehicle near the ship (especially if they leave in another)
- The same individual returning to the vessel in different capacities (passerby, fisherman, then contractor)

Some guidelines for "normal" behavior:

- Traffic—What is normal traffic for both vehicles and pedestrians?
- Workers—What do contract workers dress like? What do they usually carry? Where should they be working?
- Fishermen/Boaters—What is the normal spot for fishing on both boat and land? What is the normal rig and time for

fishing? Where do the pleasure boats normally transit near your ship?

- Access—Who is normally allowed on the pier area? What vehicles if any are allowed on the pier?
- Security—What do security forces dress like? How often do you see them? What vehicles do they drive?

WHAT TO DO IF YOU DETECT SURVEILLANCE

If you detect terrorist surveillance, you must take immediate action. Depending on the situation, there are several important points to consider. If possible, you want to apprehend the person performing the surveillance in order to prevent him from going elsewhere or putting his plan into motion. In order to accomplish this, you must be careful. The first rule is to not put yourself at risk. Never confront the individual directly and accuse him of criminal activity. At the least, this will scare the perpetrator; it could however lead to bodily harm or even death. The second rule is to alert proper authorities. Contact the VSO or Captain and if in port the port authorities. You should try and get as much information about the individual as possible. Where is he located, what does he look like, what is he wearing or driving are all important items needed to apprehend the individual. If you need to confront the individual, do so in a mild and courteous manner; never let on that you suspect him. You should give him no information and never allow him on your vessel. After you have completed your interview immediately inform the Vessel Security Officer but do not do it in front of him unless the individual is persistent and takes it to the next level.

In dealing with a vehicle you should note:

- Where it is parked
- Model
- Make
- Year
- Color
- License plate number and state of registry
- Decals
- Bumper stickers
- Damage and overall condition of the car (dirty, rusty or good condition)

In dealing with people you should note

- Where they are currently located
- Physical description (sex, race, height, weight, age)

- Clothing description
- Accent, dialect, or mannerism
- Tattoos or scars
- Disabilities
- Distinguishing peculiarities

The more information you can supply security, the easier it is for them to apprehend these individuals. It is also important to note, in case they do leave the facility, the authorities have a description of a suspicious individual or vehicle. You may feel you have a good memory, but regardless of your memory skills, it is a good idea to write all this information down as you are gathering it. It is easy to forget items or get them confused in the heat of the moment. You may also want to ask for assistance in gathering information about the individual. However, it is always important that any individual assisting you is aware not to put himself at risk.

At this point you should have a general idea of what surveillance is and how to respond. Now we go to the next phase—how do you turn your entire vessel into a "neighborhood watch"? The answer to this is simply emphasize to your crew the importance of looking out for and detecting surveillance. All the crew should be informed not to reveal any information to strangers, contractors, or visitors. They should be briefed on the unusual aspect of individuals asking these types of questions. And then the crew should be told not to confront them but to gather as much information about them as possible and relay it to the VSO or Captain.

When you receive this information from your crew, act on it accordingly. It may turn out not to be a security incident, but these positive reinforcements will lead to continued crew awareness. Some of the crew, especially ex-military or aggressive individuals, need to be counseled on not to directly confront the individuals about their suspicions. Again this can lead to problems for the confronter and the possible escape of the individual. It is easier for port police trained and responsible for this duty to respond. The crew must be made aware that this countersurveillance will make their vessel a hard target and in the long run safer and more secure.

SUMMARY

Through extensive research on criminal and terrorist operations, authorities have determined that prior to committing a crime or terrorist act the individuals conduct extensive surveillance on the selected target. It is during this phase that the vessel has the best opportunity to prevent the crime and apprehend the criminal. In order to accomplish this task, the Vessel Security Officer must brief his crew on the importance of the crew's duty of reporting any suspected surveillance. In addition the Vessel Security Officer must act on any information passed on by the crew and reinforce their actions and initiative. By getting the entire crew involved in countersurveillance, you make your vessel a "hard" target. A "hard" target is a vessel that is aware, inaccessible, and unpredictable. The criminal doing the surveillance on this type of vessel will look elsewhere. During the initial phase of surveillance is when the operatives are most obvious in their behavior.

The crew must be briefed on not confronting or trying to apprehend the individual doing the surveillance on their own. It is important that they gather as much information on the person, vehicle, or boat and pass it on to the Vessel Security Officer. The Vessel Security Officer should then inform local or port authorities so they can go out and question and possibly apprehend the individual or individuals. In accomplishing this task the crew must be encouraged to write down any information they gather. Earlier we reviewed what they should be looking for and recording. All this information will assist the authorities in catching the individuals or keeping an eye out for them in the future.

Recent intelligence has determined that individuals have photographed bridges, tunnels, and waterfront facilities. It is clear that these individuals were not merely taking photos as a pleasure trip. In addition individuals found loitering around these facilities have made it very clear that some individuals are probing for a soft target. It is in this environment that we must consider ourselves in. In addition we must consider that these people are not on any schedule and will continue to probe until they feel the time is right.

In dealing with individuals on the vessel or attempting to gain access to the vessel, the crew needs to be briefed on the importance of checking identification carefully and noting any unusual behavior or questions. Any individual aboard the vessel should have a visitor's badge and be operating in his assigned areas. The crew needs to report individuals out of their area or not wearing a visitor's badge. Any individual in the house should be scrutinized carefully. Any procedures listed in the security plan should be strictly followed.

The crew should be informed that if they stop the individuals during the surveillance phase, any further activity against the vessel will be eliminated. The last point is crucial. Terrorists and criminals have patience and may revisit your vessel even after they have been confronted by the authorities. There is no time that you should ever let your guard down. The battle against surveillance is never won, only contained. It is up to your crew and you as the security officer to present the "hard" target at all times and watch for surveillance every watch of every day.

FIVE

Threat Assessment and Analysis

February 26. Not many people can tell you what happened on February 26. That is unfortunate because if they could maybe we wouldn't have had a 9-11.

The initial bombing of the Twin Towers took place on February 26, 1993. It was a calling card or preview of things to come. Other calling cards and signals came as well. The focus is on this particular incident because ironically the target they were unable to bring down initially remained vulnerable for a second try. Had more people assessed this threat for what it was, the horror of 9-11 could have been avoided. Therefore, this chapter will show you what to look for and how to act on certain signals to prevent catastrophes before they can happen. The incidents that affect you may or may not have the consequences of 9-11. However, good threat analysis and threat assessment will prevent incidents from occurring. By practicing these procedures we can help September 11 from becoming another February 26.

In dealing with a vessel or facility, it is essential to perform a threat assessment. A threat assessment deals with identifying vulnerabilities in procedures, physical structure, and personal training. The last item is essential to eliminating threat. Any manager or ship captain will tell you that it is the crew who must know their jobs. It is not enough for the officers or mid-level managers to be competent. These officers are usually not the individuals who manually perform the job. With that said it is clear that adequate training of *all* personal is essential to the overall success of a project.

For example: I consider myself well versed on the ISPS Code and the CFRs. I sign on a ship as Second Mate; the Captain appoints me the Vessel Security Officer. I know the regulations backwards and forwards. Is the ship safe? Well if I depend on my expertise to save the day, the answer is *no*. However, if I impart my knowledge and insight to the entire crew, the answer is *yes*.

In past threat assessments the one area that continued to be identified as weak was the gangway watch. Can you blame the A/B on watch for this problem? Not really. If he is not adequately briefed and trained, how is he to know that the vendor bringing a large box onboard may actually have bad intentions for the ship. If briefed properly, he will check the vendor's I.D., inform the VSO or mate on watch, and, if required, open the box right there on the gangway. This doesn't come naturally—it must be taught.

Another area is meal breaks or using the head. It is very easy to wander away from the gangway for a short period of time and then return. This is natural, and you do have your radio, or do you? I boarded several ships and found no one at the top of the gangway when boarding. I, of course, headed straight for the mess deck for a good cup of coffee. Again I look official; I have a bag and a look of purpose so no one questions me in the mess deck, or elsewhere on the ship. Finally, the Vessel Security Officer or Captain confronts me. This is good but had I been a terrorist or criminal it would be too late. I think you see where I am going with this. The entire crew must be *aware* and also know the potential vulnerabilities in order to be vigilant. So whatever you discover in the threat assessment, inform the crew so they too can combat against the clear vulnerabilities. Certain aspects of the ship or vulnerabilities that the crew cannot control should be kept confidential.

Now let me tell you about some better experiences. I have boarded ships where my I.D. was checked, the contents of my bag was inquired about, the Mate was informed, and I was on a preapproved access list. I signed in and was issued a visitor's badge. Now the big question. Which ship would you like to sail with? If you answered the latter, then you need to pass on information, follow good standard operating procedures, and above all educate your crew or personnel.

THREAT ASSESSMENT

It is easy to confuse threat analysis and assessment. Both are important, but they occur at different times. The threat assessment is done first. It identifies vulnerabilities or weaknesses in the defensive posture of your vessel. Such weaknesses may be inherent and can't be changed. They include low freeboard, slow speed, or small crew. Even though they cannot be changed, they should be identified (this will be discussed later).

The other items to be identified are correctable vulnerabilities and these need to be corrected. The term for correcting them is protective *countermeasures*. Certain countermeasures cannot and will not be employed at all times, only during escalating security levels.

These particular countermeasures and when they are employed should be included in the vessel's standard operating procedures and your security plan. The initial threat assessment should be included in your security plan and the Vessel Security Officer is responsible to review it and conduct follow-up assessments of his vessel. Good guidance on assessments is found in United States Coast Guard NVIC 10-02. It is also defined in 33 CFR 104.305.

In order to conduct an effective threat assessment, you must first perform an on-scene survey. The on-scene survey may be conducted by someone from the company or even the vessel. However, to really get an objective view of the situation, it is suggested that you employ an outside individual, consultant, or agency. Prior to this person or persons arriving onboard to conduct the survey, they are required to be supplied with the following ten items defined in 33 CFR 104.305:

1. General layout of vessel
2. Threat assessments
3. Any previous VSA (Vessel Security Assessment)
4. Emergency and standby equipment available to maintain essential services
5. Number of vessel personnel and any security duties to which they are assigned
6. Existing personnel training requirement practices of the vessel
7. Existing security and safety equipment
8. Escape and evacuation routes and assembly stations
9. Existing agreements with private security companies
10. Existing security measures and procedures

Now with the information provided above, they are ready to perform their on-scene survey. It is important to take a minute here to emphasis that the survey is not an inspection or investigation. It is easy for Captains and crews to get defensive about their vessels. Criticism should not and cannot be the focus of the survey. As mentioned above in this chapter, if there are weaknesses, they should be identified and corrected in a professional manner. The United States Coast Guard or Port State Controls can and will board your vessel to make subsequent inspections. If deficiencies are not brought to light initially, there will be far greater consequences later on down the road. As always, it is important that not only the Company Security Officer understand this, but that he passes it along to his Masters, officers, and crew. The other aspect of the on-scene survey is that it should not be rushed. Allow adequate time for the person or team to conduct their survey. Officers and crew should be made available to the surveyor. The crew should be briefed on the inspection, but again do not play to the surveyor, go about your business as usual and let the survey take its course.

The survey should consist of an actual visit to the vessel that examines and evaluates existing vessel protective measures and procedures and operations for the following in compliance with 33 CFR 104.305.

1. Performance of all security duties
2. Controlling access to the vessel
3. Controlling embarkation of personnel, their effects, and baggage
4. Supervising the handling of cargo and stores
5. Monitoring restricted areas
6. Monitoring deck areas and areas surrounding the vessel
7. The ready availability of security communications, information, and equipment

Now that you have concluded your assessment, the first of many analyses is conducted. The surveyor should review his findings with the Captain and Vessel Security Officer. Prior to submitting his assessment, he should also review his findings with the Company Security Officer if he is not present for the survey. After this consultation is completed, he should submit the vessel security assessment to the company the ship is owned by.

The company must include a copy of the vessel security assessment in the security plan for approval to the port state control. It is easy to imagine that the company may not be happy with the assessment. Obviously some of the protective countermeasures may use valuable time that the crew is already short on. The measures may even involve additional costs that have no apparent return. It is important that everyone understand that the cost of not implementing these countermeasures can indeed be very costly. This cost is not only in terms of dollars and cents but in lives. The Coast Guard and International Community will reserve the right to fine, delay, or even detain vessels that do not comply with these regulations or protect their vessel from identified vulnerabilities (SOLAS Chapter 11-2 Regulation 9). It is easy to identify this noncompliance by simply reviewing the stated procedure in the Vessel Security Plan. If it is found in the plan, ensure the crew performs it.

After reviewing the on-scene survey along with the vessel background, the Company Security Officer should recommend the following items be included in his Vessel Security Plan.

1. Restricted areas

2. Response procedures for fire and other conditions
3. Security supervision of vessel personnel, passengers, visitors, vendors, repair technicians, dock workers, etc.
4. Frequency and effectiveness of security patrols
5. Access control systems including identification systems
6. Security communication systems and procedures
7. Security doors, barriers, and lighting
8. Any security and surveillance equipment and systems
9. Possible security threats
10. Evaluating the potential of each identified point of access

After the consultation with the Company Security Officer, the assessment is submitted. It should be clear by now that the eventual Vessel Security Plan will use the assessment as a basis. This is why an honest evaluation of the vessel is critical from the beginning. Do not depend on the first assessment to continue to keep the ship safe. It is up to the company and the Vessel Security Officer to reassess the vessel at regular intervals and make suggestions to modify the plan, if needed, accordingly. It is also possible that the initial assessment did not take into account new threats. It is important that the Vessel Security Officer not only evaluate his own vessel in the present port, but where the vessel will be called on to travel. The next responsibility of the Vessel Security Officer is to perform an adequate Threat Analysis.

An important point—the vessel security assessment and Vessel Security Plan must be kept confidential. Inform the crew in areas that they need to know and can help protect the vessel. Overwhelming them with issues will defeat the purpose. In addition they may inadvertently pass on classified information. As the Vessel Security Officer you must ensure *no one* off the ship or in the crew without a need to know is shown the security assessment or security plan. This regulation is clearly stated in the ISPS Code and in 33 CFR 104.305

THREAT ANALYSIS

A Threat Analysis is defined as the process of compiling and examining intelligence information to develop indicators of possible terrorist activities. Analysis of the terrorist or criminal threat is a difficult and challenging task. Many governments and agencies contribute information and analytical approaches in an attempt to improve understanding of the terrorist threat. Several sources are available to gather this intelligence. It is a good idea to ask for the assistance of the Company Security Officer if you are unable to obtain good intelligence on a named port. The Company Security Officer can consult with the Facility Security Officer of the port or the identified Captain of the Port if one exists.

There are four basic factors to establish information analysis and collection of information from all sources concerning the terrorist threat. These factors are used in making terrorist threat analysis on a port-by-port basis. This methodology enables both the Port Facility Security Officer (PFSO) and Vessel Security Officer (VSO) to assess the threat to his vessels posed by a terrorist using the below listed factors. These factors are:

- Capability
- Intentions
- Activity
- Operating environment of the country

If there is more than one terrorist group in the country, each one is assessed and the terrorist group with the most activity is used to set the threat level for the port. Each assessment of each factor against the backdrop of the country is being rated to produce the final threat level. The following sections discuss the threat analysis factor.

Operational Capabilities

This factor focuses on the attack methods used by the group and other measures that enhance its effectiveness, such as state sponsorship and use of technology. The key element is whether the group has the capability and willingness to conduct large casualty producing attacks, for example a suicide vehicle bomb containing thousands of kilograms of explosives timed to kill the most personnel at the target. Groups that selectively assassinate individuals or conduct late night bombings causing limited property damage pose a decreasing threat. The ability to operate on a regional or trans-national basis and the overall professionalism of the group is also analyzed. The increased capabilities of the group will require increased protective measures from the ship. The port can alert ships to problems by raising the security or MARSEC level. However, the VSO should not depend on this to take action—that is why an analysis of the ports the vessel will sail to is necessary before the vessel commences a voyage.

Intentions

This factor evaluates the stated desires of terrorist groups and the history of terrorist attacks against national interests. Recent substantial attacks in the country or the conduct of terrorist organizations in other countries is the higher end of the threat scale. The basic ideology of certain groups in question will determine if you may be a target. Tankers will be the focus of Greenpeace while British vessels in Belfast may be the target of the IRA. This factor relies on common sense if any organization states it will attack your type of vessel or your flag, be prepared. In certain situations if groups make their intention known and the option of an alternative port is available, use the alternative port. If an alternative port is not available, take proper protective measures to protect your vessel.

Activity

Is an assessment of the actions the group is conducting and whether that activity is focused on serious preparations for an attack. The highest threat is credible indications of targeting to include the movement of key operatives, final intelligence collection, and movement of weapons to the target vicinity. The media love to use the phrase "chatter" that indicates that something is likely to happen soon. Less threatening are contingency planning, training, and logistical support. Activities that would make the group less likely to attack include robust fund raising or use of area as a safe haven. Recent disruption of a group by arrests or military strikes on training camps will reduce the threat, at least in the short term. When entering an area, the recent activity is essential in determining the "risk" factor.

Operating Environment

This factor rates how the overall environment influences the ability, opportunity, and motivation to attack maritime interests in a given environment. To visualize this factor consider the home field advantage in a sporting event. The home team will always find it easier to play with a friendly crowd behind them. The fans will try to make it difficult for the visiting team to succeed in a variety of ways. Same applies to our vessel if the home team is a terrorist or criminal entity. An important element of this factor is simply the capability of the host nation's security apparatus to combat terrorism or crime. A strong nation will not allow these activities to flourish if for no other reason that it is bad for business or portrays them as weak. The other possibility could be the host nation supporting the terrorist or criminal activity. In this situation avoidance might be the best solution. If you have to go in, be very "prepared."

Another possibility may be the host nation's instability, either politically, economically, or militarily. Any instability may give opportunity for a group to attack or rob your vessel. It is important to keep abreast of changing conditions in a foreign port. If the situation dictates, it may be necessary to make a quick departure. Do not depend on the local agent or port authorities to warn you. They may have other problems or be part of the problem themselves.

RISK

The threat analysis takes into account two major factors—vulnerability and risk. Risk management is becoming a buzzword nowadays. Everyone from your credit card company to your home and life insurer will try to explain risk management to you. It's clear that the greater amount of risk you are exposed to the more protection you will need. In Bridge Resource Management, it is essential for the prudent mariner to identify potential risks before he commences a voyage. He tries to avoid these risks if possible and if not possible, take adequate preventive measures. Contingency plans are clearly stated before the voyage commences. These contingency plans are if something should go wrong. The Vessel Security Officer should do the same. Before you commence a voyage, you should identify risks the vessel may encounter. In addition the "voyage plan" should be from berth to berth and done before the ship departs. This should also be the policy for the Vessel Security Officer when doing the threat analysis. How do you perform this task?

There are several resources at your disposal to evaluate the risk of the next port. If you go on the U.S. Department of State Web site, every country in the world is described in terms of potential risk. Several agencies provide threat analysis as a service including www.tdconcepts.com. Another good way to find out information is to contact the agent of the next port. Today the agent should be able to supply you with not only the MARSEC level or security level but also any potential risks the ship may encounter. These threats may be found at anchor, transiting in, or even alongside. This initial contact with the agent should cover this material in order to perform an adequate threat analysis. Again it is essential that any information received from whatever source should be passed along to the crew. If stowaways are a problem in the next port, the fact that you are aware of it will not prevent them from coming aboard. Good vertical communication with your crew will ensure that the gangway watch at 3 A.M. watching a supposed stevedore board the vessel will take quick and effective action.

What is a credible threat? The answer is *all threats* are credible. In the initial phase of analysis, don't dismiss any threat as not being important; all the information must be collected and weighed against the vessels vulnerabilities. It is very easy to dismiss a threat as being unrealistic; it may not be if the vulnerability fits. If we look at 9-11, the expected attack was a bomb in a vehicle. Several defensive measures were in place to prevent this, even an effective I.D. policy. Unfortunately the attack came in by air. So do not dismiss any threats until they have been evaluated. In addition we know that the ship must sail. If you want a 100% guarantee that a ship will not be attacked in a foreign country, stay tied up in the United States. This, of course, is unacceptable. Therefore, a certain amount of risk must be accepted by the shipowner and Captain. Our analysis will hopefully bring that risk to a bare minimum.

Another resource overlooked in identifying threat is the local paper. Regarding the ATO Class in Freehold, N.J., the instructor mentioned that the local paper will give you the pulse of the area. It's amazing how accurate that lesson was. If you listen to what people are talking about, pick up a paper and see if those same topics are not found in the pages. One can argue that the papers create the emphasis rather than the other way around. But regardless a local paper can inform a visitor of potential risks. Input from vessels in the port can be of great use. It is up to the Company Security Officer to pass on any problems one ship in the company encounters in a port to the next inbound vessel. If a vessel has a particular problem with stowaways or attempted piracy boarding, pass that information along so the next vessel can take adequate protective measures. Good communications between the Company Security Officer and the Vessel Security Officer about future ports is essential. Do not forget to contact the Facility Security Officer also. It is important that he receives your crew list and who associated with the vessel will be coming and going. In addition he should supply you with the names or numbers of people who will be boarding or working on your ship.

Now that you have gathered all the potential threats from the resources named above, you must put them in a graph and compare them to vulnerabilities. Look at the matrix in table 5-1. On one vertical side is the threat factor. On the horizontal side is the vulnerability factor. When you combine the two, you can determine if a situation provides a high or low risk probability. After that has been determined, you must determine what action should be taken. The best case scenario would be to have low risk and no vulnerability. The Coast Guard suggests rating these factors from 1 to 3, 1 being the best case. Tables are provided in the NVIC in the appendix to assist in determining if the situation requires mitigation. The NVIC concentrates on two factors—*consequence* and *vulnerability*. In weighing these two factors, as explained in the NVIC 3, solutions are possible. These solutions are *document, consider,* or *mitigate.*

Mitigate means that mitigation strategies such as security protective measures and/or procedures may be developed to reduce risk for that scenario. These mitigation strategies should be contained in your Vessel Security Plan. The vessel should prepare

TABLE 5-1
Risk Assessment

	High	2	3	4
Vulnerability	Medium	1	2	3
	Low	0	1	2
		Low	Medium	High

Threat

Level of risk (0) low to (4) high

for these scenarios by setting effective countermeasures at each security or MARSEC level. Consider means that the scenario should be considered and mitigation strategies should be developed on a case-by-case basis. Document means that the scenario may not need a mitigation measure at this time and, therefore, needs only to be documented.

In a classroom setting it is fun to take certain scenarios and see what score you come up with. The answers may surprise you. Certain situations that you thought may require mitigation strategies do not, while other situations you thought were of no consequence may in fact require countermeasures. One must of course realize that the constant shutting down of operations may be in effect the safest solution; however, the lack of work could put the company and port out of business. As I heard several times from the Coast Guard the objective of these regulations is higher security not "the death of common sense."

SUMMARY

This chapter discussed threat assessment and analysis. It took a look at the required vessel security assessment and how it is conducted. It also looked at the job of threat analysis and gave the Security Officer some ideas on how to perform that task prior to sailing. Remember every vessel after July 1, 2004, should have had a vessel security assessment performed. In addition all vessels should have submitted a security plan. It is important to remember that these documents are not slabs of stone but living and breathing documents. It is the Company and Vessel Security Officer's responsibility to continually review and edit the plan as required. What threats a vessel may encounter may change over the years. In addition the vessel's operating area may be changed. These changes require a new threat analysis and additional mitigation strategies. It is at times when people become complacent and comfortable in their situation that problems arise.

The famous line "how could they have not noticed that" is common aboard ships that were lax in awareness. It is up to the Vessel Security Officer to ensure that this does not happen on his vessel.

SIX

Security Equipment and Defense in Depth

To achieve a greater understanding of the requirements of shipboard security and how the concepts of defense in depth strategies are integrated into those plans, Company Security Officers (CSOs) and Ship Security Officers (SSOs) should be able to describe the basic objectives or the ISPS Code as they are integrated into shipboard operations. The concept of defense in depth comes from the U.S. Marine Corp. strategy to defend bases and other positions but can also be applied to the defense of ships. The functional requirements of a Ship Security Plan is to implement antiterrorism countermeasures associated with four basic concepts: Deter, Detect, Defend, and Mitigate.

1. Deterrence: The observed presence of a dynamic and effective ship security program that reduces the probability of successful criminal action against a specific target.
2. Detection: Early and accurate identification of a threat using all means available. The critical component being alert and informed watch standers. Available technologies and equipment are also important. Early detection allows for quick response and threat delay giving the ability to better prepare and respond.
3. Defense: Physical nonlethal countermeasure to prevent criminal actions against your ship.
4. Mitigation: Planned and immediate response to a terrorist event that will limit damage and casualties.

Within these basic concepts are laced the measures required in each vessel's security plan. All ships are required to have an approved Ship Security Plan onboard. The plan should take into account the vessel type, crew size, available security assets, etc., and prescribe protective measures for increasing threats of various nature. MARSEC level implementation is only the start of a good shipboard security program. The specific measures found within each MARSEC level must be reviewed to determine which are most critical with regard to a specific threat in any given port. SSOs and CSOs must be able to quantify threats in planning for the defense of their vessel. To do this MARSEC levels, vulnerability assessments, and the ship's security plan (SSP) can be used as guidance. To effectively protect the vessel, her cargo, and crew, certain security and antiterrorism functions must be performed.

TABLE 6-1
Security Checklist

Gangway watch	✓
Access list	✓
Lighting	✓
MARSEC sign	✓
Drill conducted	✓
And so on . . .	

The SSP should be considered a living document, because changes will be made as the vessel's security program matures based on lessons learned through training, drills, exercises, and most of all experience. Continuous communication between the CSO and SSO with a constant focus on ship security is necessary to maintain a dynamic security program.

In reality your approved vessel security program will be transformed into a checklist type of program. While this is necessary and appropriate and meets the minimum requirements of the ISPS Code, it does not meet its purest intent. The professional CSO and SSO can look at each probable threat and assign one or more of the four concepts of ship security.

DETER

As an example the following deterrence measures might be considered:

- Establish and maintain visible countermeasures
- Employ measures to vary security posture to throw off the criminal planning process
- Secure and inspect spaces not in use
- Regulate lighting to best meet the threat environment
- Conduct security drills in accordance with your security plan
- Raise accommodation ladders, stern gates, ladders, etc., when not in use
- Rig hawes pipe covers and place rat guards on lines, cables, and hoses. Consider using an anchor collar

- Deter parking on the pier. Enforce centralized parking
- Consider nonlethal weapons
- Establish warning procedures to notify personnel that they are entering into a restricted area and to tell them what actions they must take and comply with
- Increase patrolling
- Mark restricted areas (English and local language)
- Establish seamless communications with all security stations
- Establish and equip a reaction force
- Identify and inspect all on-hire small craft regularly
  - Coordinate with local law enforcement
  - Monitor local communications, i.e., VHF, TV, radio
  - Consider augmenting with security teams or guards

DETECT

The most crucial concept and the one that the modern commercial ship has the most control over is detection. Identification and detection of criminal or terrorist behaviors allows for early response and possible thwarting of an attack. To maximize detection capabilities, watch standers must have maximum support from the officers onboard as well as from the company.

Awareness is a key factor of detection and a multiplier of detection capabilities. The Ship Security Officer must have knowledge of the regular behavior patterns in any waterway the vessel may sail. The professional mariners already possess this important ability through their years of sailing and experience. The effective lookout or security watch stander must also have a keen knowledge of the threats that may face the ship. This information should be specific, actionable intelligence about trends, tactics, equipment, methods, and desires of the criminal elements present. This is a requirement of both the ISPS Code and MTSA. CSO shall ". . . advise the level of threats likely to be encountered by the ship, using appropriate security assessments and other relevant information" (ISPS A11.2.1/33 CFR 104.210 C8). SSOs shall ". . . enhance security awareness and vigilance on board" (ISPS A12.2.6/33 CFR 104.215 C6).

Once you have placed qualified and knowledgeable people onboard, you must give them the proper tools to do their jobs. While there is some cost involved, it is very little compared to the cost of having even one vessel attacked.

Deck Watch Officer

The Deck Watch Officer (DWO) plays an important role in the detection portion of physical security. In addition to rounds and inspections the DWOs will perform themselves, they are also responsible for ensuring that other watch standers perform their duties in a professional manner and in accordance with the Vessel Security Plan. The SSO must ensure that all Deck Watch Officers are thoroughly familiar with their duties and responsibilities for any MARSEC level. Thorough, professional watch standing even when the threat level is negligible is the foundation of effective shipboard physical security.

TABLE 6-2
Recommended Detection Equipment

Good binoculars for all security personnel

Heavy duty flashlights

Radios for all watch standers

High intensity portable spotlight (two per ship)

Low light or infrared optics (one per ship)

Radar in good condition tuned to pick up small craft at close range

Digital video camera. Optional low light capability

Handheld metal detector (one per ship)

Adequate weather deck lighting

Searchlight on bridge

Closed-circuit television on bow and stern as well as gangway, engine room, and other high traffic, high vulnerability spaces

Gangway Watch Personnel

Personnel standing gangway watch may be the first line of defense against hostile acts and the importance of their actions must be emphasized. Alert, professional watches must be maintained at all times regardless of the threat level. These personnel must be made well aware of their specific duties and responsibilities in accordance with all pertinent instructions. Access control training has been neglected by many operating companies and is the first impression someone boarding your vessel may get whether it is a potential criminal or elements of port state control. Therefore, every effort should be made to demonstrate a professional and efficient watch. This is also a factor in threat deterrence. Gangway watch personnel should be trained in and given guidance on checking IDs, searching persons and baggage, badge issuance, and identification of hazardous devices as well as the requirements of 33 CFR part 104.220 and ISPS part B Section 13.3.

Roving Watch Personnel

Many vessels may have roving watch standers as part of their normal watch standing teams. These personnel make rounds throughout the vessel, particularly in areas unoccupied after routine working hours, to guard against fire, flooding, etc. When pier side, roving watch standers should also include the pier area as part of their routine rounds. As with all topside watch personnel, roving watch standers must exercise due diligence at all times and must be familiar with required procedures for increasing threat levels. Security rounds should be conducted at nonrepetitive intervals and should be increased as the security level is increased. It may be necessary to use outside personnel in the higher threat levels depending on the size of the vessel and crew. It may be wise to train and use other nondeck department personnel as well for implementation as security or roving patrol duties. Persons conducting roving patrols should be equipped with radios, whistles, and multi-cell heavy duty flashlights.

Security Lighting

Lighting is the most effective countermeasure for deterrence and detection for the cost. The ability of unauthorized personnel to gain access to the ship is greatly increased during the hours of darkness. Sufficient lighting will increase the effectiveness of security personnel and act as a deterrent. There is no standard security lighting formula. What equipment is available, where the threat is anticipated to come from, where the ship is located, etc., all must be considered. There is no such thing as too much lighting.

Threat Annunciation

If a threat is detected procedures must be in place to *assess the threat* and *warn the crew*. These two requirements are distinct and separate but will usually occur almost simultaneously. For example, if the gangway watch reports a potential threat approaching the vessel, the Deck Watch Officer must quickly decide (assess) whether or not the threat is serious enough to warrant sounding the security alarm (annunciation) to alert the crew and ship's reaction force. The sequence of events for these requirements will depend on the nature of the threat. At a minimum several things must be considered.

COMMUNICATIONS

Communications are extremely important between watch standers and the DWO. In most instances this will be accomplished with hand-held radios as the main form of communication with a whistle used as a backup. Those personnel detecting the threat must be able to inform the DWO, who must then assess the threat and quickly decide on a course of action.

SECURITY ALARM

Once the DWO has assessed the threat and decided on a course of action, some means must be provided for alerting both the crew and those personnel in the reaction force. The general alarm is the obvious choice. Many vessels do not use a separate and distinct code on the general alarm bell and choose to use the general alarm signal only and inform the crew to the nature of the alarm only after they have mustered at their designated locations. This could waste precious time when the crew should be taking cover not reporting to uncontrolled emergency stations. A separate security alarm signal is highly recommended. This internal alarm should not be confused with the Ship Security Alert System (SSAS).

SHIP SECURITY ALERT SYSTEM (SSAS)

When activated, the SSAS will transmit a ship-to-shore security alert to a competent authority that identifies the ship, location, and indicates a security threat. It will not send the alert to any other ship and will not raise an alarm onboard. It will continue to alert until deactivated and/or reset. Consult SOLAS XI-2, Regulation 6, for further guidance. Procedures should be established on when the ship security alert system is to be activated and by whom. The SSAS must have a secondary alarm activation point in case the bridge is lost to a hostile force.

DURESS WORDS AND CODE

Watch standers are the most likely personnel to first encounter hostile intruders. Although *overtly* spreading the alarm will be the most rapid means of calling for assistance, there may be circumstances where a more *covert* means will be the better course of action. Public address, radios, and voice or visual signals can be used to alert the crew and others without alerting the intruder. This will give you time to prepare while not forcing the intruder into aggressive or defensive actions.

DEFEND

Question: What can a merchant vessel do once a threat is detected? Answer: Not much! If raising the alarm and shooting fire hoses over the side are not enough, the typical merchant vessel has few options left. Of course, the response will change if the vessel is in port vs. at sea. At sea, the vessel's greatest defense is its mobility. Maximum speed, and evasive maneuvering are the best course of action to take to delay the threat if not prevent it. Distancing yourself gives you and your crew time to prepare and protect the ship from hostile actions, as well as call for help. Depending on the situation you may be able to delay any hostile actions until help arrives. Help does not only come in the form of a military response but may also be fellow merchants. Merchant vessels have limited self-defense capabilities that are restricted to nonlethal defensive measures except in circumstances when deadly force is appropriate. Every mariner should realize that he has the inherent right to self-defense. This is a uniform legal standard that is held up internationally. CSOs and SSOs should consider the following defensive tasks for implementation on their vessels. Keep in mind that these measure may not be required at all times, just during periods of increase threat and security levels or at various time to vary the ships security signature.

- Establish a clearly defined layered defense perimeter.
  - In port—life lines, house, restricted spaces
  - At sea—close proximity, ship, house
- Identify critical assets/targets and provide requisite security, i.e., extra security for restricted spaces or hazardous cargoes.
- Employ barricades to prevent high-speed vehicle/boat attack (must be supplied by terminal or shoreside vendor).
- Inspect vehicles and personnel.
- Train and arm crew for self-defense.
- Establish procedures for dissemination of terrorist threat information both during and after work hours.
- Establish procedures to protect against bombs/improvised explosive devices.
- Establish Chemical Biological and Radiological (CBR) plan.
- Coordinate and plan transportation for personnel departing and returning to pier/facility.
- Employ counter-swimmer measures.
- Consult with engineers to maintain ability to get under way if necessary.

MITIGATE

Mitigation strategies attempt to lessen the effects of a criminal or terrorist attack. If you cannot stop it, then you must deal with the situation. For example, if you are not successful in keeping the pirates off your vessel then maybe you can keep them out of the house by chaining all the doors shut and denying physical access to the bridge. Even if you cannot prevent the pirates from gaining access to the bridge, engine room and accommodation spaces, the early detection, evasive maneuvering, fire hoses, and locking down the ship may . . . you hope, give you enough time to allow help to arrive. By slowing down the attack, you have mitigated its effects. This tactic is called threat delay. Just as keeping your watertight doors closed and controlling vehicle access (water or land) to the ship cannot stop a bomb from exploding, damage to your ship, and potential loss of life, it will lessen the effects and increase survivability. Good mitigation strategies are often good deterrents. If your vessel demonstrates positive control of vehicle access, then a terrorist group would be more likely to target another vessel or another facility. Planning and coordination with outside entities play a key role in a strong mitigation strategy.

- Coordinate a planned medical and firefighting emergency response.
- If possible, identify support that can be provided by facility and local community.
- If in port, get under way if possible.
- At sea, call for assistance.

A sample diagram such as table 6-3 below can illustrate the measure that your vessel employees perform and how each answers on all of the four concepts of ship's defense. More importantly it may identify gaps in your security posture. By thinking of your Vessel Security Plan as a base line and integrating the concepts mentioned above, you can better meet the challenges to match the current threat. Security that is not based on current threat information is inefficient and costly.

LAYERED DEFENSE

The concept of defense in depth is similar to the global maritime strategy discussed in previous chapters. The ship's defense and security can also be looked at as a layered system on a much smaller scale. The strategy known as defense in depth gains its strength from the layering of defenses to ensure that a nearly impenetrable perimeter exists around your ship. This perimeter is seen conceptually as a defensive three-dimensional bubble around a ship. This bubble moves with the unit at all times at sea and in port. In order to properly defend and defeat a terrorist attack, the enemy force must be identified as early as possible to provide the time to make a determination of intent and to apply multiple active and passive defensive measures.

TABLE 6-3
Suggested Security Procedures

Threat	Deter	Detect	Defend	Mitigate
Stowaway	Gangway watch	Access list Badges Screening	Restricted areas Locked spaces not in use Screening of visitors	Prearrival/ departure inspections
Improvised Explosive Device (IED)	Personnel screening Inspection of cargo and stores	Check cargo and stores deliveries against manifest Training	Inspect cargo and stores off ship Authorized deliveries only	Inspect off ship Firefighting and damage control Bomb threat training
Water Born Attack	Alert watch standing Fire hoses Lights	Alert watch standing Radar Lights Intelligence AIS	Fire hoses Evasive maneuvering	Firefighting and damage control SSAS
Mar jacking	SSAS Access control Restricted areas Training	Intelligence Access control Restricted areas	Restricted areas SSAS Evasive maneuvering Self-defense	Drills SSAS Restricted areas Key and lock program

Principles

A layered defense provides no one single failure point and is comprised of three zones:

- *Assessment*—allows for initial identification of a potential threat.
- *Warning*—provides the area where the ship's crew may respond with initial and escalating measures including warnings, challenges, use of nonlethal weapons if appropriate, and if time permits, avoiding the threat.
- *Threat*—implement measures to repel the threat.

Defense in depth is achieved by identifying the threat at the earliest opportunity and employing measures to reduce or ward off the threat at a maximum range. To put in the simplest term easily understood by a mariner, defense in depth is similar to collision avoidance, except instead of trying to avoid a collision, you are attempting to detect and defend against a terrorist attack. In collision avoidance you search the horizon and beyond with all means necessary to identify any vessel that may "threaten" the ship. Once the contact is known to exist, you assess the target. Is it a threat to the ship? You may track contacts on radar, consult traffic patterns, or look at it through binoculars to make this critical assessment. If the threat is determined to exist, you will contact or warn the other vessel using radios, light, or sound signals. At some point when you are determined the threat of collision is imminent or that you are in a condition of extremis, you must take action to "defend" against a collision.

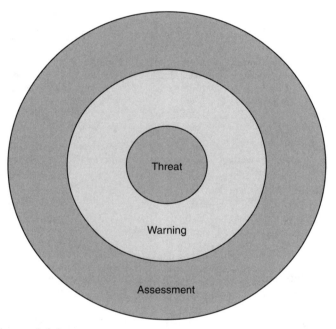

Fig. 6-1. Layered defense.

For security of ships, defense in depth should be viewed conceptually as three zones or perimeters.

- An outer perimeter distant from the ship and guarded by radar, escorts, picket boats, etc.
- A secondary perimeter consisting of the ship's hull guarded by the ship's force or augmenting forces.
- An inner perimeter of the ship itself and protected by physical security measures.

The assets that are available to the SSO or the watch officer that can be used in the assessment zone are:

- Up-to-date and current intelligence
- Sensors such as radars and night vision
- Lighting
- Alert and knowledgeable crew
- Media and open source information

Once a target has entered the warning zone, you have at your disposal

- Radios
- Signal lights
- Flares
- Loud hailers
- Signs

In the threat zone, the options are minimal which, as stated before, makes the other zones that much more important.

- Physical barriers such as the side of the ship
- Fire hoses
- Lethal or less than lethal weapons if so equipped
- Maneuverability of the vessel

"Sailors belong on ships and ships belong at sea"—at no time has this statement been more true. With little or no defensive capabilities, ships in port are at the mercy of local authorities and facility security personnel to protect them. Because a ship in port has lost its most valuable defensive asset, maneuverability, it is at its most vulnerable. However, ships also have more assets to call on, such as military and local maritime law enforcement assets, increased access to information and intelligence, as well as direct support from the Company Security Officer.

So just as the professional CSO/SSO applied the four concepts of ship's defense, you can also identify, measure, and show weaknesses in the three layers of defense in depth.

Planning Considerations

Compliance does not equal security. A responsible CSO or SSO should not relax when the VSP has been approved and the checklist is complete. The oceans and lanes of maritime commerce are a dynamic environment. Plans must be flexible to allow for the changing

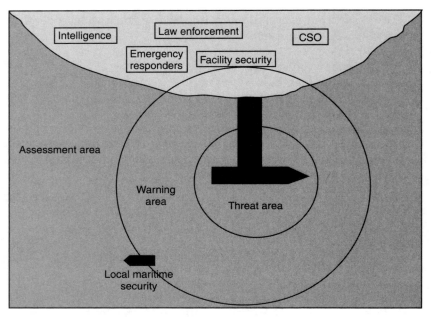

Fig. 6-2. Layered defense for a typical vessel.

environment and changing threat. As General George S. Patton, Jr., said, "One does not plan and then try to make circumstances fit those plans. One tries to make plans fit the circumstances. I think the difference between success and failure in high command depends upon the ability, or lack of it, to do just that."

In order to properly plan, the following considerations should be taken into account:

- Leverage local law enforcement assets/port facility/augmentation forces.
- Establish assessment and warning zones in order to ascertain a suspect's intent so decisions on the use of force can be made.
- Establish clearly defined perimeters.
- Establish warning system.
- Establish barrier plan to prevent high-speed attack.
- Create and maintain a reaction force.
- Conduct random patrols.
- Employ sensors, i.e., radar and thermal imagers.
- Use nonlethal weapons when available and appropriate.

Every day the threat changes, as a student of current events CSOs and SSOs attempt to minimize the vulnerability of their ship

TABLE 6-4
Examples of Layered Defense Planning

Threat/Zone	Assessment	Warning	Threat
Stowaway	Intelligence Watch standers Liaise w/facility	Signs Access control procedures Restricted areas	Inspections

Improvised
  Explosive Device
  (IED)
	Intelligence
	Watch standers
	Training
		Inspection of cargo
		  and persons
		Vehicle access
		Gov't security
			Search procedures
			Local law enforce-
			  ment
			Damage control

Water Born Attack	Intelligence Watch standers Training	Radar Lookouts Lights Radios Light/sound signals	Maneuver Call for assistance Damage control Flares

while maintaining efficient operation of the ship. Keeping in mind how the security plan allows for a layered defense in three zones and uses the four concepts of ships defense (deter, detect, defend, and mitigate) will enable the SSO and CSO to identify and fill gaps in the security plan that may not have otherwise been addressed. It may be useful to think planning considerations from the threat perspective, or where the threat may come from. The four areas you will want to consider are Sea, Land, Subsurface, and Air.

SEA

Attacks from the water are the first priority in the maritime industry, because that, of course, is where most time is spent and because little can be done about defending against a land-based attack where land attacks must rely on facility and port state security assets. As a CSO or SSO, you must first do your homework and consider the port you will be calling on, or the body of water you will be transiting. Since today's vessels are mostly on scheduled runs, this need only be done once for each port; then if necessary, a simple review and editing will suffice.

Conduct an initial harbor survey using all available resources and determine if the pier area is controlled, as well as the date of the last search, if not under continuous screening. The CSO may contact the Port Facility Security Officer (PFSO) to determine the current security level of the facility and port. He may also want to identify the security measures in place that may affect the ships in port security posture. Deployment of water barriers and warning signs are essential and may be required in some ports depending on the

MARSEC level. You should identify who will provide these, who will pay for these, and who is the supplier if the shipping company is the responsible party.

The Vessel Security Plan will establish procedures for surveillance and watch keeping to enhance vessel security. Review to ensure the following are being done in a professional manner:

- Plan to establish surveillance of surroundings to include land and water.
- Ensure the use of radar, visual, electro-optical surveillance, and communications considerations are covered by the plan.
- Create a plan for search of vessels and structures in close proximity of the ship.
- Modify engineering and firefighting readiness based on anticipated threat level.
- Create a warning procedures plan.
- Conduct a vessel inspection and search visitor boarding the vessel.

LAND

Many of the same measures are the same for threats that originate from shore as those that originate from the sea. The implementation of those measures does change. Consider the following considerations for land threats:

- Obtain a pre-arrival port assessment from the CSO.
- Determine what physical barriers and signage are required.
- Establish entry control points.
- Coordinate with facility security for vehicle searches.
- Use access control lists for vetting and continuous control of husbanding services. This may include issuing badges to the local workforce.
- Maintain watch and conduct surveillance of surrounding area.
- Modify engineering and damage control readiness based on the anticipated threat level.
- Review warning and alarm procedures.

SUBSURFACE

One area that is sometimes neglected by both the shore- and ship-based security personnel is the threat from swimmers and underwater explosives such as mines. While there is very little a merchant ship can do to prevent such an attack, you must be aware of the threat. Look for any signs that may be consistent with underwater attacks and report these as soon as possible. Some port facilities may be equipped with underwater surveillance gear to detect such a threat. In some cases, ships are required to conduct underwater hull surveys either prior to leaving or entering a port. This is one of the security measures that may be imposed by port state control. Planning for such a requirement and identifying service providers prior to will prevent costly delays in the ship's schedule and manage unnecessary costs. Anticipate environmental conditions affecting swimmers such as temperature, current, heavy sea state, and visibility in the water. Any factor that makes scuba diving more difficult will make underwater attacks less likely. But not impossible! The illegal drug trade has perfected the use of underwater magnetic containers that are attached and retrieved by divers to transport drugs. This expertise could easily be transformed to the use of explosives. Ensure the following considerations are included in plan for subsurface terrorist style attack:

- Coordination for an underwater sweep of pier prior to arrival. This may improve planning for the use of unmanned underwater vehicles, remotely operated vehicles, and/or divers.
- Configure ship lighting to deter and detect swimmers.
- Create a plan for the random cycling of ship's systems such as the screws and other systems that will deter an underwater attack.
- Plan for or coordinate with facility security for random pier and hull sweeps.
- Plan for visual, underwater sensors, and swimmer detection systems surveillance.

AIR

Threats from the air are almost never considered, probably because there is so little merchant mariners can do about it and the overwhelming belief that it will never happen. Well, whoever thought that airliners would be used as missiles to attack buildings? High-level intelligence officials warned of airliners being used to attack cruise ships. Also Palestinian elements had planned to use model airplanes to fly explosives into Israeli checkpoints. Ensure the following considerations are in a plan against air threat. Possible air threats could be from radio-controlled, general aviation, commercial aircraft, to sophisticated missile attack. No possibility should be excluded.

- Be aware of normal air traffic patterns.
- Establish communications with local air control.
- Create a warning procedures plan.
- Report all suspicious air activity. Give specific account including tail number and in the case of remote control look for base station.

WEAPONS OF MASS DESTRUCTION (WMD)

Weapons of mass destruction (WMD) present unique planning considerations for merchant ships. Most vessels do not have a plan to deal with operating in a contaminated environment. Merchant vessels need not prepare for chemical, biological, or radiological defense (CBR-D) such as a navy vessel will; however, with a little planning, some preparation, and some small costs, a merchant vessel can use its inherent capabilities to minimize exposure and escape a contaminated environment. These capabilities are, ability to maneuver and escape, ability to close the ship to outside air and adequate water discharge via the existing firefighting system. Regardless if an incident is the result of a terrorist attack or industrial accident, preparation for a vessel with non-CBR defense capabilities should include:

- Inspect all accesses and ventilation to the house for proper closure.
- Review procedures for shutdown of ventilation.
- Inventory all protective clothing including raingear and industrial respirators and masks.
- Identify deep shelter, two bulkheads separation from the weather decks.
- Inspect breathing apparatus such as SCBAs for possible use in getting underway in a contaminated environment.
- Review procedure for wetting down the ship without being outside by pre-staging firehouses using low velocity fog. Secure nozzles by any means available for maximum coverage.

HIJACKING

Also referred to as Mar-Jacking, this unfortunately is a relatively common occurrence. Hijacking of a ship sometimes leads to the disappearance of the ship and crew. Then the cargo is sold off under false pretenses and the crew is never heard from again. This is categorized as piracy. This also demonstrates a vulnerability that could be exploited by terrorist. The same techniques could be used to gain control of the ship, then the ship could be used to ram other vessels, bridges, or sink in a channel of a major port to disrupt commerce. For the crew the end goal of the attacker is not a concern. The important point is to keep the perpetrator off the ship by all means necessary. The *Dewi Madrim,* a chemical tanker, was hijacked by machinegun-bearing pirates in speedboats off the coast of Sumatra in 2003. These were not pirates. These were terrorists learning how to drive a ship. They also kidnapped officers in an effort to acquire expertise on conducting a maritime attack. Without the use of deadly force, planning to avoid a hijacking situations starts with a good threat assessment. The best single sources for this information is the International Maritime Bureau weekly piracy report and the Office of Naval Intelligence (ONI) Threat to World Wide Shipping. Once you have a good idea where an attack is most likely to occur and what to look for, you can increase your defensive posture at the appropriate time for an efficient security program. Beyond awareness, other planning considerations include:

- Voyage planning, Stay out of the dark alleys.
  - Avoid high risk areas at night if possible.
  - Maneuver to avoid any suspicious target at appropriate distance.
- All eyes on deck.
  - Use bow and stern lookouts, well equipped.
  - Extra deck officer or Master on bridge.
  - Have 3 cm radar tuned for small targets close aboard.
- Access control.
  - All hatches dogged and locked from entry. Use only one entrance.
- Communicate. Stay in contact with all stations at regular intervals.
  - Test emergency communications.
- Lights, Camera, Action. 360° search at periodic intervals.
  - Supply lights, whistles, and radios to all watch standers.
- Coordinate with Engine Department.
  - Have engines ready for evasive maneuvers.
  - Practice procedures if vessel is taken.
    - Disable main engine.
    - Secure lights and power.
    - Secure fuel.
    - Deny control.
  - Fire pump online, hoses rigged to repel boarders.
- Keep crew informed.
  - Instruct crew on emergency procedures.
  - Ensure all crew knows how to call for help in an emergency.
  - Ensure crew understands actions to be taken in case the vessel is boarded.

Prior to 9-11 you were told that not fighting back against pirates was the best action to take for survival. Pirates were simply interested in financial gain. If you left them alone, they would leave you alone. Today that is still mostly true. However, you must consider the unpleasant possibility that the "attackers" are not pirates with goals of financial gain but terrorists. You must decide at the time of capture, who are the individuals and what is your best course of action, much like the passengers of Flight 93 on that fateful day in September 2001. Having been taken hostage, they followed the old rules. Cooperate, do not resist, and you will survive. But having learned the fate of the two other airlines, they faced the unpleasant decision of die now or die later. Armed with the new information, the passengers fought back and gave their lives to save countless others.

SUMMARY

The Vessel Security Plan is the minimum standard requirement for ISPS compliance. The concepts of shipboard defense—Deter, Detect, Defend, and Mitigate—are the milestones of the greater goal, which is protecting your ship and keeping global commerce safe! Considering ship security as a concept will help identify gaps in security that could be exploited by criminals and terrorists. Understanding the measures as they are layered in the Assessment, Warning, and Threat Zones will help the Company and Ship Security Officer to implement and maintain a comprehensive strategy for ship security. Only through vigorous and consistent effort, with international partners in governments, at the port facilities and with other ships, will you be successful in the mission as CSO and SSO to protect the ships from the threat of worldwide terrorism. By preventing terrorist attacks on the maritime industry, we protect our economy, our industry, and our shipmates.

SEVEN

Bomb Threat Planning

In the early 90s as a Navy bomb disposal officer, I was assigned to the Office of Naval Intelligence (ONI) to provide intelligence support to our naval and maritime special operations forces. ONI had a well-established and respected merchant ship analytical division that had long kept an eye on the capabilities and operations of the world's merchant fleets. On this particular day one of the merchant analysts called me and told me that an Israeli newspaper had received an anonymous call stating that a bomb, possibly attached to the hull, was onboard a U.S. flag vessel that had departed from Texas and was enroute to Haifa, Israel. The analyst asked my advice as to what to do. Many questions ran through my mind: where was the ship now? What was the cargo? What ports had it visited, was there any previous threats or terrorist capabilities in the previous ports, was the company aware of the threat, did we have communications with the ship, did the Master and crew have any bomb incident training?

This was before Al Qaeda was a household word and as far as I knew incidents like this were rare. It was agreed that the major U.S. agencies involved including State, Justice, Defense, and the NSC should convene a video conference at the National Military Command Center to formulate plan in response to the bomb threat. I was invited because of my EOD experience and intelligence background. Upon arriving at the Pentagon, I found my way to the NMCC and the conference. Suffice it to say that the level of knowledge concerning merchant ships by the civilian and Army and Air Force Officers in attendance was understandably minimal. As I sat and listened to the briefings, I learned the ship was 800 miles east of Bermuda still heading east. The Department of Justice representative said that groups sympathetic to Palestinian causes existed in Texas, but they had no hard intelligence indicating a possible maritime attack. There was a pregnant pause in the room as everyone contemplated the situation. As is common in bomb threat situations, there is often little hard information to make a decision. You are damned if you do and damned if you don't take action. Realizing this, I thought the prudent course of action was to conduct a thorough search of the ship. It would bear some considerable cost and disrupt the ship's schedule, but considering the source of the threat it was the least we could do. The only other action was to ignore it and hope nothing happened. I then wrote a note that said:

- Turn the ship back to Bermuda for a safe harbor
- Request the Master to conduct a search onboard the vessel for suspicious items
- Fly an EOD team to Bermuda to conduct an underwater search of the hull and provide technical support

An Air Force Colonel took the note read it and handed it to an Army General who read it aloud to the group. They agreed to the plan.

The ship was prevented from entering Bermuda waters but the Navy EOD team did arrive by air and eventually conducted a thorough search of the hull. Luckily neither the crew nor the EOD divers found anything.

Although there was some initial confusion in the beginning, the sentiments later expressed by the participants was that the effort was the right thing to do considering the threat information that was available. The lessons learned from the incident provided a basis for future response actions and the need to train and exercise for threats to maritime assets wherever they are located.

INTRODUCTION

Bombing or the threat of being bombed is a reality in today's maritime environment. Bombs and explosive devices have been and remain the most common and most deadly method of terrorist attack. Past incidents, interrogations with captured terrorists, and information gleaned from documents and intelligence sources all indicate that terrorists have used or intend to use explosive devices to damage or destroy vessels.

Al Qaeda and other terrorist groups have shown the capability and intent to successfully attack ships with explosives in a variety of methods. Some recent examples include attack by explosive laden boats (USS *Cole,* S/T *Limburg*), sinking of the Super Ferry in Manila 2004, attacking oil terminals with suicide boats (Basra Iraq 2004), and hiding suicide bombers in containers (Ashdod, Israel 2004). Other possible attack scenarios planned or discussed have included use of bombs against facilities and establishments frequented by crewmembers, truck bombs on piers, attacking large vessels with explosive laden aircraft, attacking vessels with swimmers and limpet mines, using floating explosive or mine-like devices in ports and ramming ships with other explosive laden ships. The means and methods of attack are nearly endless and are limited only by the imagination and capability of the attacker.

This does not mean a vessel is defenseless. A point that is constantly emphasized by law enforcement and security authorities is the value of being prepared. By developing a plan dealing with bomb and explosive incidents, a ship can significantly reduce the threat and mitigate damage in the event of an attack. A crew trained to screen personnel and cargo, monitor the perimeter of the ship, and keep a good lookout above, on, and below the surface of the water in threat areas is key to prevention. This chapter will discuss basic principles and identification features of bombs and hazardous devices and provide guidelines for actions to take in an explosives incident situation.

TERRORIST USE OF IMPROVISED EXPLOSIVE DEVICES (IEDS)

Terrorists often use homemade explosive devices (improvised explosive devices or IEDs) in carrying out their attacks. IEDs are ideal terrorist weapons. They are constructed of common items that are readily available and difficult to trace and cost relatively little. IEDs may be large or small and can be designed to be transported to the

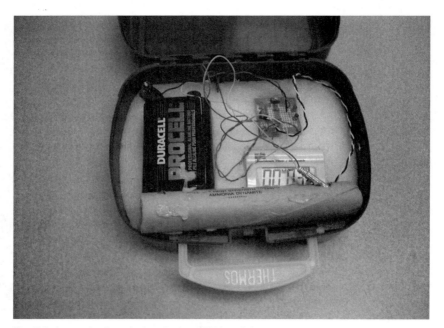

Fig. 7-1. Improvised explosive device (IED) lunch box.

target in components ready for last minute assembly. Bombs can be constructed to look like almost anything and can be placed in any number of ways. Such design concepts make detection more difficult and thereby provide an additional increment of safety to the terrorist.

The use of IEDs can enhance the qualities of violence that give terrorist groups their ability to intimidate or coerce their target. The detonation itself creates a highly visible and newsworthy scene even hours after it has occurred. The use of bombs in a terror campaign emphasizes the authorities' inability to safeguard their personnel and maintain law and order. A bomb or threat of a bomb onboard a vessel is very disruptive and can shut down a ship or a port until the situation is safely brought to a conclusion.

BOMB THREATS

A bomb threat message can be delivered in a variety of means including telephone, mail, audiotape, or the Internet. The majority of threats are called into the target; occasionally the information is passed through a third party. The threat may or may not specify location of a bomb, include the time of detonation/ignition, or contain an ultimatum related to the detonation/ignition or concealment of a bomb.

Often the question arises why would someone call in a bomb threat. There are two logical explanations that can be considered.

The caller has knowledge of an explosive device or incendiary device and wants to minimize personal injury or property damage. The caller may be the perpetrator or someone who has become aware a bombing situation.

The caller wants to create anxiety and panic that will result in a disruption of the normal activities of a facility where the device is reportedly placed. Generally, no matter what the reason, there will probably be a reaction to it. Through proper planning a wide variety of potentially damaging reactions can be greatly reduced. A majority of bomb threat messages turn out to be hoaxes. However, until an actual device can be ruled out, it is important that all threats must be evaluated and proper actions taken. There have been recent incidents where bomb threats were received on passenger ferries. No bombs were found or detonated. The manner in which the company and the crew responded to the incidents will have a lasting effect on the public's confidence or lack of confidence in the system.

IMPROVISED EXPLOSIVE DEVICES (IEDs)

A bomb is often referred to as an IED or improvised explosive device. An IED is any device capable of producing damage to material and injury or death to personnel when it is detonated or ignited. Bombs may be of any degree of sophistication and may be placed to destroy equipment, cause fires or casualties, etc. Generally, the IED will consist of an energetic, lethal, noxious, or pyrotechnic material and an initiation device or fuse.

The majority of IEDs, though lethal, normally contain only a small amount of explosives. In the past several years large explosive devices delivered by package or contained in vehicles (VBIED, vehicle borne improvised explosive device) have been used against domestic and overseas U.S. targets. IEDs can be categorized as Weapons of Mass Destruction (WMDs) in certain cases of large bombs with thousands of pounds of explosive material or designed to disburse lethal/noxious agents.

Types of IEDs

IEDs are generally categorized by the type and effect of main charge. The three main types are:

- Explosive—Causes damage by fragmentation, heat, and blast wave. Heat produced will often cause a secondary incendiary effect.
- Incendiary—Generates fire, producing heat without substantial explosion when ignited.
- Dispersal Devices—Improvised chemical, biological, radiological, and nuclear devices that are designed to disburse lethal/noxious agents, i.e., "dirty bombs" or RDDs radiological dispersal devices.

Characteristics and Classification of IEDs

IEDs normally consist of a filler (explosive, incendiary, or chemical), container, fuse, detonator, and power source depending on the method of initiation. The predominant numbers of IEDs are homemade or specifically assembled for an intended target. Use of military munitions, i.e., a bomb, as an IED would not be unusual. It is not unusual for international terrorists to use military explosives, especially malleable plastic explosives such as Semtex in the construction of an IED. Detection and recognition of an IED is becoming steadily more challenging (i.e., shoe bomb) because of the variety of devices being assembled. The sophisticated designs, clever packaging, and the imaginative use of commonly available materials make identification a daunting task. Improvised explosive devices can also be categorized by the methods of packaging or container, by the fusing system, or by the delivery method.

Secondary Devices and Booby Traps

Secondary devices and booby traps have long been used in terrorist operations. A secondary device is predominantly a device that initiates due to an action by responding personnel. Whenever an area is suspected of containing an IED or where one has detonated, responders must be mindful and exercise caution for such devices. When confronting a suspected IED, the situation should only be handled by qualified bomb squad or military Explosive Ordnance Disposal (EOD) personnel.

Packaging of IEDs

Bombs can be packed and concealed in an almost endless variety of ways. The purpose of the packaging is to conceal the device and facilitate the delivery to the target area. Some examples of packing to disguise IEDs include:

• Briefcases	• Fire extinguishers	• Tool boxes
• Duffel bags	• Vehicles	• Stores
• Shoes	• Mail	• Ordnance
• Vests	• Electronic devices	• Pipes
• Flashlights	• Trash bins	• Toys
• Beverage containers	• Tanks	• Anything

Methods of Delivery

Improvised explosive devices can be delivered to a ship or a port facility in a wide variety of methods that include:

- Hand delivery
- Mail
- Vehicle (car/truck/boat/plane)
- Projected (mortar or shoulder fired)
- Swimmer delivery
- Floating explosive object/mines
- Hidden in stores or cargo shipments

Fusing Systems

A fusing system is designed to actuate the explosive device. Fusing systems are usually electrical or non-electrical, mechanical electrical, or mechanical nonelectrical. The simplicity or sophistication of a fusing system is only limited by the resources and skill of the bomber. Many terrorist bomb makers have received some training in their trade including the publication of an Al Qaeda bomb manual.

Mechanical/Nonelectrical (Pipe Bombs)

This type of device does not incorporate electronic circuitry into the system. The firing system uses a nonelectric blasting cap or initiator, time fuse, percussion primers spring-loaded strikers, trip wires, pressure devices, booby traps, or firing devices. The "shoe bomber" used a homemade fuse he attempted unsuccessfully to light and detonate a bomb hidden in his shoe while onboard an airliner over the Atlantic Ocean. Pipe bombs usually have a time fuse inserted in an end cap to initiate the device.

Electrical Fusing Systems (Briefcase IED)

These systems incorporate some kind of switch to complete a circuit and provide power to an electrical blasting cap or initiator. Electronic systems have become more sophisticated with the rapid development of integrated circuits that use little power and can operate over a long period of time. Miniaturized circuits can be easily concealed and are very reliable.

IEDs can be initiated electrically in a myriad of ways. A common method seen more today uses command activation using cell phone, pagers, or a wire. A device can also be designed to activate by a push or a pull, environmental and physical actions such as temperature, light, sound, and changes in barometric pressure. Time delays can also be included by using mechanical or electronic clocks. Examples of electrical device used to initiate bombs include:

- Mercury switches
- Alarm systems
- Photo cells
- Electronic timers
- Integrated circuit chips
- LED wristwatches
- Cell phones
- Pagers
- Musical greeting card circuits
- E-cell timers
- Electronic initiating devices

IED Explosives

The type of explosives terrorists can employ or manufacture varies greatly. Terrorists have used military explosives procured from state sponsors or bought on the black market; high explosives removed from conventional ordnance; modified or booby trapped mines, grenades, etc.; stolen commercially available explosives; or improvised explosive mixtures. Examples include:

- Plastic explosives C-4/Semtex
- TNT
- Ammonium nitrate fertilizer and fuel oil (ANFO)
- Black powder
- Smokeless powder
- Potassium/Sodium chlorate (incendiary mixture)
- Modified munitions
- Liquid explosives/incendiary mixtures
- C-4 and Semtex
- Plastic explosive

SUICIDE BOMBERS

Historically, Al-Qaeda has used explosives in nearly every attack, but as of this writing, explosive belts and suicide bombers have not been used in attacks in the United States. The attack on the USS *Cole* and MV *Limburg* did use suicide bombers in boats. FBI Director Robert Mueller in 2005 stated that suicide bombers are inevitable here in America and, of course, overseas. SSOs and law enforcement community must remain vigilant to this potential threat. The law enforcement community has developed the acronym, "ALERT," that can help identify a possible suicide bomber.

Potential bomber indicators:

- Alone and nervous.
- Loose or bulky clothing.
- Exposed wires.
- Rigid mid-section (explosive device location).
- Tightened hands (person may be holding a detonation device).

Suicide bombers target any public location where large groups gather. The explosive device usually consists of 10–30 lb of explosives that can be hidden in clothing or other packaging systems. Bombers will add nails, bolts, ball bearings, hazardous chemicals, and other materials to augment the effect of the explosives. The result of a suicide bombing is devastating. Members of the law enforcement community and watch standers must be vigilant to this potential threat. Recognition of any of the ALERT indicators could help divert a deadly attack. Any suspicious activity or persons should be reported immediately to the port authorities.

MAIL BOMBS

Bombs can be planted onboard a vessel in many ways. They can be hand carried aboard, attached to the hull, hidden in stores and cargo, or sent in the mail. Personnel who handle and receive mail should be aware of the indicators of mail bombs in the course of their duties. If a suspect package is discovered, it should immediately be set aside and reported to authorities. Mail bombs have exhibited the following unique characteristics that may assist crewmembers in identifying a suspect package or letter:

- Mail bombs may bear restricted endorsements such as "personal" or "private."
- The addressee's name and/or title may be inaccurate or misspelled.
- Mail bombs may have distorted handwriting or the name and address may be prepared with homemade labels or cut-and-paste lettering.
- Package or mail bombs may have protruding wire, aluminum foil, or oil stains visible and may emit a peculiar odor.
- Mail bombs may have an excessive amount of postage stamps affixed.
- Letter-type bombs may feel rigid or appear uneven
- Parcel bombs may be unprofessionally wrapped and endorsed
- Packages or parcel bombs may have an irregular shape, soft spots, or bulges.
- Packages or parcel bombs may make a buzzing, ticking, or sloshing sound.
- Pressure or resistance may be noted when removing contents from an envelope or package.

PREPARATION AND RESPONSE TO A BOMB INCIDENT

Proper preparation is paramount in handling bomb threats and actual bombs. Every vessel should have a section of their security plan devoted to bomb incident procedures, including periodic drills and exercises. If a bomb incident occurs, proper planning will instill confidence in the leadership, reinforce the notion that those in charge do care for the welfare of crew and passengers, and reduce the possibility of casualties, damage, and reduce the threat of panic, especially if passengers are embarked. Elements of a bomb incident plan should include the following:

- Establish a simple procedure for the person receiving the threat.

- Designate a chain of command.
- Establish a command center.
- Establish communication procedures.
- Establish clearly how and by whom the bomb threat will be evaluated.
- Determine availability and communication with support agencies ashore.
- Provide an evacuation plan for crew and passengers.
- Designate search teams and areas to be searched.
- Establish search techniques.
- Establish procedures to report and track progress of search.
- Standby with firefighting and damage control capabilities.

RECEIPT OF BOMB THREAT

Any individual aboard a ship who has received a bomb threat should immediately notify the Master or watch officer. Upon notification, a designated individual will then notify the facility security officer, base commander, operational commander, company representative, and local authorities. To ensure all appropriate agencies are notified, a Bomb Threat Action Check-off List should be included in the vessel's security plan.

The Master or his designated representative should begin analyzing the situation for appropriate action.

TELEPHONE BOMB THREATS

Personnel should respond calmly to a bomb threat call. If possible, get more than one person to listen to the call. Keep the caller on the line as long as possible. Ask the caller to repeat the message and record every word spoken by the caller. Use of a Telephonic Threat Complaint sheet should be available at the gangway or other areas that may receive incoming call. In particular, the person receiving the call should:

- Remain calm. Rarely has a bomb threat caller failed to allow ample time for evacuation.
- Listen for voices or speech peculiarities and try to distinguish background noises that might help identify or locate the caller.
- Keep caller on the line as long as possible.
- Be alert for repeated use of certain words or phrases.
- Listen for accents—national or regional.
- Tape record the conversation if possible.
- Record the date and precise time the threat is received.

- Try to get the caller to answer as many questions as possible pertaining to the location or time of possible detonation.
- Do not hang up the phone.
- Write all information down and pass it on to the chain of command.

WRITTEN BOMB THREAT

With written bomb threats, save all materials, including any envelope or container. Once the message is recognized as a bomb threat, unnecessary handling should be avoided. Every possible effort must be made to retain evidence such as fingerprints, handwriting or typewriting, paper, and postal marks that are essential to tracing the threat and identifying the writer.

While written messages are usually associated with generalized threats or extortion attempts, a written warning of a specific device may occasionally be received. It should never be ignored.

BOMB INCIDENT RESPONSE DECISION MAKING

If a bomb threat is received, the Master will need to evaluate the threat and decide further actions. His decisions will be based on the best available information and advice from law enforcement authorities, port authorities, and company policy. The Master's decision will determine if a search will be conducted, if an evacuation is necessary, and other emergency actions. Essentially there are three alternatives when faced with a bomb threat.

- Ignore the threat
- Evacuate immediately
- Search and evacuate if warranted

The decisions should be based on available intelligence, threat, and security situation of the vessel, port, and crew. The Master should consider the physical security of his vessel, have other bomb threats been received, have there been crew or labor problems, how and where could a bomb been delivered? Consultations with officers, crew, and local authorities can assist in the decision making process.

Ignoring the threat completely can result in added difficulties. While a statistical argument can be made that few bomb threats are real, it cannot be overlooked that bombs have been associated with threats. If passengers or crew learn that threats have been received and ignored, it could have a negative effect on business and morale. Also, it is possible that a bomber being ignored will actually plant a bomb.

Evacuating on every bomb threat may appear to be the preferred approach. However, there are negative factors that must be considered. The obvious is that a bomb threat caller may know this is your policy and bring your vessel to a standstill. This is a favorite tactic of a disgruntled employee. Also a bomber could plant a bomb near exits and wait for an evacuation to detonate it.

Initiating a search after a threat is received and evacuating after a suspicious device is found is perhaps the best alternative. It is not as disruptive as an immediate evacuation and will provide a sense of security that action is being taken. If a device is found, the evacuation can usually be accomplished while avoiding the potential danger area.

The Master's decision should determine what type and areas are to be searched. Generally it is recommended that unless there is clear evidence that the bomb threat is false, a low-key search of vulnerable or public areas should be accomplished.

If a search is to be accomplished at sea, the Master should advise passengers of a "security alert" and ask passengers and crew to stand fast or muster at designated locations while the search is being conducted. There should not be a reference to the word "bomb" in order to keep calm and order.

It should be noted that bomb squads and EOD personnel do not generally conduct searches; they are few in number and are not familiar with the vessel and its cargo. They can provide technical advice and support to assist during the incident. Usually bomb personnel notified of a threat will stand by in case a suspect device is located. The ship should be prepared to assist any arriving bomb disposal personnel if a suspect device is discovered.

SHIP SEARCH PROCEDURES

In order to accomplish an efficient and orderly search, specific plans should be prepared and drilled on each vessel. There are two types of searches conducted for hazardous devices.

Preventive Searches

These are security searches conducted to deter and detect the smuggling of bombs or arms onboard a ship or terminal. These types of searches should be conducted before people and goods embark the vessel. These searches can be greatly enhanced with the use of technology including metal detectors, X-ray machines, and explosive detection equipment. The use of trained dogs is an excellent technique in preventive searches.

Checking of cargo and stores manifests, passenger lists, and vetting of personnel, vehicles, and baggage are important preventive measures. No person or vehicle should be allowed to break out of an area once searched. All cargos should be secured and put under surveillance once they are screened. The percentage of goods and persons searches will be dictated by the security plan and the threat level.

Reactive Searches

These type of searches are conducted in response to a specific bomb threat or intelligence that a bomb or weapons have been placed aboard. It can also be used during times of a high threat. The following guidelines are provided for reactive searches:

- If a decision is made to search the ship, generally the ship's crew familiar with its spaces will conduct a preliminary search for any suspicious items.
- The Master should brief his department heads accordingly and they in turn should brief their own search teams as to specific areas to be searched.
- High risk and open unsecure areas should be searched first.
- Searchers should be trained to recognize bombs and hazardous devices.
- There must be a system to record and mark searched areas.
- A command and control point with a designated alternative should be established.
- Searchers should be able to communicate with the Master or search controllers.
- Searchers must know what to do if a suspect device is found
- Ship officers and crew must be prepared to conduct orderly evacuations of nonessential personnel and passengers if a device is found.
- Communication with support organizations and vessel's chain of command must be established and maintained.

Search Teams

It is advisable to use more than one individual to search spaces. Search teams should be made up of personnel familiar with the areas they are searching. Using crew's to quickly search their own areas for any suspect items will contribute to a thorough and quicker search. The decision as to who should conduct searches lies with ship's management and should be considered and incorporated into the vessels security plan.

Search Guidelines

Personnel made up into two-person teams should conduct detailed searches. The following techniques in searching for a bomb can be used as guidelines:

- Move first to various parts of the space and stand quietly, with eyes shut and listen for clockwork device. Frequently a clockwork mechanism can be quickly detected without the use of special equipment. Even if no clockwork mechanism is found, the search team is now aware of the background noise level of the space itself.
- The team leader should look around the space and determine how it is to be divided for searching. Division should be based on the number and type of objects in the space, not the size of the space.
- Start from the bottom and work up.
- Search from bulkheads to the center of the space.
- After the space has been searched, conspicuously mark the space.
- Do not rely on conducting random or spot-checking of logical threat areas when conducting a detailed search. The bomber may not be a logical person.
- When searching outside areas, thoroughly check trash receptacles, deck drains, and storage lockers.
- Personnel familiar with the space shall do searches of machinery spaces and other specialized spaces. Be alert for small charges placed to rupture the hull, high pressure piping, or electrical cables.
- Have the occupants of the space stand by to open lockers, desks, and cabinets if deemed necessary.

Suspicious Device Found

It is critical that personnel involved in a search be instructed that their job is search for and report a suspicious device or object. Under no circumstances should anyone move, jar, or touch a suspicious object or anything attached to it. The determination that a suspect device is hazardous and the rendering safe and removal of a bomb or hazardous device must be left to a professional bomb squad or EOD personnel. When a suspicious device is discovered the following procedures are recommended:

- Do not touch a suspicious object or device.

- Report its location and description to the Master or watch officer. Take a picture if possible while minimizing exposure to the device.
- Evacuate and isolate the immediate area including spaces above, below, and adjacent to the suspect device.
- Avoid use of radios in the vicinity of the device. RF energy can cause premature detonation of an electric initiator (blasting cap).
- Isolate steam, water, ventilation, and power cables to the area if possible.
- Consider opening doors and hatches to vent the force of the blast overboard.
- Set emergency stations, stand by for detonation. Issue a warning to all hands when threat exists.
- If a device is found while the ship is in port, the Master or watch officer should consider evacuating nonessential crew and passengers, retaining only sufficient crew to provide damage control and support to emergency responders.
- If a device is found while a vessel is at sea, the Master's response should be based on the location and size of the device and an estimation of damage should the device detonate, the ship's location, and time for assistance to arrive.

Actions if a Device Detonates

If a bomb explodes onboard or near the ship, the Master should:

- Initiate damage control and firefighting precautions.
- Render first aid to any casualties.
- Muster personnel to establish number and names of casualties.
- Inform crew and passengers of situation as necessary.
- Inform local authorities, company, and make distress call if necessary.
- Be prepared to handle inquiries from the press and next of kin.

Reporting Guidelines

All bomb threats or bomb incidents are considered security incidents and should be reported immediately to the USCG National Response Center and local authorities as appropriate. Even if no device was found or if a threat is evaluated as a hoax, knowledge and analysis of such incidents will allow law enforcement authorities to assess the situation in case of further incidents.

Inquiries from the News Media

All inquiries from the news media should be directed to an appointed ship or company spokesperson. All other crew should be instructed not to discuss the situation with outsiders especially the news media. The reason for this provision is to furnish the news media with accurate information and to see that additional bomb threats are not precipitated by statements from uninformed persons.

CONCLUSION

This chapter serves only as a guide in the identification and response to bombs and hazardous devices. The ultimate decision of how to handle a bomb threat must be made by the Master or responsible officer. A vessel's security plan must be clearly understood and exercised by all responsible officers and crew that have responsibilities. Consult and draw upon any expertise available to you from law enforcement and bomb specialists. The best way to handle a bomb threat is to practice good physical security and access control measures to deter and prevent the introduction of bombs or hazardous devices on your vessel. Your life and others may depend on it.

EIGHT

Weapons of Mass Destruction (WMD)

Since 1945 the world has not seen a nuclear explosion. In recent years the use of chemical weapons and/or biological weapons have been limited and with minimum casualties. With this recent history, it is hard to imagine why this topic generates so much attention and fear. The answer lies in what one successful release of a WMD could do. The result would be catastrophic in both casualties and economics. It is for this reason why so much effort is being spent to see that it never happens. If it should, the containment is essential to limit the consequences. In order to accomplish this, you must first have a thorough understanding of what the elements are and how they would affect you. This chapter takes a look at those elements and studies them further.

In the merchant industry and navy the dealing with WMD is known as CBR-D. Vessels that may be exposed to these elements are equipped with essential CBR-D gear and have aboard a decontamination station that is used to decontaminate crewmembers before they re-enter the vessel. The history of CBR-D goes back to the Second World War when the first atomic bomb was detonated in Hiroshima, Japan. After that explosion dealing with the atomic bomb was paramount. With the introduction of the hydrogen bomb the name was changed to NBC or Nuclear-Biological-Chemical warfare. Later, NBC was changed to CBR-D or Chemical-Biological-Radiological to recognize the threat of a chemical attack as opposed to a nuclear attack. Nuclear was changed to radiological to cover the all-encompassing radiological threat. We list the elements by threat with the chemical threat being the most likely. Special recognition is given to a terrorist's desire to use a biological element to cause fear and death.

The use of chemical weapons against ships was practiced in Operation "Southern Breeze" near Charleston, South Carolina. The results clearly show that although the threat is real and consequences to a vessel are great that proper precaution and knowledge can limit those consequences. Several municipalities have performed exercises in order to test the areas preparation for biological or chemical terrorist attack. Top-Off conducted in 2005 in New

York and elsewhere was such an exercise. In reviewing the lessons learned from these exercises, we acknowledge that although we have good procedures and policies in place, running these exercises to adapt to the changing threat is essential. With that in mind the Vessel Security Officer should include a brief on these weapons to his crew. Also consider their potential use or transport in the vessels drills and exercises.

HISTORY OF CBR WARFARE

There are several examples of CBR warfare in both recent and past history. The Romans used to throw diseased bodies into besieged cities by catapult. This would infect the inhabitants of the city with the disease. During the Crusades and also in Roman times advancing troops had to deal with infected wells contaminated with diseased bodies. The troops drinking from this water became sick and sometimes died.

During the French and Indian War, the Indians were provided blankets infected with smallpox. The Indians having little or no resistance to this disease became sick and several eventually died. We know that several Indian tribes were wiped out by white settlers not due to battle wounds but their inability to fend off diseases that the Europeans had built resistance to. In recent years we have seen the use of anthrax as a terrorist biological weapon. From the American Indians, we have learned how little or no resistance to a disease can have devastating consequences. Today we can vaccinate individuals against these diseases thus providing them with that essential immunity to the disease.

Chemical weapons were first used in mass scale during the First World War. Anyone who has seen a late night WWI movie cannot help noticing the use of gas masks. These gas masks were needed to survive in the gas-laced battlefields of Europe. The Germans were the first to use the gas but eventually both sides made common use of chlorine and mustard gas. Chemical weapons caused many casualties on both sides. In the Geneva Convention following the war, the use of chemical weapons in future conflicts was strictly forbidden. Amazing as it seems, given the characters of the dictators in WWII gas was not used in a large way as a weapon. We do know that Cyclone-B was used in the concentration camps. This, however, was simply murder rather than warfare. Today chemicals are used in gas and injection form for execution. The reason the dictators of the second war did not use chemical weapons can be traced to the fact that all sides had ample stock piles of chemical weapons that they would release if attacked by chemical weapons. This balance of possession also worked in the Nuclear Age that will be discussed next. This balance of possession will not prevent terrorist organizations or individuals from using these weapons in the future. As we have seen in Iraq, certain individuals are more than happy to use chemical weapons on their own citizens. The use of chemical weapons in the Iraq/Iran war was well documented by the U.N. It is for this reason the chemical weapons are considered the biggest threat.

Fig. 8-1. Chemical protective gear in a chemical warfare environment.

Nuclear weapon usage against individuals has been limited to two instances: Hiroshima and Nagasaki both in Japan in August 1945. The use of these two bombs effectively ended the war with Japan and conceivably saved hundreds of thousands of lives. The devastation and consequent radioactive fallout was so horrific that the future use of these weapons has never happened. The testing of these weapons, very common in the cold war era, has also been discontinued. Nuclear weapons and the radioactive fallout caused by their release is something the civilized world has worked very hard to prevent. Again certain individuals do not share that view. It is these individuals that given the chance may release these weapons. It is up to all of us to see that this does not happen. In order to accomplish that vigilance is required from the Vessel Security Officer and all crewmembers. Your vessel may be used as a transportation device for such a weapon. These weapons will be examined more closely.

NUCLEAR AND RADIOLOGICAL WARFARE

The following examines the characteristics of a conventional weapon. A conventional explosion releases a fireball, shock, light, and heat. Depending on the size of the bomb will determine the amount of each of the elements mentioned here. In a nuclear explosion fission and fusion are used instead of a chemical reaction to produce a significantly larger explosion. A nuclear explosion will release a fireball, shock, light, and heat just like a conventional explosion. In addition it will also release an electromagnetic pulse, thermal radiation, and most importantly radiation in the form of "fallout." The destructive potential of a nuclear weapon is determined by making a comparison to the amount of a conventional weapon trinitrotoluene (TNT) it would take to produce the same amount of destruction. Nuclear devices are rated at kiloton or megaton. A kiloton bomb would have the destructive power of 1,000 tons of TNT while a megaton bomb would equal one million tons of TNT. The devices dropped on Hiroshima and Nagasaki were in the 20 kiloton range. Today we have 5 megaton nuclear missiles. That would produce the destructive power of 5 million tons of TNT! As you can see the release of such a device would cause massive casualties and long-term consequences. However even a smaller device say a suitcase bomb in the 1 kiloton range is enough to cause extensive casualties and long-term major disruption. It is, therefore, essential that we do not let the wrong people get access to these weapons.

The fireball of a nuclear explosion will generate a temperature in the vicinity of the detonation (ground zero) in the tens of millions of degrees Celsius. This of course will immediately vaporize anything or anyone in that area. The fireball will emit a visible light for about one minute following the explosion. This initial flash is brilliant and within milliseconds, the fireball will become brighter than the sun at noon. Do not look at this light as permanent eye injury can result even at great distances. The thermal blast will travel at the speed of light and will probably reach the vessel before other side effects. The energies frequency excites the molecules of whatever it strikes, converting the electromagnetic energy into heat energy. The result will be spontaneous combustion of flammable materials and paint blistering several miles from ground zero. This radiation can also cause first, second, and even third degree burns to crew unprotected on deck. To counter this thermal radiation the vessel is encouraged to have its crew in CBR-D protective suits and use water through the CMWD system that will be discussed later to shield the vessel with water. Initial radiation passing through the atmosphere interacts with gaseous atmospheric molecules producing an ionized region. A strong energy surge, peaking in a millisecond is created called an electromagnetic pulse. Electromagnetic pulses induce high-voltage electrical currents that can disrupt the vessel's navigation and communication systems. Any individual touching this equipment at that time will receive a severe shock. In addition the equipment may become inoperative. An air blast or shock wave is found in both conventional and nuclear explosion but in a nuclear explosion the blast is much more severe. The winds are in excess of 180 mph and cause a sudden increase in air pressure called overpressure. It is a moving wall of compressed air causing extensive damages and injuries. Underwater detonations can also cause large water waves in the form of a tidal wave. An underwater bubble formed by such an explosion will cause a ship to sink straight down. An underwater shock can cause structural damage to the vessel. The last effect is one that needs to be examined closely, nuclear radiation.

Initial radiation is only created in the first minute following the detonation. Five elements are released; they are called X-rays, alpha and beta particles, gamma rays and neutrons. Of the five the most dangerous are gamma rays and neutrons due to their longer ranges and penetrating powers. Alpha particles travel only an inch or two and cannot penetrate normal clothing or unbroken skin. Beta particles travel about ten feet and cannot penetrate heavier clothing. Gamma radiation can travel thousands of yards through the air and have substantial penetrating capability. Gamma Rays can penetrate anything; you must try to slow it down or absorb it. Multiple layers of steel, lead, concrete, wood, earth, and even sea water can be used. One foot of sea water has the same protective characteristics as one inch of steel. Subatomic particles that have been expelled from the nucleus during fission or fusion are called neutrons. They travel at very high speed, can cover thousands of yards, and have good penetrating capability. Neutron radiation is an internal and external hazard. As it passes through living tissue, it destroys the nuclei of cell structures. When struck by neutron radiation, regardless of source, living matter will die. Neutron radiation does not depend on the massive explosion associated with the nuclear detonation. Its ability to kill living organisms can be used with tank shells, hand grenades, or even your suitcase bomb. For this reason it is an excellent choice for potential terrorists. Before discussing residual radition, here are the four types of bursts.

A burst that takes place at an altitude of 100,000 feet or more is known as a high altitude burst. The greatest threat of this type of burst is the electromagnetic pulse (EMP). This can disrupt navigation and communication satellites if detonated in orbit. The second is and air burst. The air burst is below 100,000 feet usually at a height of 2,000 feet. This blast will create EMP and limited radioactive fallout due to its height. The most dangerous of the bursts is the surface burst. The detonations at Hiroshima and Nagasaki were surface bursts. These bursts produce EMP, thermal radiation, air blast, and shock wave that can cause massive casualties. In addition we need to worry about the spread of nuclear fallout that depending on the wind can spread many miles. Surface blasts can cause severe damage to merchant and navy ships if not sinking them immediately.

A vessel is well advised to put as much distance between a nuclear surface or subsurface detonation and their ship. A subsurface burst is one conducted below the ground. This type of burst produces no air blast or EMP. Depending on the depth of the detonation this blast is potentially the least dangerous.

In a nuclear reaction, the material vaporized is sent skyward in the fireball that produces the legendary mushroom cloud. As the fireball cools, these fragments descend to earth. These particles that descend to earth are radioactive and create a situation known as fallout. This fallout is a danger to both the crew and ship. Its avoidance is paramount to the survival of your crew. In order to gauge the danger to your crew, it is essential to understand exposure and dose. Exposure is the amount of gamma radiation an object or person is subjected to. Exposure can be measured by either a cumulative (accumulated exposure) or over a specific period of time (exposure rate). Roentgens-R is a measure of total exposure to gamma radiation. This exposure is usually measured by the hour giving R/hr. Dose is the amount of radioactive energy that a body absorbs. This can be measured in a unit of time (dose rate) or over a specific time period (accumulated dose).

It is important to remember that individual or separate exposures are cumulative. An individual requires a long period of time to release any radioactivity he has been exposed to. Therefore it is essential to keep all crew away from any radioactivity unless the mission specifically calls for them. The best area on the ship for this would be deep shelter. Deep shelter is located well inside the ship and as far down as possible. All nonessential personal should be located there after a radioactive incident.

There are several instruments available to monitor radioactive areas. These instruments are either personal devices or radiacs for general areas. The two most popular personal devices are the DT-60/PD that is a nonself-reading dosimeter and an IM-143/PD that is a self-reading dosimeter. Both devices will display how much gamma radiation the wearer has been exposed to. For measuring areas, the AN/PDR-43 radiac is used for rapid internal and external surveys. It will give you the concentration of gamma radiation in a specific area.

The AN/PDR 27 is used for subsequent or detailed follow-up surveys. The instrument is more sensitive than the AN/PDR 43 and can pinpoint the radioactive area for washdown teams. The AN/PDR 65 radiac is a very high-range gamma survey instrument and due to its bulk is usually mounted in a permanent position possibly in the house or bridge.

There are four methods of radiological control. They are:

1. Contamination avoidance
2. Radiation mitigation
3. Shipboard decontamination
4. Decontamination of personnel, clothing, and portable equipment

The easiest way to practice contamination avoidance is to get as far away as possible from the suspected detonation site. Another possibility would be to use the vessel's countermeasure washdown system. This system uses the vessel's fire main to provide a water shield. The water is sprayed out from predetermined positions on the ship via hoses or fixed nozzles. In addition to the CMWD system, it is essential to button up the vessel. Close all doors, hatches, and vents. Radiation mitigation is achieved by placing crew in deep shelter as discussed before. You should also rotate ship crew through other areas of the ship and deep shelter to limit exposure for all crew. Personnel decontamination is accomplished by passing through the vessel's DECON station that will be discussed later in the chapter. It is also essential to decontaminate all portable equipment and clothing. Please view table 8-1 as a rough guideline to the effects of exposure to radiation.

BIOLOGICAL WARFARE

Biological weapons are designed, produced, and used in order to reduce or eliminate an adversary's ability to wage war or conduct a mission. The biological attack can be disguised as a normal outbreak or to coincide with the intended time of attack. As we have heard earlier, the most successful attack will be those conducted against a population with limited, if any, immunity to the disease. Although the focus recently has been on chemical weapons, history has shown that biological agents have been used successfully and over a wider area. It is, therefore, essential that the Vessel Security Officer takes some time to study the basics of biological warfare and pass it on to his crew.

There are two categories of biological agents. Casualty agents are designed to cause death or serious illness. This will make the vessel unable to perform its mission over a long period of time. Several

TABLE 8-1

Acute Clinical Effects of Single High Dose Rate Exposures of Whole-Body Irradiation to Healthy Adults

Phase of Response	0–100 Rads (Subclinical Range)	LD_0–LD_5 Range ~100–800 Rads (Low Lethal Range)			LD_{50} Over 800 Rads (Supralethal Range)	
		100–200 Rads	*200–600 Rads*	*600–800 Rads*	*800–3,000 Rads*	*Over 3,000 Rads*
Initial Response						
Incidence of nausea and vomiting	None –5%	5–50%	50–100%	75–100%	100%	100%
Time of onset	—	~3–6 hours	~2–4 hours	~1–2 hours	<1 hour	<1 hour
Duration	—	<24 hours	<24 hours	<48 hours	<48 hours	<48 hours
Combat effectiveness	100%	>80%	Can perform routine tasks; sustained combat or comparable activities hampered for 6–20 hours	Can perform only simple routine tasks; significant incapacitation in upper part of range; lasts more than 24 hours	Progressive incapacitation following an early capability for intermittent heroic response	Progressive incapacitation following an early capability for intermittent heroic response
Latent Phase						
Duration	—	More than 2 weeks	Approximately 7–15 days	None to approximately 7 days	None to approximately 2 days	None
Secondary Response						
Signs and symptoms	—	Moderate leukopenia	Severe leukopenia; purpura, hemorrhage; infection; epilation after about 300 Rads and above		Diarrhea; fever; disturbance of electrolyte balance	Convulsions; tremor; ataxia; lethargy
Time of onset, post-exposure	—	2 weeks or more	Several days to 2 weeks		2–3 days	—
Critical period, post-exposure	—	None	4–6 weeks		5–14 days	1–48 hours
Organ system responsible	None	Hematopoietic system			Gastrointestinal tract	Central nervous system
Hospitalization						
Percentage	None	<10%	Up to 90%	100%	100%	100%
Duration	—	45–60 days	60–90 days	90–120 days	2 weeks	2 days
Incidence of Death	None	None	0–80%	80–100%	90–100%	90–100%
Average Time to Death	—	—	3 weeks to 2 months		1–2 weeks	2 days
Therapy	None	Hematologic surveillance	Blood transfusion, antibiotics, and rest		Maintenance of electrolyte balance	Supportive treatment

pathogens and toxins can be used for this purpose. The incapacitating agent will make personnel on the vessel incapable of conducting their mission for a short period of time. Examples of this are food poisoning strands. This may make the individual incapable of performing the mission immediately following the exposure but able to return after a short period of time. This agent is nonlethal to healthy adults. We should note here that casualty and incapacitating agents are used in chemical agents as well. Other similarities in the two are agent persistency and stability. Persistency refers to how long the biological agent will continue to be effective after its release in the environment. If an agent breaks down rapidly, it is considered to be non-persistent. The other consideration is the route of entry. If the agent can enter the body through unbroken skin it is known as percutaneous. If it requires broken skin or inhalation for infection, it is known as nonpercutaneous.

Biological agents are classified as either pathogens or toxins. Pathogens are microscopic organisms that can cause diseases in humans, animals, and plants. These organisms enter the body and reproduce themselves. This massive reproduction pushes out existing cells and organisms this will cause illness and if left unchecked eventual death. Depending on the pathogen, the incubation period or time from infection to sickness will vary. However unlike toxins, it will require a certain period of time and the effects will not be immediate. The microbes of pathogens are living organisms and therefore require all the elements that living organisms need to survive. These microbes can be transported to their victim by other living organisms known as "vectors." These vectors are usually immune to the microbe but through the victim's contact with the vector will acquire the disease. The microbes will need water, food, and oxygen. If you eliminate these requirements, the microbe will die. Unfortunately eliminating those elements will also kill the host person. A good example of vectors are insects and rodents. Biological agents can also be classified as quick acting or delayed acting depending on how fast the agent will produce the desired effect on unprotected personnel. Pathogens are generally delayed acting while toxins are generally quick acting.

The five major types of pathogens are:

1. Bacteria—These are single-cell microscopic organisms. Humans have no natural immunity to many animal bacteria and, therefore, cannot defend against them. These bacteria can be used as weapons against personnel. Popular examples of bacteria used as biological agents are anthrax, tularemia, and plague. These agents can be introduced directly or by vectors. A good example of vectors

are the rats that ran wild in medieval Europe carrying the Bubonic Plague or Black Death. It was actually the fleas on the rats that carried the plague.

2. Viruses—These microorganisms are smaller than bacteria. Viruses cause about 60% of all infectious diseases. The virus will enter a living cell and take over the biological process of the cell. There they demonstrate the characteristics of a living organism only when in contact with the host and can reproduce only through the use of a host's cells. These viruses eventually displace the host cells causing massive infection and if unchecked eventual death. Viruses are small enough to pass through most protective filters on masks, including the MCU-2/P used frequently by MSC contract vessels. Examples of viruses are Yellow Fever, Smallpox, Ebola, Encephalitis, and a major killer this century, Influenza.

3. Rickettsiae—These microbes are parasites that require living tissue from which they draw nutrients and an environment that is helpful to life and reproduction. These microbes generally live in the intestinal lining of blood-sucking and nonblood-sucking insects. The transfer to man occurs during biting or when in contact with their excrement. Examples of rickettsiae are Q Fever, Typhus, and Rocky Mounted Spotted Fever.

4. Fungi—These agents are members of the plant kingdom and include molds, mildew, yeasts, and mushrooms. Most members of this family are bigger than bacteria and can be seen by the naked eye. Although fungi cause few infections the next section in this chapter will show how deadly they can be as toxins. The most common form of fungi is athletes foot.

5. Protozoa—Very few of this type of species are pathogens. Protozoa will appear again in the toxin section. Although not recommended for use against ships at sea, this species include Malaria and Amoebic dysentery, both can become fatal if untreated. They are good candidates to contaminate food and water and in this venue can reach the entire crew.

In choosing a pathogen agent to be used by a bioterrorist a few qualities are desirable. How well the agent lives in storage and then reproduces itself after dissemination is an important consideration. This is known as "viability." "Communicability" is also desirable. This is the ability to be transferred from person thereby easily reaching a larger number of crew. Obviously the best agent will reach the desired population and kill or incapacitate its members.

Toxins are poisonous by-products of microorganisms, plants, and animals that can be harmful to humans and animals. They are at full strength at delivery and require no incubation period like pathogens. An important fact to remember is that toxins are not living organisms and, therefore, do not require food, water, and oxygen like pathogens do. Toxins can be synthetically produced. A few qualities desirable for the terrorist in his toxin of choice include:

- Stable in storage
- High toxicity
- Persistent regardless of the environment
- Economic in large quantities
- Able to be aerosolized
- Undetectable by sensors

The following is a review of the five types of toxins:

1. Bacterial—Bacteria release toxins during the normal function of the waste elimination process and when they begin to die. Of these two those produced as normal waste are more likely to be used as biological agents because of their potency.
2. Fungi—Compounds produced by fungi are most frequently only dangerous when inhaled or ingested. Several types of this toxin can be produced in militarily significant quantities by chemical synthesis or fermentation. Perfection is not needed as the crude mixtures are often more potent.
3. Algae—Several types of fresh and saltwater algae produce toxins. Saltwater algae produces one of the most potent neurotoxins known. Humans acquire this toxin by eating shellfish that feed on this particular type of algae. Algae toxins are desirable to terrorists because they are easily produced in mass quantity.
4. Venom—Certain species of fish reptiles and animals produce venoms highly toxic to man. Animal toxins are less stable than those produced by plants or fungi. Snake bites are a good example of venom.
5. Plant—This is one of the oldest forms of biological agents and can be used to paralyze and kill adversaries. Ricin is one of the most potent type of this toxin and is abstracted from castor beans.

Weather is a major consideration when biological agents are disseminated as aerosols. Both pathogens and toxins are affected by conditions that determine movement and strength. The five most important factors are sunlight, humidity, wind, pollutants, and temperature. The ideal condition for release are night, humidity based on use of dry or wet agent, no wind, no pollutants and temperature depending on agent used. Given these conditions, a subway station might be a good place for release. A subway station was used in Tokyo for fatal results.

In addition to weather, a population immunity and duration of incubation period must be considered. Population with no immunity and an incubation within about 24 hours is most desirable. Chemical agents can be disseminated by bursting devices such as missiles, rockets, and bombs. They can also be delivered by spray via a plane or helicopter. For ships a good way would be to contaminate the food and water or local sources via communicability.

The ways of detecting the release of a biological agent include illness in crew, provided intelligence, warning devices, and biological samplings. Detection units are known as IBADS (Interim Biological Agent Detection System). In addition you may employ active or passive defense. An active defense would be an air strike or attack on the facility producing the agents itself. A passive defense is what you on the ships can use and includes all other measures used to protect the vessel and crew. Some examples of good passive defense include good hygiene by all crew and general cleanliness of all spaces. Sanitation is also important, the old adage "a clean ship is a safe ship" is true here. Later in the chapter, individual protective equipment will be discussed, which is also important, and the last possibility is "quarantine" of all potentially infected individuals. Table 8-2 shows some potential biological agents.

CHEMICAL WARFARE

A chemical agent is a substance that through chemical reactions in the human body produces lethal or damaging effects on personnel. You'll find several similarities between biological agents and chemical agents in regards to describing characteristics. To review a few, a casualty agent either kills or incapacitates an individual for a long period of time. An incapacitating agent prevents personnel from performing duties over a short period of time. Persistency is the measure of the duration of an agent's toxic effect after release. Volatility is a measure of how readily the agent evaporates. Nonpercutaneous agents can only enter the body through inhalation, open wounds, or ingestion. Percutaneous agents can enter the body through unbroken skin or injure the skin directly. Quick acting agents act immedi-

Table 8-2
Biological Agents

Disease / Agent	Routes of Infection	Untreated Mortality (%)	Incubation Period	Infective Dose	Treatment
(B. anthracis)	S, D, R	S: 5 to 20 R: 80 to 90	12 hours to 5 days	8,000 to 10,000 spores/man	Antibiotics (limited effectiveness after severe symptoms develop)
Plague (Yersinia pestis)	V, R	Bubonic: 50 Pneumonic: 100	A couple of hours to 12 days	10 organisms/ man	Antibiotics
Q fever (Coxiella burnetii)	V, R	<1	2 to 10 days	1 organism/ man	Antibiotics
Smallpox	R	High 30s	7 to 17 days	10 to 100 organisms	Supportive
Viral hemorrhagic fevers (Ebola, Marburg, Lassa, Rift Valley, Dengue, etc.)	DC,V, R?	Up to 90 (depends on virus)	3 to 21 days	Ebola 1 to 10 PFU	Symptomatic (some may respond to Ribavirin)
Venezuelen equine encephalitus (VEE)	R, V	Low, <1	1 to 5 days	25 viral particles/man	Supportive
SEB	D, R	<1	2 to 8 hours	30 nanogm/ person	Symptomatic
Botulinum neurotoxins	D, R	60	18 to 36 hours	001 mcg/Kg	Antitoxin early
Ricin	D, R	High	2 hours to several days if ingested 1 to 3 days if inhaled	3 to 5 mcg/Kg	Symptomatic

ately on the individual after exposure. Delayed acting agents need a period of time to act.

Most chemical agents are stored as liquids, though some may be stored or disseminated in solid form. Agents used as weapons may arrive on target as liquid droplets, aerosols, and vapors. Chemical agents are toxic in any form. Weather affects chemical agents in a similar fashion to biological agents. Rain dilutes and disperses the agent. Wind is also bad as it greatly increases the rate of evaporation. Temperature is the main environmental influence. The higher the temperature, the faster the agent evaporates. Again the CMWD system is effective in preventing the agent from sticking to the vessel and for removing it from the deck. Some agents have a characteristic color and odor and can be detected by sight and smell. This is not a recommended means of detection for obvious reasons. Your *mask* is the best protection against these agents.

Let us first look at the incapacitating agents. They are:

- Psychochemical agents
- Physiochemical agents
- Riot control agents (RCA)—tearing and vomiting agents

The symptoms of psychochemical agents affect the individual psychologically. They either suppress or stimulate the nervous system. This results in bizarre or irrational behavior. Effects last hours or days and no permanent damage results physically. Physiochemical agents give false alarm signals to the body. The body responds with strong emotional and physical reaction such as fear or rage that interferes with judgment and control. Tearing agents cause tears to flow and may also irritate the skin. Other effects of tear gas are itching, stinging, and burning and may irritate the nose and throat. Vomiting agents produce nausea and vomiting. You may also have tightness in the chest and severe chest pains. In rare instances when coupled with lack of oxygen this incapacitating agent may result in death.

The casualty agents are:

- Nerve agent
- Blood agent
- Blister agent
- Choking agent

Nerve agents disrupt the transmission of nerve impulses and produce systemic effects. They affect the entire body and not just exposed areas. The primary effects are primarily on body functions rather than on body tissue. Examples of nerve agents are Tabun (GA), Sarin (GB), Soman (GD), GF, and VX. All quick acting and delivered by liquid. Mild exposure will result in headaches, muscle twitching, tightness in chest, and secretion of mucous from the nose and saliva from the mouth. Moderate exposure results in difficulty breathing and nausea. Severe exposure will yield involuntary defecation and urination, convulsions, paralysis of the respiratory muscles, and mental impairment, followed by death within minutes. Blood agents attack an enzyme that is important for the transfer of oxygen from the bloodstream to the cells of the body, causing cells to be starved for oxygen. This condition is known as anoxia. Examples of blood agents are Hydrogen Cyanide (AC), Cyanogen Cyanide (CK), and Arsine (SA). Symptoms include convulsions and low pulse rate. Breathing may become labored or rapid. This phase will be followed by lack of energy and difficulty breathing, ending with cessation of breathing and death. This agent is dispersed as a gas and is quick acting except for Arsine, which is delayed. Blister agents produce both damage to body tissue in the area of contact and systemic effects. Blister agents may be delayed acting. This damage to body tissue occurs both externally and internally. The damage progresses from redness and irritation to blisters then decay. Initial symptoms are runny nose, sore throat, and hoarseness, followed by paralysis of the vocal cords and difficulty in breathing. Other symptoms include vomiting, exhaustion, pain, and possibly shock. Death will occur from complications caused by damage to tissues. Examples of blister agents are Distilled Mustard (HD), Nitrogen Mustards (HN), Lewsite (L), Mustard Lewsite (HL), and Phosgene Oxime (CX). This agent is mainly disseminated in liquid form. Choking agents include Phosgene (CG) and Diphosgene (DP). Symptoms include tears, dry throat, coughing, nausea, and vomiting. After 2–6 hours of exposure, the lungs begin to fill with body fluid that excludes air from the air sacs. This causes breathing to become rapid and shallow and also coughing up large quantities of fluid. Victim dies within 24 hours. If they survive the 24 hours, they are likely to recover. Please review table 8-3 for more information on chemical agents.

PROTECTIVE EQUIPMENT AND DECONTAMINATION

In dealing with nerve agents there are two countermeasures: the taking of tablets such as NAPP tablets (Nerve Agent Pyridostigmine Pretreatment) or CANA (diazepam) tablets prior to exposure and the second is the use of injections after exposure. These injections are atropine and 2 PAMCI taken together. These injections should contain the symptoms in order for personnel to vacate the area. It is also possible to have your crew provided with protective equipment. This chemical protective clothing can either be a Chemical Protective Overgarment (CPO) or an Advanced Chemical Protective Garment (ACPG). This includes a smock or jacket and pants. For your feet, you can use Chemical Protective Foot Covers (CPFC). Your hands will have inner cotton gloves and outer rubber gloves specifically made for use in a chemical environment. The most important piece of equipment is the mask. The mask used on MSC contract vessels is the MCU-2P. It comes in three sizes (small, medium, and large) and should be fit tested prior to use. It is necessary to get an airtight fit so facial hair with the mask is prohibited. The mask comes with a C_2 canister that attaches to the mask to be used in a chemical environment and also a carrying case that allows the crewmember to carry the mask with him if potentially needed. If there is any risk of chemical agent exposure, the mask must be carried with the crewmember and used when necessary.

Decontaminating the ship is a detailed process that won't be covered here. What needs to be covered is the decontamination station. The decon station is set up between the outside deck and the vessel's house. Any crewmember returning from outside the house in a chemical, biological, or radiological environment must pass through this station before re-entering the house. There are five stages to the decon station. They include the area just outside the station, outer clothing area, inner clothing area, shower, and medical check area. In the outer area, outside the decon station, you decon by washing your gloves, mask, and boots. This is done with water possibly mixed with calcium hypochlorite. After you complete this, enter the outer

Table 8-3
Chemical Agent and Riot Control Agent Summary

Agent and Symbol	Physiological Effects	Military Use	Duration of Effectiveness	Physical State at 68°F	Normal Route of Entry	Onset of Symptoms
Tabun (GA)	Nerve	Casualty	Persistant	Liquid	Eye-respiratory Skin hazard	Quick acting
Sarin (GB)	Nerve	Casualty	Nonpersistant	Liquid	*Eye-respiratory	Quick acting
Soman (GD)	Nerve	Casualty	Persistant	Liquid	Skin hazard Eye-respiratory	Quick acting
GF	Nerve	Casualty	Persistant	Liquid	Skin hazard Eye-respiratory	Quick acting
VX	Nerve	Casualty	Persistant	Liquid	Skin hazard Eye-respiratory	Quick acting
Distilled mustard (HD)	Blister	Casualty	Persistant	Liquid	Skin hazard Eye-respiratory	Delayed
Nitrogen mustards (HN 1, 2, and 3)	Blister	Casualty	Persistant	Liquid	Skin hazard Eye-respiratory	Delayed
Lewisite (L)	Blister	Casualty	Persistant	Liquid	Skin hazard Eye-respiratory	Quick acting
Mustard-lewisite	Blister	Casualty	Persistant	Liquid	Skin hazard Eye-respiratory	Quick acting
Phosgene oxime (CX)	Blister	Casualty	Nonpersistant	Solid or liquid	Skin hazard Eye-respiratory	Quick acting
Hydrogen cyanide (AC)	Blood	Casualty	Nonpersistant	Gas	Eye-respiratory	Quick acting
Cyanogen chloride (CK)	Blood	Casualty	Nonpersistant	Gas	Eye-respiratory	Quick acting
Arsine (SA)	Blood	Casualty	Nonpersistant	Gas	Eye-respiratory	**Delayed
Phosgene (CG)	Choking	Casualty	Nonpersistant	Gas	Eye-respiratory	Delayed
Diphosgene (DP)	Choking	Casualty	Nonpersistant	Liquid	Eye-respiratory	**Delayed
BZ	Psycho-chemical	Incapacitating	Nonpersistant	Solid	Eye-respiratory	Delayed
Adamsite (DM)	Vomiting	Riot control	Nonpersistant	Solid	Eye-respiratory	Quick acting
O-chlorobenasimal-ononitrile (CS)	Tear	Riot control	Nonpersistant	Solid	Skin irritant Eye-respiratory	Quick acting
O-chloroarsine (DA)	Vomiting	Riot control	Nonpersistant	Solid	Skin irritant Eye-respiratory	Quick acting
Chloropicrin (PS)	Tear	Riot control	Nonpersistant	Liquid	Skin irritant Eye-respiratory	Quick acting

* Normally encountered as a vapor, but liquid form could be present and highly toxic to skin.
** There are prompt effects, but major effects are delayed.

clothing area. In the outer clothing area, you remove your smock, pants, outer gloves and boots (CPFC). You should pass through the station in teams of two as it is important not to touch any of the potentially contaminated clothing. In the inner clothing area, you remove all clothing and place it in bins found also in the outer clothing area. You enter the shower area completely naked except for your mask. In the shower area you are completely washed down. Remember to pay close attention to any hairy areas that may retain residue of an agent. It is also important to cover your canister on your mask so as not to get water in there. After the shower stage you enter the medical check area; if all is clear in this area you re-enter the house, remove your mask, and put it in a plastic bag. The mask will need to be decontaminated before re-issue. If there are any problems in the medical check area, the crewmember is returned to the shower stage.

Other items that are used to detect chemical agents are M8 paper, M9 paper, an M256 kit, and the chemical agent point detection

Fig. 8-2. MCU-2/P protective mask.

system (CAPDS). We will give a brief overview of these items; however, it is advised that anyone using this equipment in a position of authority take a course. A recommended course is the MSC 6 day CBR-D Officer Course that will examine these items more closely. There are also several CBRNE courses available. M8 chemically treated paper can be dipped in an unknown liquid to determine if it is a liquid nerve or blister agent. The paper will change color accordingly. M9 paper can be affixed outside the house or in potential release areas. It has a sticky back that will adhere to steel or a chemical protective ensemble suit.

This paper will also change color when exposed to a chemical agent. The specific agent cannot be determined by M9 paper. An M256A1 Detector kit will identify the agent for you. This kit similar to M8 paper will require you to actually put a sample of the liquid on paper. There are several sensor detector devices and more being developed. Currently we have the Chemical Warfare Directional Detector

Fig. 8-3. Survey team with chemical protective overgarments (CPO).

(CWDD) AN/KAS-1. This sensor can detect a nerve agent several miles from the ship. Draeger tubes are used to detect phosgene. In all cases where an agent has entered the house, purging is recommended. Six air exchanges will remove 99.9% of any existing agents.

It will be necessary to send teams out to survey for CBR agents. Any survey team should have a preassigned survey route and return into the house as soon as possible. Before re-entering the house, they must pass through the decon station. If they find any agents, subsequent scrub down teams should be sent out to remove the agent by water and calcium hypochlorite.

It is important to note three items essential for CBR survival:

1. Time
2. Distance
3. Shelter

If possible, place as much distance between you and the site of the agent release. Allow as much time as possible before going out on deck or back into the area of release. If not needed for mission completion, do not return to the area at all. Keep your crew inside and in deep shelter if possible. Inform your crew that if several become sick at once or exhibit any symptoms, vacate the area immediately, seek shelter, and inform the Vessel Security Officer. Prior warning before the release of an agent will give the best chance of survival. As the Vessel Security Officer you cannot always depend on receiving that information. This chapter gave you some insight into how to deal with the release of an agent near your ship. Share it with your crew if appropriate and be aware of the possibility yourself. Terrorist organizations have clearly stated that given the opportunity, they will release weapons of mass destruction.

NINE

Vessel Security Plan

The Vessel Security Plan is the backbone of the success in a vessel maintaining security. Prior to submission and approval, an On-scene Security Assessment must be conducted. The responsibility of developing the security plan lies with the Company Security Officer. The implementation of the approved security plan lies with both the Company and Vessel Security Officers. As of July 1, 2004, nearly all vessels have an approved Vessel Security Plan in the United States or a Ship Security Plan on foreign vessels. A side note—the Vessel Security Plan equates to the Ship Security Plan on foreign ships and the Vessel Security Assessment equates to the Ship Security Assessment. The general description of the plan is defined in 33 CFR 104.400, while the format of the plan is outlined in 104.405. The submission and approval process is described in 104.410, while any amendments and auditing of the plan is covered in 104.415. NVIC 10-02 (Chapter 10) and the ISPS Code give helpful insights into both the Vessel Security Assessment and Vessel Security Plan. The plan once approved is good for five years from date of approval. Access to the plan should be restricted to those persons with an operational need to know.

COMPANY SECURITY OFFICER (CSO) AND VESSEL SECURITY OFFICER (VSO)

The Vessel Security Plan (VSP) must identify the Company Security Officer and Vessel Security Officer by name or position and provide 24-hour contact information. The Company Security Officer is usually identified by name due to the permanency of the shoreside position. The Vessel Security Officer is usually identified by position due to the rotation aboard merchant vessels. In the case of the Company Security Officer, it should be an individual who will be staying with the company for awhile. Constantly changing the name of the CSO in the VSP is awkward and eliminates any gained knowledge or experience. It may be necessary to have more than one CSO due to the number of vessels in a given company. If this is the case, one CSO will have to be the primary CSO who the others report to. It is important not to assign excessive numbers of vessels to a given CSO or assign excessive additional duties that will not allow him to perform his CSO duties effectively. The VSO will generally be a given Deck Officer position but that is not a requirement. The Captain, Chief Mate, and Second Mate are the most common positions for Vessel Security Officer. Training of these individuals as VSOs is usually supplied through union schools or maritime colleges. Again proper training of these individuals and allowing them adequate time to perform their duties is essential in the job being done correctly and keeping the vessels safe.

VESSEL SECURITY PLAN (VSP)

The VSP must be written in English. A translation of the VSP in the working language of vessel personnel may also be developed. It is not uncommon for two plans to be onboard foreign vessels. Under the ISPS Code, the plan may be written in English, French, or Spanish. In the United States having certain sections translated into Spanish may assist in explaining the security duties to some of the crew.

The VSP should contain a clear statement emphasizing the Master's authority as described in 104.205. This is also defined in ISPS Code Part A as well as the SOLAS Regulation 8 Chapter 11-2. In this regard, the Master is ultimately responsible for the security of the vessel. He must support the VSO in any way possible regarding security. The company must also support the Captain and vessel in regards to security as well. The Captain is holding a double-edged sword here. If he takes no action and a security incident occurs, he will be held responsible. If he takes action and a security incident does not occur, the company may not be too happy. That is why you as the Vessel Security Officer must provide the Master with as much information possible before a decision is made. In matters where security and safety conflict, the Master is responsible to take measures to ensure that safety is maintained. In order to accomplish this, additional measures may be required. The Vessel Security Officer must not conduct or implement security evolutions that will endanger the safety of the crew.

The VSP must address all vulnerabilities identified in the Vessel Security Assessment. Prior to writing the plan, the CSO will be given a copy of the Vessel Security Assessment identifying vulnerabilities. That assessment will also be included in the plan as Section 17. The major purpose of the on-scene assessment is to determine the inherent vulnerabilities of a vessel and what countermeasures should be taken to prevent any security incidents. As described in NVIC 10-02, the VSP may address procedures to mitigate threats in the Vessel Security Assessment. The level of the perceived threat will determine the number of countermeasures that would be necessary.

This process is codified by describing security measures for each MARSEC level. If you analyze the format of the plan, you will see that there are 17 sections. Each section will be reviewed later in the chapter. For further guidance on security levels internationally, check ISPS Code A Section 7. It is important to note here that Sections 10–14 deal specifically with "Security Measures." The level of these security measures depends specifically on the MARSEC level. As the MARSEC level increases, the number of security measures and procedures will increase. Therefore, how the vessel deals with MARSEC level 1 and MARSEC level 2 is different. To determine what the differences are and what remains the same requires the VSO to review the security plan.

From what has been described so far, you can see that the security plan is not a short or frivolous document. It is important that the VSO takes the time not only to read the Vessel Security Plan but understand what is expected at each MARSEC level. Considering the security plan may be 100 pages or more, the time required to read and understand the plan may take several hours or even days. The good news is that once you have read and understand one Vessel Security Plan other security plans will generally follow the same format. If you return to the same vessel, it will remain the same plan except for any amendments. Something the VSO should check for. For this reason it is important that a new VSO takes the time and effort when first signing on to read and understand the Vessel's Security Plan, spending the time early on will eliminate anxiety and confusion that will eventually occur when you are asked about what to do according to the security plan. Has this been overemphasized? After conducting audits and talking with Vessel Security Officers, it is pretty clear that some never read the plan. So if you are the Vessel Security Officer for a given vessel *read the security plan.* In addition know exactly where it is kept and refer back to the plan before training, drills, and exercises.

Here is what you will read.

FORMAT OF THE VESSEL SECURITY PLAN

It is required under 33 CFR 104.405 that the owner or operator must ensure that the VSP consists of the individual sections listed below. If the VSP does not follow the order as it appears in the list, the vessel owner or operator must ensure that the VSP contains a table of contents identifying the location of each of the following sections. To avoid confusion, for the port state controls and new Vessel Security Officers, it is a good idea to follow this list in order and also to have a table of contents to identify sections. Earmarking the sections by number or name is another common practice. This allows the reader to focus in on the section in question quickly. From what you have already heard, the easier you can make the plan the better.

The required sections are as follows with 33 CFR reference:

1. Security Organization of the Vessel—104.200, 104.205, 104.210, 104.215
2. Personnel Training—104.215, 104.220, 104.225
3. Drills and Exercises—104.230
4. Records and Documentation—104.235
5. Responses to Changes in MARSEC Level—104.240
6. Procedures for Interfacing with Facilities and Other Vessels—104.250
7. Declaration of Security (DoS)—104.255
8. Communications—104.245
9. Security Systems and Equipment—104.260
10. Security Measures for Access Control—104.265
11. Security Measures for Restricted Areas—104.270
12. Security Measures for Handling Cargo—104.275
13. Security Measures for Delivery of Vessel Stores and Bunkers—104.280
14. Security Measures for Monitoring—104.285
15. Security Incident Procedures—104.290
16. Audit and Vessel Security Plan (VSP) amendments—104.415
17. Vessel Security Assessment (VSA) report—104.300, 104.305, 104.310

From what you can see above, the plan format is covered in 33 CFR Part 104 pretty much sequentially. It certainly makes it easy to read and teach the material.

33 CFR Part 104 is found in appendix C. If you have a question on Section 8 of the plan, Communications, simply open the text to the appendix with Part 104 and turn to 104.245. In addition thorough knowledge of Part 104 and being able to show it to USCG inspectors will certainly help in the inevitable unannounced inspection. Now you need to examine what should be included in the plan under each section.

Section 1, Security Organization of the Vessel, should clearly state the Master's authority and which position will act as Vessel Security Officer. The Company Security Officer must be named as well as 24-hour contact information. The qualifications and responsibilities of each of these positions is clearly spelled out in Part 104. It is a good idea for a VSO to keep a copy of the 33 CFR Parts 101–106 handy for quick reference. The VSO should review 104.215 carefully before and during his time as VSO.

Section 2, Personnel Training, is covered in Chapter 10. It is important to clearly establish in the plan how you intend to train the crew, personnel with security-related duties, and the Vessel Security Officer. In reviewing this section, ensure the vessel is still in compliance. It won't take long for a port state control or USCG to determine no training has been done either by inspection of records or simply speaking with the crew.

Section 3, Drills and Exercises, is covered in Chapter 10. Remember drills occur every three months while exercises are an annual event. If any of these are not recorded according to a port state control, they did not occur. It is important to document all drills and exercises immediately following the drill or exercise.

Section 4, Records and Documentation, is covered in Chapter 10. Ensure that the entries are legible, initialed, and kept in a secure place. The records must be maintained for two years and made available for inspection. The eight items that must be recorded are listed in Part 104.235. If you feel additional entries should be made by all means enter them. There is a provision to maintain the records in electronic format. If this option is chosen, the VSO must ensure the electronic entries are not deleted, destroyed, or amended without authorization.

The three MARSEC levels are covered in Section 5 of appendix C. In addition the 12-hour time limit necessary to comply with the new MARSEC level is addressed. For example if you receive notification at 1000 to set MARSEC level 2, you have 12 hours to ensure that all MARSEC level 2 requirements in your plan are met. Properly reviewing the plan will determine if this is possible. It is the Vessel Security Officers responsibility to ensure what is in the Plan for MARSEC levels 2 and 3 can be accomplished in a 12-hour period.

An important note here is that if a facility is operating at a higher MARSEC level than the vessel, the vessel should set the higher MARSEC level without undue delay. Therefore, prior knowledge of the MARSEC level the facility is operating under should be passed on to the vessel. This is accomplished by Section 8 (Communications).

Procedures for interfacing with facilities and other vessels are covered in Section 6 of appendix C. The risk that the vessel is exposed to depends on the vessel's location. The security of a facility or vessel with which your vessel is located alongside must be addressed. Any measures for interfacing are covered under their respective MARSEC levels. The best way to ensure this to both parties satisfaction is covered in the next section, "Declaration of Security."

Section 7 of appendix C covers Declaration of Security. A model Declaration of Security is found in appendix B. It is essential that the VSO reviews the vessel's DoS to ensure compliance. In addition several copies should be available for the VSO to use. The VSO is required to keep the last 10 ports of call DoS for inspection. If a vessel visits a port that was under MARSEC level 2, the potential for increased scrutiny is possible. It is important to review who can sign the DoS. From the ship side, it must be the Master, Vessel Security Officer, or their designated representative. From the facility side, it must be the Facility Security Officer or his designated representative. Under MARSEC level 1, the DoS can be effective for 90 days. Under MARSEC level 2, the DoS can be effective for 30 days. There are no time provisions given to a DoS under MARSEC level 3. Remember the DoS is the time to establish communications with the facility or vessel.

Section 8 of appendix C covers Communications. Clear, continuous, and defined lines of communication need to be established between the facility and vessel, two vessels, and with the shipboard personnel. Radios, signs, or PA announcements should all be covered in the plan and reviewed when signing the DoS. It is also important to establish clear policies on who to contact in case of a security incident. The plan should include notifying the Coast Guard and National Response Center at 800-424-8802 or 202-267-2675 in addition to the facility and shipboard personnel. This procedure should also be established in Section 15, Security Incident Procedures.

Section 9 of appendix C covers security systems and equipment maintenance. In this section you define how equipment will be maintained, tested, and calibrated. The recognized procedure is to follow the manufacturer's recommendation. Therefore, it is essential to have the manufacturer's manuals onboard. Records of testing, maintaining, and calibrating is one of the eight required items to be written in the security log. This section must also address procedures for responding to malfunctions and failures in the equipment or systems. Backup plans must be clearly identified.

Section 10 addresses access control. If you review 33 CFR Part 104, you'll see this section 104.265 is by far the longest. There is a reason for that—proper access control is essential to a vessel's security. In addition this is one of the easier sections for any port state control to identify that you are not following your plan. If the gangway is unmanned and the plan states it should be, you are in clear noncompliance of your Vessel Security Plan. This section also should give clear guidelines on what additional measures should be implemented at each raise of MARSEC level. This section more than any other gives clear guidelines of what the Coast Guard wants to see in the plan. Three items are of paramount concern and must be addressed in this section.

1. Controlling access to the vessel.
2. Detering the unauthorized introduction of dangerous substances and devices.
3. Securing dangerous substances that are authorized to be onboard.

Screening personnel and baggage is addressed in this section. Badges to be issued for visitors (escorted and unescorted) and recognized identification for personnel. It is important that the VSO review this section carefully and that all items identified are being practiced.

Section 11 of appendix C addresses restricted areas. It is important for the plan to clearly identify restricted areas. The Vessel Security Officer must be fully aware of those areas identified in the plan. These areas must be clearly labeled with a placard or sign. In addition any crew who operates in that area must be made aware that it is restricted and access is limited to only those that have been cleared by the VSO. The three MARSEC levels are identified here as to monitoring and searching these spaces. The recommended areas are defined in 104.270.

Cargo handling is addressed in Section 12 of appendix C. In this section you see methods to deter tampering with cargo. Store only identified cargo onboard. Identify cargo prior to loading and coordinating security measures with the shipper. Again guidelines for all three MARSEC levels should be included. Loading contraband cargo that may be a bomb, drugs, or WMD material should always be in the mind of the VSO when reviewing this section.

It is also important to maintain those standards when the months and years go by and no incident occurs. Tampering with cargo is one of the easiest ways to get something onboard.

Delivery of vessel stores and bunkers is covered in Section 13 of appendix C. Here again, you must check for tampering. Receive only stores that have been ordered and inspect prior to receiving. In addition establish recognized suppliers and ensure that they arrive at the ship to allow you to comply with your security plan before receiving the stores or bunkers. The VSO must be familiar with the procedure identified in the Plan for each MARSEC level.

Security measures for monitoring are covered in Section 14 of appendix C. This section involves the entire crew. Your initial training should incorporate parts of this section. Proper lighting is addressed in this section. Stowaway and contraband searches are also addressed. Procedures to identify any equipment or system failures or malfunctions are identified and corrected. Guidelines for all three MARSEC levels should be included and the VSO should be aware of them.

Security incident procedures are identified in Section 15 of appendix C. This section covers initial notification of essential authorities. Part 101.305 provides good guidance in this area. This section also addresses notifying your own crew and how best to respond. This section should be unique to the vessel and requires the VSO to review it carefully.

Section 16 of appendix C addresses audits and VSP amendments. This section is covered in Part 104.415. Any amendments to the Vessel Security Plan must be approved by the Marine Safety Center (MSC). The Coast Guard may decide an amendment is needed after an inspection. If that is the case, the Coast Guard will give the owner or operator written notice and request the owner or operator to propose amendments addressing the matters in the notice. Under this situation, the owner or operator has 60 days to submit its proposed amendments. Until the amendments are approved, the owner or operator must ensure temporary security measures are implemented.

If the owner or operator through audit or personal inspection decides changes in the plan are required, the owner or operator has 30 days to submit an amendment. Nothing in the regulations will limit the owner or operator from implementing additional security measures not mentioned in the VSP in order to address exigent security situations. The MSC should be informed of your initiating these measures and for how long.

If the owner or operator changes for a particular vessel, it is the responsibility of the VSO to amend the existing Vessel Security Plan.

The VSO or CSO must ensure an audit is performed annually on the VSP. Any alterations to the vessel requires an audit. Any changes of owners or operators for the vessel or company requires an audit. If the audit reveals that amendments are necessary for the plan, the VSO or CSO must submit an amendment to the MSC for review and approval in 30 days.

Section 17 is the Vessel Security Assessment (VSA) report. The assessment covered in chapter 5 earlier in this book is a crucial part of the formation and existing VSP. This assessment is kept with the plan and reviewed by the VSO on a regular basis. Addressing the issues mentioned in the VSA will keep the vessel secure.

SUMMARY

Now that you have reviewed the plan, it is important for the VSO to become familiar with the plan. In order to accomplish this, the VSO must continually review sections of the plan and propose amendments if he feels that they are required. It has been stated from several sources that the Vessel Security Plan is a living document and not set in stone. As conditions and your vessel change, ensure that your plan supplies the maximum security possible. Only the VSO at the ship can gauge these changes and new risks. Use the plan as a guideline and comply with it. If it's found in the plan, it must be done. Therefore, it is important that the VSO is familiar with the VSP of his ship.

TEN

Training Drills, Exercises, and Record Keeping

Now that you have covered the Security Plan and have it approved, is the job done?

Absolutely not—in fact for the Master, Vessel Security Officer, and crew, it is just beginning. Do not expect a document, no matter how well written, to protect you from danger. It is only through proper training, drills, and exercises that you can achieve that goal. In the front line appears the Vessel Security Officer. How he or she conducts the training and drills will be a direct reflection on how safe the vessel will be. The annual exercise should give a clear indication where the crew stands in preparation. Do not rule out the occasional visit from the U.S. Coast Guard or port state control to ask questions of your crew or try to gain access to your vessel with either false or no identification. The vessel passing these unannounced inspections will be a direct result of the Vessel Security Officer doing his job in proper training and drills.

The Vessel Security Officer will also be responsible for record keeping. 33 CFR Part 104.235 clearly defines the eight events that must be recorded by the VSO. These records must be maintained for two years. They also must be made available to the Coast Guard on request. It would be prudent to keep the security log with the Vessel Security Plan in a secure place. As with the plan, the information must be kept confidential. If you choose not to keep a log, remember to keep any loose papers together for if the events are not documented, their ever occurring is called into question. You may keep the security records in electronic format. If you choose this option, they must be protected against unauthorized deletion, destruction, or amendment. Good practice would be to have any computer files backed up on hard disk and stored with your plan. It is difficult on a working vessel to ensure that a computer will not decide to "crash" some day.

In order to comply with the regulations concerning training, drills, exercises, and record keeping, you must first be completely aware of what the requirements are. You can find the regulations clearly defined in 33 CFR Part 104.230 for drills and exercises.

Training is covered in 33 CFR Part 104.210 for the Company Security Officer, 33 CFR Part 104.215 for the Vessel Security Officer, Part 104.220 for personnel with security duties, and Part 104.225 for all other vessel personnel. Record keeping is found in 33 CFR Part 104.235. It is important for the Vessel Security Officer to refer back to these sections if he has any doubts in implementation or practice. It is also important for the VSO to periodically review these sections prior to conducting training, drills, or exercises. The proper implementation of training, drills, and exercises, in addition to proper record keeping procedures, will be the Vessel Security Officer's responsibility. If there are any problems in any of these areas, he should immediately inform the Master and/or the Company Security Officer.

Given the demands of a merchant vessel coupled with the reduction in crew size should indicate that at some point the Vessel Security Officer will need help. In performing these duties, don't hesitate to ask for help early and let the Master know what assistance you need. Not performing the above duties or not recording it properly is not an option for excessive ship work. This not only will lead to problems with the Coast Guard or port state control but will put your ship in danger.

TRAINING

When does security training start? Those of you reading this book have already started your security training that will eventually end in your being a Vessel Security or Company Security Officer. The fact that you are fully aware of the regulations and have knowledge in detecting suspicious activity and limiting your vessels vulnerabilities will not be enough to protect your vessel. It is a given that you will not be on all spaces on the ship at all times. However, one of the crew may be in a position at some point to prevent a terrorist activity or maritime crime. How they react at that time will determine the fate of the ship.

There is a joke about an out-of-towner visiting New York for the first time and attempting to get directions from a local. The street he is looking for is Broadway and he asks the local. "How do I get to Broadway?" The local responds, "Practice." This response certainly did not help the out-of-towner reach Broadway that day. But if he had any intentions of reaching the Great White Way in theatre or music, the answer was right on the mark.

So how do you make your ship safer—*practice*. Practice starts the minute a crewmember signs onboard. In 33 CFR 104.225 it states, all other vessel personnel, including contractors, whether part-time, full-time, temporary, or permanent, must have knowledge of, through training or equivalent job experience in the following, as appropriate:

(a) Relevant provisions of the Vessel Security Plan (VSP)
(b) The meaning and the consequential requirements of the different Maritime Security (MARSEC) levels, including emergency procedures and contingency plans
(c) Recognition and detection of dangerous substances and devices
(d) Recognition of characteristics and behavioral patterns of persons who are likely to threaten security
(e) Techniques used to circumvent security measures

How can you be assured that a new crewmember has the above knowledge? In order to guarantee this, an initial security brief should be given to each new crewmember. This can be accomplished during the required STCW familiarization time frame or other appropriate time according to company's policy. Regardless of when it is carried out, certain elements of above is fair game for Coast Guard or port state controls questions during an inspection. In order to pass, the crew must be briefed. It is required that the MARSEC level of the ship be known by all aboard (33 CFR Part 104.240). You are also responsible to "brief all personnel of identified threats, emphasize reporting procedures, and stress the need for increased vigilance." In order to accomplish this crew must be aware of what the MARSEC levels stand for. The initial brief should incorporate the existing Homeland Security Advisory System (HSAS) that anyone who watches television would see and relate it to MARSEC levels. This is found in 33 CFR 101.205.

As a quick review MARSEC level 1 covers HSAS green, blue, and yellow. Thus the sign for MARSEC level 1 is yellow. MARSEC level 2 covers HSAS orange. Use an orange sign for MARSEC level 2. MARSEC level 3 covers HSAS red thus MARSEC level 3 sign is red. The terms for MARSEC level 1, 2, and 3 are elevated, high, and severe, respectfully. As just described here, all crew must also be able to understand. It is a good idea to post the vessel's MARSEC level in a public place in addition to how the MARSEC levels correspond to HSAS levels.

If the crewmember is responsible for any security duties as described in the Vessel Security Plan, he must be briefed at that time on what those duties are. As stated before, the Vessel Security Plan is a confidential document; however, relevant parts that relate to the crewmembers' responsibilities can be shown or paraphrased with the clear understanding that they are part of the success of the security plan. Inform the crew that if you see a suspicious object, inform the Mate or VSO immediately. As discussed earlier in the bomb chapter, it is important that they know not to move the object, touch it, or use a radio near it. Discuss the potential individual conducting surveillance or attempting to place something onboard. Also discuss the risk of someone attempting to stowaway or steal from the ship. The schedule of the ship should dictate what the brief should emphasize. The last element should be made clear that these individuals who threaten the security of the vessel may try to circumvent existing security measures and any observation the crewmember may see to improve the security of the vessel should be reported to the Vessel Security Officer.

In dealing with the lower crew, it is imperative that they feel as if they are part of the security team and an intricate part of the success of the security plan. If the brief accomplishes the concept of "empowering" the crewmember in the area of security, it was a successful brief. It is not always possible to give your usual great briefing every time. That is why it might be a good idea to write down both the general security brief and personnel with security duties down in order to go over the same material each time a brief is given. A handout to the crew is also a good idea. With all the information being piled on them the first day, not all information may get through. Having a written document to refer back to would be helpful. This written brief is a good item to show the Coast Guard to ensure compliance. Update the brief when needed.

The second level of Training deals with personnel with security duties. 33 CFR 104.220 states that company and vessel personnel responsible for security duties must have knowledge, through training or equivalent job experience, in the following, as appropriate:

(a) Knowledge of current security threats or patterns;
(b) Recognition and detection of dangerous substances and devices;
(c) Recognition of characteristics and behavioral patterns of persons who are likely to threaten security;
(d) Techniques used to circumvent security;
(e) Crowd management and control techniques;
(f) Security related communications;
(g) Knowledge of emergency procedures and contingency plans;
(h) Operation of security equipment and systems;
(i) Testing and calibration of security equipment and systems, and their maintenance while at sea;
(j) Inspection, control, and monitoring techniques;

(k) Relevant provisions of the Vessel Security Plan (VSP);

(l) Methods of physical screening of persons, personal effects, baggage, cargo, and vessel stores;

(m) The meaning and consequential requirements of the different Maritime Security (MARSEC) levels.

In reviewing the above you can see there are 13 elements that the CFR calls for. You may be thinking that the writers of the regulations went a little overboard—not really. If you take a close look at the 13 elements, you will see that 5 are covered in the training for all vessel personnel. So if you look at it that way, there are only 8 new elements to deal with.

First, any personnel dealing with security duties should know what to look for. That is why they require the VSO to inform them of any security threats or patterns they may encounter. If they know what to look for, they will identify the threat quicker. They must be aware of crowd management and control techniques. Obviously in a situation with an agitated crowd, the VSO and Master must be informed but the initial contact will still be in the hands of the crewmember. Being able to handle the situation was covered in chapter 4. The crewmember does not need to be an expert crowd negotiator, but he should have some basic knowledge on what to do and what not to do while he informs the VSO. The crewmember needs to be briefed on any communication a crewmember is responsible for. It is a common mistake to assume a new crewmember is radio savvy.

The time for the crewmember to learn about the radio is before he assumes the duty, not when an emergency arises. Where crewmembers fit into the emergency or contingency plan should also be made clear to them. At this level, it is not uncommon for them to be shown a segment of the security plan that references their duties. Try not to overload crewmembers, but seeing their duties as part of the VSP may make it clearer to them why it is important.

Whatever security equipment and systems crewmembers are responsible for, they need to be briefed. The equipment is only as useful as the operator. If the operator does not know how to use it, the equipment is useless. Testing and calibrating the equipment is the responsibility of the VSO, but the crewmember handling the equipment must also be aware of testing and calibration techniques. Crewmembers must also be aware of inspection, control, and monitoring techniques that apply to their duties. The final element of physical screening of persons, personal effects, baggage, cargo, and stores must be covered in an adequate fashion that the crewmember can handle those duties he is called upon to perform. He must also be briefed on his limitations and respect for human privacy and dignity.

These precautions must not stop him from doing his job effectively. Only adequate training will accomplish this goal.

As you can see, assuming security-related duties is not something that should be assigned lightly or arbitrarily. It is important for the VSO to be familiar with any background history of the crew that might make the crewmember better suited for certain duties. Any equivalent job experience or prior training should be taken advantage of to provide for a safer vessel. This will also expedite the security brief for the VSO. However, it is important to note if such a crewmember is not available, the security training to gain that knowledge becomes even more important. How long should these training sessions last? The security training for all personnel can be very brief if the crewmember indicates a good knowledge in all the areas. The same holds true for personnel with security-related duties. If a lack of knowledge is evident, the briefing can be anything but brief. On the bright side, as the timeline from July 1, 2004, increases, you should encounter fewer of this type of crew.

And now the Vessel Security Officer. In 33 CFR 104.210 this knowledge-based proficiency is identified under Qualifications. The initial segment listed under number 1 consists of all of the Company Security Officers knowledge-based proficiencies. They include:

(i)   Security administration and organization of the company's vessels;
(ii)   Vessel, facility, and port operations relevant to that industry;
(iii) Vessel and facility security measures including the meaning and consequential requirements of the different MARSEC levels;
(iv)   Emergency preparedness and response and contingency planning;
(v)   Security equipment and systems and their operational limitations;
(vi)   Methods of conducting audits, inspection, and control and monitoring techniques; and
(vii) Techniques for security training and education, including security measures and procedures.

. . .

i   Relevant international conventions, codes and recommendations;
ii   Relevant government legislation and regulations;

iii Responsibilities and functions of other security organizations;

iv Methodology of Vessel Security Assessment;

v Methods of vessel security surveys and inspections;

vi Instruction techniques for security training and education, including security measures and procedures;

vii Handling sensitive security information and security-related communications;

viii Knowledge of current security threats and patterns;

ix Recognition and detection of dangerous substances and devices;

x Recognition of characteristics and behavioral patterns of persons who are likely to threaten security;

xi Techniques used to circumvent security measures;

xii Methods of physical screening and nonintrusive inspections;

xiii Security drills and exercises, including drills and exercises with facilities; and

xiv Assessment of security drills and exercises.

In addition to those found in 33 CFR 104.210, the following are found in 33 CFR 104.215:

(2) Vessel layout;

(3) The VSP and related procedures, including scenario-based response training;

(4) Crowd management and control techniques;

(5) Operations of security equipment and systems; and

(6) Testing and calibration of security equipment and systems, and their maintenance while at sea.

It is clear that the knowledge base for the Vessel Security Officer is wide. Several elements are found in both the security training for all personnel as well as the security training for personnel with security duties. It is important that as the VSO you are familiar with the above-mentioned areas. This book along with a certified Coast Guard–approved course should ensure you receive that knowledge. Keep this book with you along with any pertinent information as you embark as the Vessel Security Officer. It is not always important to memorize all the components of the regulations as long as you know where to look to find the answer. In conclusion, a thorough knowledge on the part of the Vessel Security Officer is essential to conduct proper training and answer questions from the crew as they arise.

DRILLS

In order to ensure that the training reaches the crew and they understand and can perform their duties as described in the Vessel Security Plan, the VSO must conduct drills. Drill requirements are found in 33 CFR 104.230. The emphasis is placed on the Vessel Security Officer to identify any related security deficiencies that need to be addressed. Holding a drill and then returning to work without a critique eliminates one of the most important reasons for the evolution. It is important that after a drill you perform an evaluation and identify what lessons were learned from the drill. This is not always a fault finding mission. Some drills will go smoothly. This should be noted and confirm that your plan and crew are prepared. However, do not be afraid to identify drills that fail to go well. This may identify the need for specific or additional training. It also may identify weaknesses in the security plan that need to be amended. 33 CFR 104 allows for these needed changes by amendments to the plan, which will be discussed later in this chapter.

One security drill must be conducted every three months. If a vessel is out of service due to repairs or seasonal suspension of operations (ex—Great Lakes), a drill must be conducted within one week of the vessel's reactivation. Another good example of that would be a breakout situation for a vessel in lay-up status. In addition, a security drill must be conducted when the percentage of personnel aboard the vessel who have never participated in a security drill on a vessel of similar design and owned or operated by the same company exceeds 25 percent. Be careful not to confuse this with returning crew. Despite the fact you may have a large crew turnover due to completion of contract, if the crew are returning from vacation and have been aboard before during a drill, this drill is not required. If you are dealing with a change of company or contract situation, you may encounter this situation. If so, a drill must be conducted within one week of such time.

The drill must test individual elements of the Vessel Security Plan. As was described in the previous chapter, the plan encompasses a series of elements. Take one of the elements, "Restricted Areas" and run a drill. Identify a restricted area on the ship and attempt to gain access. If the security plan calls for the space to be locked, is it in fact locked. If it calls for placards to be posted, are they in fact posted and legible. By going through this with the crew, you reinforce the importance of keeping restricted areas off limits to unauthorized personnel. The crew will be reminded of what the restricted areas aboard the vessel are and inform the VSO in the future if they see someone in the area or trying to gain access to the area.

Vary your drills; don't get in the habit of running drills that the crew are good at and will expedite the process. Work through the plan and try to run drills on sections you suspect the crew need a review.

Security drills may be held in conjunction with nonsecurity drills where appropriate. If you run a drill on a "suspicious" package, you may follow up with the package exploding and run a fire drill. This type of drill not only reinforces the potential consequences of a "suspicious" package, it prepares crew mentally for a worse case situation. In your debrief do not jumble both drills. Review each segment separately. Focus the security drill on how you handled the package in question. Then move on to the fire drill and how you put out the fire or contained it. You are already saving time by not assembling the crew twice; ensure that during that time period the crew get the most from both drills.

A favorite drill with significant benefits would be simply to raise the MARSEC level aboard. You are aware from previous readings that this must be accomplished in 12 hours. Checking to see if the vessel can do this before it is actually required is a great idea for a drill or even an exercise. In section 2 of 33 CFR 104.230 it states that if your vessel is required to raise the MARSEC level, this can count as a drill or exercise, provided that the Captain of the Port is notified of attainment of heightened security level. Be aware that raising the MARSEC level may take considerable effort and interfere with ongoing operations. Ensure that the drill does not conflict with any safety issues for the crew. You may discover that operating at MARSEC level 2 in 12 hours is unobtainable on your vessel. Required modifications should immediately be performed.

It is encouraged but not required to participate with the facility on security drills and exercises. This benefits both you and the facility. Working with each other in this area will help if an actual security incident occurs. The familiarization with each other's capabilities and limitations will benefit both vessel and facility. If your schedule coincides with a facility drill or exercise event, why not take advantage. In conclusion, drills must test the proficiency of vessel personnel in assigned duties at all MARSEC levels and the effective implementation of the Vessel Security Plan. They must enable the VSO to identify any related security deficiencies that need to be addressed.

EXERCISES

Exercises must be conducted at least once each calendar year, with no more than 18 months between exercises. An exercise is a full test of the security program and must include the active participation of the relevant company and vessel security personnel and may include facility security personnel and government authorities depending on the scope and nature of the exercises.

Four possibilities for an exercise are:

1. Full scale or live
2. Tabletop simulation or seminar
3. Combined with other appropriate exercises
4. A combination of the elements in 1 through 3

Again the focus of the exercise is to test the applicability of the Vessel Security Plan. If the plan does not work well during the exercise, changes may be required. If the crew does not perform well, additional training will be required. Do not run an exercise without a debrief or self-evaluation. Areas for improvement should be noted as well as areas where the crew performed well. Exercises may be vessel-specific or as part of a cooperative exercise program to exercise applicable facility and Vessel Security Plans or comprehensive port exercises. Each exercise must test communication and notification procedures, elements of coordination, resource availability, and response.

The exercise is a clear indication of how effective your security plan works. It is important for the VSO to consider what type of exercise he wants to run and schedule it accordingly. Remember if port facility or local law enforcement is to be used, they need adequate warning. Scheduling exercise months in advance will not only ensure that your schedule and office can adjust accordingly but that shoreside personnel can adjust accordingly. Trying to plan the exercise to take advantage of the 18-month grace period may have dire consequences if actual operational needs arise. Try to run the exercise on an annual basis and leave the last 6 months for the inevitable operational emergency situation. In addition it may be nice to see how the vessel does in an exercise.

In conclusion similar to the drills, the Vessel Security Officer is responsible for the security exercise and should start planning for it as early as possible. Run any ideas past the Captain and Company Security Officer. Some companies may have already arranged exercises. The VSO should review these scenarios and prepare the vessel to get the most out of the exercise. Above all the VSO should be prepared to submit a lessons learned report and record it as required.

RECORD KEEPING

The VSO is required to keep records on a variety of events. This being said it would be prudent for the VSO to keep these records in a folder or even better a security log. This log may be kept with the security plan. This will guarantee protection from unauthorized access or disclosure and make it readily available for port state control inspections. It is important to note early on that these records are required to be kept for two years. Some computer savvy VSO's may retain records in electronic format. This is fine but to avoid the inevitable computer crash back up your records on a disk periodically and keep that disk in a secure place. If records are kept in an electronic format, they must be protected against unauthorized deletion, destruction, or amendment. Vessel keeping requirements are found in 33 CFR 104.235

The following records must be kept:

- Training
- Drills and Exercises
- Incidents and breaches of security
- Changes in Maritime Security (MARSEC) levels
- Maintenance, calibration, and testing of security equipment
- Security threats
- Declaration of Security (DoS)
- Annual audit of the Vessel Security Plan

It is important to re-emphasis here that all the above records must be protected from unauthorized access or disclosure.

Under training, refer to the training required in 104.225. The required entry should include the date of the training, the duration, description, and list of attendees. This is no different than what is required for most company logbook entries for drills and training. Be careful that your initial training sheet or log entry covers this description accurately as subsequent training sessions will be recorded in that format. It is a good idea when making your first entry in the security log to ensure that it complies with 104.235.

Drills and exercises are similar. It requires date, description, and list of participants and, in addition, best practices or lessons learned that may improve the Vessel Security Plan.

As discussed earlier, the main focus of the drills and exercises is to see how effective the Vessel Security Plan is. It is a good idea to record the drills and exercises immediately following the event. If the event isn't recorded, the actual occurrence may be called into question. In addition, as time goes by the lessons learned become less clear.

Incidents and breaches of security is a serious matter. What needs to be recorded is the date and time of occurrence, location within the port, location within the vessel, description of incident or breaches, to whom it was reported, and description of the response. As described earlier, you must clearly identify a security incident or breach of security. Documentation in this section may be reviewed by several law enforcement agencies so try to be as thorough and neat as possible. Do not get caught up in telling the world and not document the incident while it is still fresh.

Any time your vessel encounters a change in MARSEC level, it must be recorded. You must record the date and time notification was received and time of compliance with additional requirements as per your Vessel Security Plan. It is easy to remember to record when a MARSEC level is raised, but also remember it needs to be recorded when the level is returned to "elevated" or 1.

Each occurrence of maintenance, calibration, and testing of equipment must be recorded. In addition, the date and time and the specific security equipment involved must be recorded. This record may be easy to leave out because it may not be as exciting as the four above. However, as the VSO, you must ensure that it finds its way into the security logbook for the port state control to see.

Any security threat must be recorded. Included in record are date and time of occurrence, how the threat was communicated, who received or identified the threat, description of threat, to whom it was reported, and description of the response. It is essential in the aftermath of this occurrence that it is properly documented and retained for two years.

Manned vessels must keep onboard a copy of the last 10 DoSs and a copy of each continuing DoS for at least 90 days after the end of its effective period. These DoSs may be kept with the Captain's papers. If that is the case, make sure your log book reflects that. You do not want to be checking the bridge and elsewhere for the DoSs especially if you are in the middle of a port state control inspection.

The last item required to be recorded is the annual audit of the VSP. For each annual audit, a letter certified by the Company Security Officer or the VSO stating the date the audit was completed. It is important to keep this audit with the plan or in the security log. Port state controls will check for it, and you will be able to determine when your next audit will be required. It is also a good idea for the VSO to review the audit when he assumes his duties onboard a vessel.

Keeping adequate and legible records is always a good indication of the competence of a ship's officer. Once you know what is required to be retained, you must go about the business of recording and retaining. If you have any questions, review 33 CFR 104.235 or this chapter. Remember if you retain too much, it will not be held against you but not recording the above eight events will be in noncompliance with the regulations. A final note—unless you are informed otherwise by the USCG or port state control, records over two years old should be discarded. As time goes by you will acquire a lot of useless paperwork and documents. This may interfere with your locating what's important.

Now you are ready to assume the duties of Vessel Security Officer. Keep this book with you—it contains 33 CFR Part 104—and also carry the ISPS Code for your continuing review. Remember the crew will come to you with problems and questions. Stay aware and keep your vessel secure.

ELEVEN
Security Challenges of the Cruise Industry

In the area of maritime security, the cruise industry presents the greatest challenges. The number of factors present in a risk matrix is greater than any other form of marine transportation. The risk is somewhat reduced when comparing cruise vessels with ferries. This discussion will center on cruise ships with some of the factors being germane to other types of passenger carrying vessels.

A cruise ship is a high visibility target of opportunity. An incident, no matter how minor, if connected to an act of aggression would most certainly make headlines for days. This alone would enhance the stature of the group claiming responsibility. Such an act overtly committed would have the potential of causing severe economic damage to the bookings within the industry. Collateral damage would extend to the vast infrastructure supporting the industry. It would also produce economic damage to local and national economies that depend on tourism for a significant portion of their revenue. It would take a significant amount of time for the cruising public to return to ships as a vacation.

The cruise industry as a whole was security conscious prior to the events transpiring on 9-11. With internal security it was a matter of increasing vigilance and adding training and technology. There is also a very high level of cooperation between the ship's staff and agencies with jurisdiction over vessel and passenger operation. These agencies include and are not limited to: USCG, U.S. Customs Service, Immigration and Naturalization Service, Federal Bureau of Investigation, INTERPOL, Federal Department of Agriculture, United States Public Health Service, CDC, as well as state and local police agencies.

The basics of vessel security have been in place for years prior. The impact has been felt primarily with port operations. The new levels of security have been problematic in the areas of provisioning and storing.

It will be noted in this discussion there are differences between management and officers, the difference being officers are licensed by the flag state and are legally responsible for the vessel and its operation. Examples of officers would include the master and mates as

162

well as engineers. Managers on the other hand are nonlicensed supervisory staff. They are responsible for running the food, beverage, hotel, and casino functions of the vessel. They have no legal authority in the operation of the vessel.

There are a number of factors present that make cruise ship security a more challenging area than other modes of marine transportation. These factors are:

- Vessel size
- Passenger and luggage screening
- Crew screening
- Contractor screening
- Percent of crew turnover
- Security at nondomestic ports
- Screening of stores and supplies
- Availability of chemicals and noxious agents onboard
- Ease of obtaining information regarding both the vessel and the route sailed
- Crowd control with limited trained staff
- Availability of help when under way or berthed at a port with limited facilities

VESSEL SIZE

As cruise lines have economized, ships have grown significantly. Several years ago, a ship with a passenger capacity of 2,400 persons and a crew of 900 was considered large. Growth in the size of vessels has accelerated considerably. A ship carrying 5,000 passengers and 1,400 crew is now classed as large. There are vessels being built that will have a combined passenger-crew size of over 8,000 persons. In theory these vessels can be evacuated in a timely fashion. In practice there has never been an evacuation of a vessel of this size in a real situation. There is also a difference between evacuating a vessel while in port with multiple gangways available as well as a large pier area and evacuating a vessel at sea.

ONBOARD SECURITY

All cruise ships have a dedicated security staff embarked. The size and makeup of the staff is determined by the company's policy. In practice the staff is headed by a security officer; normally that person will have a police or military background and is a European, American, or Israeli national. The security staff under him will vary due to the nature of the company recruiting practice. Most will have a military or security background. It is a practice of some companies to hire a more professional staff from a country that is not representative of the rest of the crew. An example would be Nepalese Ghurkas used by some lines. This limits crew fraternization with the security staff. All security as well as all of the crew is required to be trained in crowd management. All officers, managers, and security receive additional training in crisis management.

All cruise ships have up-to-date screening technology aboard. This includes metal detectors and portable X-ray units for crew and passenger screening.

There are no firearms onboard cruise vessels as per industry policy. If a passenger or crewmember is unruly, the method to subdue would be verbal, followed by physical with pepper spray used as a last resort. Ships security would be the only personnel authorized to take these steps.

PASSENGER SCREENING

Ideally the screening of passengers is a twofold process. The initial screening is done at the time of checking in to board the vessel. Passengers who are U.S. citizens are required to present either a valid or expired U.S. passport or photo identification and a birth certificate. Non-U.S. citizens must possess a valid passport and a valid, unexpired U.S. Multiple Re-Entry Visa. Starting on 12/31/2006 all U.S. citizens must possess a valid passport. These policies are communicated to passengers upon booking.

This documentation is checked by cruise line personnel upon check-in. If the requirements are not satisfied, the passenger is denied boarding. The check-in process begins on the day of the vessel's departure and continues up to sailing. At the time of check-in, a passenger is photographed and, depending on the cruise line, a photo ID is issued. This acts as identification as well as a room key and a shipboard credit card. The ID issued facilitates the re-boarding of a passenger during port visits. It also generates onboard and off ship lists and passenger lists.

A passenger's luggage is normally checked in at this time and is subject to screening similar to the process used by airlines. The luggage is X-rayed and screened for explosives. This is done prior to loading and is accomplished by private contractors rather than the TSA. Any problematic luggage is set aside for further examination and possible confiscation of items considered to be contraband. Usual items confiscated are dive knives, spear guns, and liquor purchased for personal consumption. These items are retained onboard the vessel by the security staff and returned to the passenger at the conclusion of

Fig. 11-1. Passengers preparing to board vessel.

the voyage. Items considered to be dangerous are set aside and authorities notified. The passenger is identified and further action is taken by shore authorities.

At the conclusion of the check-in process, the passenger and any carry on baggage are subject to search prior to boarding. This is accomplished by passing through a metal detector by the passenger and an X-ray of the baggage. After this screening, the passenger is free to board the vessel.

When the vessel calls at ports during the cruise, passengers are subject to screening upon re-boarding the ship. This consists of passing through a metal detector as well as the X-raying of all packages. This is accomplished by shipboard security in most cases. In the case of U.S. ports it is sometimes contracted out to local security firms. Any items considered to be contraband are confiscated at this time.

Prior to arrival at the debarkation port the passenger and crew lists are transmitted to the Coast Guard via the COTP or the NVMC (National Vessel Movement Center). Information required includes:

- For passengers: The list must include full name, date of birth, nationality, and passport number.
- For crew: Full name, date of birth, nationality, passport number or mariner's document number, and position or duties on the vessel.

This information must be transmitted 96 hours prior to arrival with exceptions made for short voyages where it must be transmitted 24 hours prior.

This information is shared among law enforcement agencies and has resulted in passengers being arrested upon arrival for outstanding warrants.

Upon arrival all passengers and disembarking crew are subject to customs and immigration inspection.

Problems in Passenger Screening

The most challenging aspect of passenger screening is the numbers of persons being screened within a small time window. The normal stay at the embarkation port is between 10 and 12 hours. A cruise vessel will arrive at its embarkation port between 0500 and 0600. The ship will sail between the hours of 1700–1800 the same day. In that time window all disembarking passengers need to be processed off the ship, usually during the hours of 0800–1100. Embarking passengers will be allowed to board at 1200. This may entail, on a large vessel, processing over 10,000 passengers (5,000 each embarking and disembarking). This also entails moving and inspecting over 20,000 pieces of luggage. This is for one vessel. During the start of a vacation period a port will experience a particularly heavy volume of traffic. The busiest sailing day in Miami during 2003 had a total of 40,340 passengers embarking. The Port of Ft. Lauderdale experienced a one day passenger embarkation count of 39,646 passengers.

CREW SCREENING

With the vast majority of crewmembers being foreign nationals, all cruise companies require them to have a multiple entry visa prior to the commencement of employment. These visas are issued at the U.S. embassy in the crewmember's home country with the cruise line assisting in providing a letter of employment. The ability to get a visa would be the initial screening of the crewmember. When the crewmember arrives in the U.S. he or she is given the same screening that all foreign nationals receive at the airport. Prior to boarding, the crewmember, as well as personal effects, is searched. This is done either by contract or ship's security. Anytime a crewmember enters or exits the vessel, he or she is subject to search by metal detector and X-ray for packages.

Problems in Crew Screening

Cruise ships normally experience a high turnover in personnel. This is due to both the nature of the jobs and crew cycling out for vacations, etc. With a large percentage of the crew originating from less developed nations, there is always the possibility of a financial incentive. Usually it involves smuggling. It can involve gathering data about the vessel or conspiring to do harm. In practice cruise companies rely on the vigilance of managers, officers, and the security staff to look for suspicious activity. All managers and officers are required under IMO regulations to undergo ISPS training. This has served to highlight the importance of vigilance on the part of the crew in taking responsibility for the vessel's internal security.

In practice any areas of the vessel considered to be critical are restricted to crewmembers working in that area. Locked and monitored areas include the bridge, engine and associated machinery spaces, all chemical storage area, all communication and computer areas, and any area considered to be critical. Any crewmember who does not normally belong in those areas would be intercepted and questioned. All of these areas, as well as any crew areas, are off limits to passengers. Any passengers found would be questioned by security.

CONTRACTOR AND VISITOR SCREENING

All contractors and corporate visitors are subject to pre-screening. A list must be submitted to the port 24 hours prior to arrival containing a list of those persons. If a person's name is not on the list, that person will not be allowed to enter the terminal area, let alone the vessel. There are no blanket approvals granted for companies with an ongoing relationship with the cruise company. This has been proven to be problematic if a vessel is in need of last minute repairs while in port.

All persons visiting, whether corporate, VIP, or contractor, is subject to the same search as passengers or crew.

SCREENING OF STORES

Any commodity brought on the vessel is subject to screening. The commodities are all checked for explosives, usually by dogs, prior to loading. This is done at the pier apron after the supplies are delivered and prior to loading. In addition all crew mail and packages are normally X-rayed. Contract security and screening services are normally used, relieving the shipboard security staff of that burden. The usual practice, dictated by economic, logistical, and public health regulations, is to take stores and supplies at U.S. ports exclusively. From a security standpoint, it makes that part of the operation more protected.

In practice stores, especially ones that may be flammable or hazardous should be stowed into their respective areas onboard. There is usually a time lag in this because any perishable products will

Fig. 11-2. Contractor access control.

take precedence during the stores evolution. Hazardous material may be left unsupervised for periods of time prior to the checking and stowing. This practice represents an opportunity for persons wishing to do harm to the vessel.

SECURITY AT NON-U.S. PORTS

At foreign ports, security is performed exclusively by the shipboard security staff. They will process all passengers and crew on and off the vessel. Upon re-boarding all are subject to passing through a metal detector and an X-raying of all packages again looking for banned items such as weapons and items considered contraband by the cruise operators.

It is considered common practice to offload trash at foreign ports due to the high disposal costs associated with U.S. regulations. This is done by the vessel's crew and is nominally supervised by ship's security or an officer. The trash is offloaded either pier side into dumpsters or on the offshore side into a barge. This practice is considered a weak point in the overall security of the vessel. It is easy for contraband to be brought onboard with the co-operation of a crewmember. It has served as a popular smuggling venue in the past.

Security at non-U.S. ports goes from professional to nonexistent depending on the country visited. In practice all vessels are kept away from cruise ships at U.S. and European ports. This is not the case in many of the ports visited. In many of the cruise ports harbor security is lacking making the vessel vulnerable to attack.

Response reaction time will vary with the security infrastructure of a given port. The ISPS Code was promulgated to address some of these issues but in practice the budgetary and cultural realities of different countries will dictate the actual level of security present as well as a unified response to an incident onboard a ship.

RISK ASSESSMENT

The risk of an event happening to a cruise vessel has been minimized internally with the aforementioned practices. The external risk has been minimized externally in U.S. and European ports. At present the remaining risks are not controllable without draconian security measures that would negatively impact both the industry and traveling public.

Examples of risk not addressed would be a missile or suicide attack delivered either while the vessel is under way or at a cruise port.

Fig. 11-3. Access control security perimeter established.

This is a risk that is not controllable by the industry or U.S. authorities outside domestic waters.

There is a real risk of a crewmember either being bribed or having his family held hostage to inflict internal damage using materials and chemicals easily available onboard the vessel. The mixing of chlorine, used for sanitation, and a strong acid would produce a toxic cloud. If done in a public area panic would ensue.

There exists a real risk of biological contamination through the spread of an easily communicable disease. This could be accomplished by one person mingling in the crowded environment onboard a ship. The ease of this method is demonstrated every year by the communicability and spread of the Norwalk and Norwalk like viruses onboard vessels.

The real risk of an incident onboard a cruise vessel, no matter how small, is the potential for severe economic disruption to the industry. If an act is committed and panic, injury, or loss of life is experienced even on a small scale the economic disruption would be enormous. This disruption would include not only the cruise companies themselves but the network of suppliers, businesses, and ports dependent on that income.

The partial recovery of the aviation industry following the acts of 9-11 was due to the fact that people need air transportation for business and personal reasons. The cruise industry provides a vacation and leisure activity that is not a necessary transportation function. The vessels themselves are part of the destination. A high visibility act would take the industry years to recover from. The key in preventing such acts is constant vigilance and rapid response. Given the vulnerabilities there can be no guarantees that an incident will not happen. Proper scenario planning can mitigate the risks and help in preparation and recovery but due to the nature of the industry, travel by cruise ship can never be made risk free. It is the Vessel Security Officer's duty to minimize that risk.

Suggested Vessel Security Course Outline

- All courses need to be approved by the Port State Control in order to get official certification.
- Course length is 14 hours. If you include lunches and breaks you would probably need 2 full days.
- If you teach it as part of a 3 credit course (given 42 hours for 3 credits), it should be half your semester. This leaves time for the PFSO Course or CBR-D training.

The official course outline must be purchased from the International Maritime Organization. Below are suggested topics for the Vessel Security Officer.

TOPICS

Section 1 Introduction

1.1 Course Overview
1.2 Competencies to be Achieved
1.3 Historic Perspective
1.4 Current Security Threats and Patterns
1.5 Ship and Port Operations and Conditions
- 1.5 hours

Section 2 Maritime Security Policy

2.1 Relevant International Conventions, Codes, and Recommendations
2.2 Relevant Government Legislations and Regulations
2.3 Definitions
2.4 Legal implications of action or nonaction of Ship Security Officer
2.5 Handling Sensitive Security-Related Information and Communications
- 1.0 hour

Section 3 Security Responsibilities

3.1   Contracting Governments
3.2   Recognized Security Organizations
3.3   The Company
3.4   The Ship
3.5   The Port Facility
3.6   Ship Security Officer
3.7   Company Security Officer
3.8   Port Facility Security Officer
3.9   Shipboard Personnel with Security-Related Duties
3.10 Port Facility Personnel with Security-Related Duties
3.11 Other Personnel
    • 1.5 hours

Section 4 Ship Security Assessments

4.1   Risk Assessment Methodology
4.2   Assessment Tools
4.3   On-Scene Security Surveys
4.4   Security Assessment Documentation
    • 1.5 hours

Section 5 Security Equipment

5.1   Security Equipment and Systems
5.2   Operational Limitations of Security Equipment and Systems
5.3   Testing, Calibration, and Maintenance of Security Equipment
      and Systems
    • 1.0 hour

Section 6 Ship Security Plan

6.1   Purpose of the Ship Security Plan
6.2   Contents of the Ship Security Plan
6.3   Confidentiality Issues
6.4   Implementation of the Ship Security Plan
6.5   Maintenance and modification of the Ship Security Plan
    • 1.5 hours

Section 7 Threat Identification, Recognition, and Response

7.1   Recognition and Detection of weapons, dangerous substances,
      and devices
7.2   Methods of physical searches and nonintrusive inspections
7.3   Implementing and coordinating searches
7.4   Recognition, on a nondiscriminatory basis, of persons posing
      potential security risks

7.5 Techniques used to circumvent security measures
7.6 Crowd management and control techniques
  • 1.5 hours

Section 8 Ship Security Actions
8.1 Actions required by different Security Levels
8.2 Maintaining security of the ship/port interface
8.3 Usage of the Declaration of Security
8.4 Implementation of Security Procedures
  • 1.0 hour

Section 9 Emergency Preparedness, Drills, and Exercises
9.1 Contingency Planning
9.2 Security Drills and Exercises
9.3 Assessments of Security Drills and Exercises
  • 1.0 hour

Section 10 Security Administration
10.1 Documentation and Records
10.2 Reporting Security Incidents
10.3 Monitoring and Control
10.4 Security Audits and Inspections
10.5 Reporting Nonconformities
  • 1.0 hour

Section 11 Security Training
11.1 Training Requirements
11.2 Instructional Techniques
  • 1.5 hours

  • Total 14 Hours

APPENDIX B

Declaration of Security

_____	_____
(Name of Vessel)	(Name of Waterfront Facility)

This _Declaration of Security_ is valid from _____ until _____, for the following _vessel/waterfront facility interface_ activities under Security Level _____:

The vessel and waterfront facility agree to the following security responsibilities.

	(Initial blank or circle responsible party)	
Activity	Vessel	Facility
1. Communications established between the vessel and waterfront facility:		
a. Means of raising alarm agreed between vessel and waterfront facility.	_____	_____
b. Vessel/waterfront facility report/communicate any noted security nonconformities and notify appropriate government agencies.	_____	_____
c. Port specific security information passed to vessel and notification procedures established (specifically who contacts local authorities, National Response Center, and Coast Guard).	_____	_____
2. Responsibility for checking identification and screening of:		
a. Passengers, crew, hand carried items, and luggage.	Vessel / Facility	
b. Vessel's store, cargo, and vehicles.	Vessel / Facility	
3. Responsibility for searching the berth/pier directly surrounding the vessel.	Vessel / Facility	
4. Responsibility for monitoring and/or performing security of water surrounding the vessel.	Vessel / Facility	
5. Verification of increased MARSEC level and implementation of additional protective measures.	_____	_____
6. Establish protocol to coordinate response between Vessel/Waterfront facility to acts that threaten either the Vessel and/or Waterfront facility.	_____	_____

The signatories to this agreement certify that security arrangements for both the vessel and the waterfront facility during the specified _vessel/waterfront facility interface_ activities are in place and maintained.

Date of issue: _____

_____	_____
(Signature of Master or _Vessel Security Officer_)	(Signature of Facility Security Officer or authorized designee)
_____	_____
Name and Title, _Vessel Security Officer_	Name and Title, Facility Security Officer
Contact information _____	Contact information _____
IMO number:	Mailing address:

APPENDIX C

33 CFR Part 104

Subpart A—General

§ 104.100 Definitions.

Except as specifically stated in this subpart, the definitions in part 101 of this subchapter apply to this part.

§ 104.105 Applicability.

(a) This part applies to the owner or operator of any:

(1) **Mobile Offshore Drilling Unit (MODU), cargo, or passenger vessel subject to the International Convention for Safety of Life at Sea, 1974, (SOLAS), Chapter XI-1 or Chapter XI-2;**

(2) **Foreign cargo vessel greater than 100 gross register tons;**

(3) **Self-propelled U.S. cargo vessel greater than 100 gross register tons subject to 46 CFR subchapter I, except commercial fishing vessels inspected under 46 CFR part 105;**

(4) **Vessel subject to 46 CFR chapter I, subchapter L;**

(5) **Passenger vessel subject to 46 CFR chapter I, subchapter H;**

(6) **Passenger vessel certificated to carry more than 150 passengers;**

(7) **Other passenger vessel carrying more than 12 passengers, including at least one passenger-for-hire, that is engaged on an international voyage;**

(8) **Barge subject to 46 CFR chapter I, subchapters D or O;**

(9) **Barge subject to 46 CFR chapter I, subchapter I, that carries Certain Dangerous Cargoes in bulk, or that is engaged on an international voyage;**

(10) **Tankship subject to 46 CFR chapter I, subchapters D or O; and**

(11) **Towing vessel greater than eight meters in registered length that is engaged in towing a barge or barges subject to this part, except a towing vessel that—**

(i) **Temporarily assists another vessel engaged in towing a barge or barges subject to this part;**

(ii) **Shifts a barge or barges subject to this part at a facility or within a fleeting facility;**

(iii) **Assists sections of a tow through a lock; or**

(iv) **Provides emergency assistance.**

(b) An owner or operator of any vessel not covered in paragraph (a) of this section is subject to parts 101 through 103 of this subchapter.

(c) **Foreign Vessels that have on board a valid International Ship Security Certificate that certifies that the verifications required by part A, Section 19.1, of the International Ship and Port Facility Security (ISPS) Code (Incorporated by reference, see § 101.115 of this subchapter) have been completed will be deemed in compliance with this part, except for §§ 104.240, 104.255, 104.292, and 104.295, as appropriate. This includes ensuring that the vessel meets the applicable requirements of SOLAS Chapter XI-2 (Incorporated by reference, see § 101.115 of this subchapter) and the ISPS Code, part A, having taken into account the relevant provisions of the ISPS Code, part B, and that the vessel is provided with an approved security plan.**

(d) Except pursuant to international treaty, convention, or agreement to which the U.S. is a party, this part does not apply to any foreign vessel that is not destined for, or departing from, a port or place subject to the jurisdiction of the U.S. and that is in:

(1) Innocent passage through the territorial sea of the U.S.; or

(2) Transit through the navigable waters of the U.S. that form a part of an international strait.

[USCG-2003-14749, 68 FR 39302, July 1, 2003, as amended at 68 FR 60513, Oct. 22, 2003; USCG-2004-18057, 69 FR 34925, June 23, 2004]

§ 104.110 Exemptions.

(a) **This part does not apply to warships, naval auxiliaries, or other vessels owned or operated by a government and used only on government non-commercial service.**

(b) **A vessel is not subject to this part while the vessel is laid up, dismantled, or otherwise out of commission.**

[USCG-2003-14749, 68 FR 60513, Oct. 22, 2003]

§ 104.115 Compliance dates.

(a) On July 1, 2004, and thereafter, vessel owners or operators must ensure their vessels are operating in compliance with this part.

(b) On or before December 31, 2003, vessel owners or operators not subject to paragraph (c)(1) of this section must submit to the Commanding Officer, Marine Safety Center, for each vessel—

(1) The Vessel Security Plan described in subpart D of this part for review and approval; or

(2) If intending to operate under an approved Alternative Security Program, a letter signed by the vessel owner or operator stating which approved Alternative Security Program the owner or operator intends to use.

(c) On July 1, 2004, and thereafter, owners or operators of foreign vessels must comply with the following—

(1) Vessels subject to the International Convention for Safety of Life at Sea, 1974, (SOLAS), Chapter XI-1 or Chapter XI-2, must carry on board a valid International Ship Security Certificate that certifies that the verifications required by part A, Section 19.1, of the International Ship and Port Facility Security (ISPS) Code (Incorporated by reference, see § 101.115 of this subchapter) have been completed. This includes ensuring that the vessel meets the applicable requirements of SOLAS Chapter XI-2 (Incorporated by reference, see § 101.115 of this chapter) and the ISPS Code, part A, having taken into account the relevant provisions of the ISPS Code, part B, and that the vessel is provided with an approved security plan.

(2) Vessels not subject to SOLAS Chapter XI-1 or Chapter XI-2, may comply with this part through an Alternative Security Program or a bilateral arrangement approved by the Coast Guard. If not complying with an approved Alternative Security Program or bilateral arrangement, these vessels must meet the requirements of paragraph (b) of this section.

[USCG-2003-14749, 68 FR 60513, Oct. 22, 2003, as amended by USCG-2004-18057, 69 FR 34925, June 23, 2004]

§ 104.120 Compliance documentation.

(a) Each vessel owner or operator subject to this part must ensure, on or before July 1, 2004, that copies of the following documents are carried on board the vessel and are made available to the Coast Guard upon request:

(1) The approved Vessel Security Plan (VSP) and any approved revisions or amendments thereto, and a letter of approval from the Commanding Officer, Marine Safety Center (MSC);

(2) The VSP submitted for approval and a current acknowledgement letter from the Commanding Officer, MSC, stating that the Coast Guard is currently reviewing the VSP submitted for approval, and that the vessel may continue to operate so long as the vessel remains in compliance with the submitted plan;

(3) For vessels operating under a Coast Guard-approved Alternative Security Program as provided in § 104.140, a copy of the Alternative Security Program the vessel is using, including a vessel specific security assessment report generated under the Alternative Security Program, as specified in § 101.120(b)(3) of this subchapter, and a letter signed by the vessel owner or operator, stating which Alternative Security Program the vessel is using and certifying that the vessel is in full compliance with that program; or

(4) For foreign vessels, subject to the International Convention for Safety of Life at Sea, 1974, (SOLAS), Chapter XI-1 or Chapter XI-2, a valid International Ship Security Certificate (ISSC) that attests to the vessel's compliance with SOLAS Chapter XI-2 and the ISPS Code, part A (Incorporated by reference, see § 101.115 of this subchapter) and is issued in accordance with the ISPS Code, part A, section 19. As stated in Section 9.4 of the ISPS Code, part A requires that, in order for the ISSC to be issued, the provisions of part B of the ISPS Code need to be taken into account.

(b) Each owner or operator of an unmanned vessel subject to this part must maintain the documentation described in paragraphs (a)(1), (2), or (3) of this section. The letter required by each of those paragraphs must be carried on board the vessel. The plan or program required by each of those paragraphs must not be carried on board the vessel, but must be maintained in a secure location. During scheduled inspections, the plan or program must be made available to the Coast Guard upon request.

[USCG-2003-14749, 68 FR 39302, July 1, 2003, as amended at 68 FR 60513, Oct. 22, 2003; USCG-2004-18057, 69 FR 34925, June 23, 2004]

§ 104.125 Noncompliance.

When a vessel must temporarily deviate from the requirements of this part, the vessel owner or operator must notify the cognizant COTP, and either suspend operations or request and receive permission from the COTP to continue operating.

[USCG-2003-14749, 68 FR 60513, Oct. 22, 2003]

§ 104.130 Waivers.

Any vessel owner or operator may apply for a waiver of any requirement of this part that the owner or operator considers unnecessary in light of the nature or operating conditions of the vessel. A request for a waiver must be submitted in writing with justification to the Commandant (G-MP) at 2100 Second St., SW., Washington, DC 20593. The Commandant (G-MP) may require the vessel owner or operator to provide additional data for determining the validity of the requested waiver. The Commandant (G-MP) may grant, in writing, a waiver with or without conditions only if the waiver will not reduce the overall security of the vessel, its passengers, its crew, or its cargo, or facilities or ports that the vessel may visit.

§ 104.135 Equivalents.

For any measure required by this part, the vessel owner or operator may propose an equivalent as provided in § 101.130 of this subchapter.

§ 104.140 Alternative Security Programs.

A vessel owner or operator may use an Alternative Security Program as approved under § 101.120 of this subchapter if:

(a) The Alternative Security Program is appropriate to that class of vessel;

(b) The vessel is not subject to the International Convention for Safety of Life at Sea, 1974; and

(c) The Alternative Security Program is implemented in its entirety.

[USCG-2003-14749, 68 FR 39302, July 1, 2003, as amended at 68 FR 60513, Oct. 22, 2003]

§ 104.145 Maritime Security (MARSEC) Directive.

Each vessel owner or operator subject to this part must comply with any instructions contained in a MARSEC Directive issued under § 101.405 of this subchapter.

§ 104.150 Right to appeal.

Any person directly affected by a decision or action taken under this part, by or on behalf of the Coast Guard, may appeal as described in § 101.420 of this subchapter.

Subpart B—Vessel Security Requirements

§ 104.200 Owner or operator.

(a) Each vessel owner or operator must ensure that the vessel operates in compliance with the requirements of this part.

(b) For each vessel, the vessel owner or operator must:

(1) Define the security organizational structure for each vessel and provide all personnel exercising security duties or responsibilities within that structure with the support needed to fulfill security obligations;

(2) Designate, in writing, by name or title, a Company Security Officer (CSO), a Vessel Security Officer (VSO) for each vessel, and identify how those officers can be contacted at any time;

(3) Ensure personnel receive training, drills, and exercises enabling them to perform their assigned security duties;

(4) Ensure vessel security records are kept;

(5) Ensure that adequate coordination of security issues takes place between vessels and facilities; this includes the execution of a Declaration of Security (DoS);

(6) Ensure coordination of shore leave for vessel personnel or crew change-out, as well as access through the facility of visitors to the vessel (in-

cluding representatives of seafarers' welfare and labor organizations), with facility operators in advance of a vessel's arrival. Vessel owners or operators may refer to treaties of friendship, commerce, and navigation between the U.S. and other nations in coordinating such leave. The text of these treaties can be found on the U.S. Department of State's Web site at http://www. state.gov/s/l/24224.htm;

(7) Ensure security communication is readily available;

(8) Ensure coordination with and implementation of changes in Maritime Security (MARSEC) Level;

(9) Ensure that security systems and equipment are installed and maintained;

(10) Ensure that vessel access, including the embarkation of persons and their effects, are controlled;

(11) Ensure that restricted areas are controlled;

(12) Ensure that cargo and vessel stores and bunkers are handled in compliance with this part;

(13) Ensure restricted areas, deck areas, and areas surrounding the vessel are monitored;

(14) Provide the Master, or for vessels on domestic routes only, the CSO, with the following information:

(i) Parties responsible for appointing vessel personnel, such as vessel management companies, manning agents, contractors, concessionaires (for example, retail sales outlets, casinos, etc.);

(ii) Parties responsible for deciding the employment of the vessel, including time or bareboat charters or any other entity acting in such capacity; and

(iii) In cases when the vessel is employed under the terms of a charter party, the contract details of those documents, including time or voyage charters; and

(15) Give particular consideration to the convenience, comfort, and personal privacy of vessel personnel and their ability to maintain their effectiveness over long periods.

[USCG-2003-14749, 68 FR 39302, July 1, 2003, as amended by USCG-2003-14749, 68 FR 60513, Oct. 22, 2003]

§ 104.205 Master.

(a) Nothing in this part is intended to permit the Master to be constrained by the Company, the vessel owner or operator, or any other person, from taking or executing any decision which, in the professional judgment of the Master, is necessary to maintain the safety and security of the vessel. This includes denial of access to persons—except those identified as duly authorized by the cognizant government authority—or their effects, and refusal to load cargo, including containers or other closed cargo transport units.

(b) If, in the professional judgment of the Master, a conflict between any safety and security requirements applicable to the vessel arises during its operations, the Master may give precedence to measures intended to maintain the safety of the vessel, and take such temporary security measures as seem best under all circumstances. In such cases:

(1) The Master must, as soon as practicable, inform the nearest COTP. If the vessel is on a foreign voyage, the Master must promptly inform the Coast Guard **via the NRC** at 1-800-424-8802, direct telephone at 202-267-2675, fax at 202-267-2165, TDD at 202-267-4477, or E-mail at **lst-nrcinfo@comdt.uscg.mil** and if subject to the jurisdiction of a foreign government, the relevant maritime authority of that foreign government;

(2) The temporary security measures must, to the highest possible degree, be commensurate with the prevailing Maritime Security (MARSEC) Level; and

(3) The owner or operator must ensure that such conflicts are resolved to the satisfaction of the cognizant COTP, or for vessels on international voyages, the Commandant (G-MP), and that the possibility of recurrence is minimized.

[USCG-2003-14749, 68 FR 39302, July 1, 2003, as amended at 68 FR 60513, Oct. 22, 2003]

§ 104.210 Company Security Officer (CSO).

(a) *General.* (1) Each vessel owner or operator must designate in writing a CSO.

(2) A vessel owner or operator may designate a single CSO for all its vessels to which this part applies, or may designate more than

one CSO, in which case the owner or operator must clearly identify the vessels for which each CSO is responsible.

(3) A CSO may perform other duties within the owner or operator's organization, **including the duties of a Vessel Security Officer,** provided he or she is able to perform the duties and responsibilities required of a CSO.

(4) The CSO may delegate duties required by this part, but remains responsible for the performance of those duties.

(b) *Qualifications.* (1) The CSO must have general knowledge, through training or equivalent job experience, in the following:

(i) Security administration and organization of the company's vessel(s);

(ii) Vessel, facility, and port operations relevant to that industry;

(iii) Vessel and facility security measures, including the meaning and the consequential requirements of the different Maritime Security (MARSEC) Levels;

(iv) Emergency preparedness and response and contingency planning;

(v) Security equipment and systems and their operational limitations;

(vi) Methods of conducting audits, inspection and control and monitoring techniques; and

(vii) Techniques for security training and education, including security measures and procedures.

(2) In addition to knowledge and training in paragraph (b)(1) of this section, the CSO must have general knowledge through training or equivalent job experience in the following, as appropriate:

(i) Relevant international conventions, codes, and recommendations;

(ii) Relevant government legislation and regulations;

(iii) Responsibilities and functions of other security organizations;

(iv) Methodology of Vessel Security Assessment;

(v) Methods of vessel security surveys and inspections;

(vi) Instruction techniques for security training and education, including security measures and procedures;

(vii) Handling sensitive security information and security related communications;

(viii) Knowledge of current security threats and patterns;

(ix) Recognition and detection of dangerous substances and devices;

(x) Recognition of characteristics and behavioral patterns of persons who are likely to threaten security;

(xi) Techniques used to circumvent security measures;

(xii) Methods of physical screening and non-intrusive inspections;

(xiii) Security drills and exercises, including drills and exercises with facilities; and

(xiv) Assessment of security drills and exercises.

(c) *Responsibilities.* In addition to those responsibilities and duties specified elsewhere in this part, the CSO must, for each vessel for which he or she has been designated:

(1) Keep the vessel apprised of potential threats or other information relevant to its security;

(2) Ensure a Vessel Security Assessment (VSA) is carried out;

(3) Ensure a Vessel Security Plan (VSP) is developed, approved, and maintained;

(4) Ensure the VSP is modified when necessary;

(5) Ensure vessel security activities are audited;

(6) Arrange for Coast Guard inspections under 46 CFR part 2;

(7) Ensure the timely or prompt correction of problems identified by audits or inspections;

(8) Enhance security awareness and vigilance within the owner's or operator's organization;

(9) Ensure relevant personnel receive adequate security training;

(10) Ensure communication and cooperation between the vessel and the port and facilities with which the vessel interfaces;

(11) Ensure consistency between security requirements and safety requirements;

(12) Ensure that when sister-vessel or fleet security plans are used, the plan for each vessel reflects the vessel-specific information accurately;

(13) Ensure compliance with an Alternative Security Program or equivalents approved under this subchapter, if appropriate; and

(14) Ensure security measures give particular consideration to the convenience, comfort, and personal privacy of vessel personnel and their ability to maintain their effectiveness over long periods.

[USCG-2003-14749, 68 FR 39302, July 1, 2003, as amended at 68 FR 60513, Oct. 22, 2003]

§ 104.215 Vessel Security Officer (VSO).

(a) *General.* (1) A VSO may perform other duties within the owner's or operator's organization, provided he or she is able to perform the duties and responsibilities required of the VSO for each such vessel.

(2) For manned vessels, the VSO must be **the Master or** a member of the crew.

(3) For unmanned vessels, **the VSO must be an employee of the company, and** the same person may serve as the VSO for **more than** one unmanned vessel. If a person serves as the VSO for more than one unmanned vessel, the name of each unmanned vessel for which he or she is the VSO must be listed in the Vessel Security Plan (VSP).

(4) The VSO of any unmanned barge and the VSO of any towing vessel interfacing with the barge must coordinate and ensure the implementation of security measures applicable to both vessels during the period of their interface.

(5) The VSO may assign security duties to other vessel personnel; however, the VSO remains responsible for these duties.

(b) *Qualifications.* The VSO must have general knowledge, through training or equivalent job experience, in the following:

(1) Those items listed in § 104.210 (b)(1) and (b)(2) of this part;

(2) Vessel layout;

(3) The VSP and related procedures, including scenario-based response training;

(4) Crowd management and control techniques;

(5) Operations of security equipment and systems; and

(6) Testing and calibration of security equipment and systems, and their maintenance while at sea.

(c) *Responsibilities.* In addition to those responsibilities and duties specified elsewhere in this part, the VSO must, for each vessel for which he or she has been designated:

(1) Regularly inspect the vessel to ensure that security measures are maintained;

(2) Ensure maintenance and supervision of the implementation of the VSP, and any amendments to the VSP;

(3) Ensure the coordination and handling of cargo and vessel stores and bunkers in compliance with this part;

(4) Propose modifications to the VSP to the Company Security Officer (CSO);

(5) Ensure that any problems identified during audits or inspections are reported to the CSO, and promptly implement any corrective actions;

(6) Ensure security awareness and vigilance on board the vessel;

(7) Ensure adequate security training for vessel personnel;

(8) Ensure the reporting and recording of all security incidents;

(9) Ensure the coordinated implementation of the VSP with the CSO and the relevant Facility Security Officer, when applicable;

(10) Ensure security equipment is properly operated, tested, calibrated and maintained; and

(11) Ensure consistency between security requirements and the proper treatment of vessel personnel affected by those requirements.

[USCG-2003-14749, 68 FR 39302, July 1, 2003, as amended at 68 FR 60513, Oct. 22, 2003]

§ 104.220 Company or vessel personnel with security duties.

Company and vessel personnel responsible for security duties must have knowledge, through training or equivalent job experience, in the following, as appropriate:

(a) Knowledge of current security threats and patterns;

(b) Recognition and detection of dangerous substances and devices;

(c) Recognition of characteristics and behavioral patterns of persons who are likely to threaten security;

(d) Techniques used to circumvent security measures;

(e) Crowd management and control techniques;

(f) Security related communications;

(g) Knowledge of emergency procedures and contingency plans;

(h) Operation of security equipment and systems;

(i) Testing and calibration of security equipment and systems, and their maintenance while at sea;

(j) Inspection, control, and monitoring techniques;

(k) Relevant provisions of the Vessel Security Plan (VSP);

(l) Methods of physical screening of persons, personal effects, baggage, cargo, and vessel stores; and

(m) The meaning and the consequential requirements of the different Maritime Security (MARSEC) Levels.

§ 104.225 Security training for all other vessel personnel.

All other vessel personnel, including contractors, whether part-time, full-time, temporary, or permanent, must have knowledge of, through training or equivalent job experience in the following, **as appropriate:**

(a) Relevant provisions of the Vessel Security Plan (VSP);

(b) The meaning and the consequential requirements of the different Maritime Security (MARSEC) Levels, including emergency procedures and contingency plans;

(c) Recognition and detection of dangerous substances and devices;

(d) Recognition of characteristics and behavioral patterns of persons who are likely to threaten security; and

(e) Techniques used to circumvent security measures.

[USCG-2003-14749, 68 FR 39302, July 1, 2003, as amended at 68 FR 60513, Oct. 22, 2003]

§ 104.230 Drill and exercise requirements.

(a) *General.* (1) Drills and exercises must test the proficiency of vessel personnel in assigned security duties at all Maritime Security (MARSEC) Levels and the effective implementation of the Vessel Security Plan (VSP). They must enable the Vessel Security Officer (VSO) to identify any related security deficiencies that need to be addressed.

(2) A drill or exercise required by this section may be satisfied with the implementation of security measures required by the Vessel Security Plan as the result of an increase in the MARSEC Level, provided the vessel reports attainment to the cognizant COTP.

(b) *Drills.* (1) The VSO must ensure that at least one security drill is conducted at least every 3 months, except when a vessel is out of service due to repairs or seasonal suspension of operation provided that in such cases a drill must be conducted within one week of the vessel's reactivation. Security drills may be held in conjunction with non-security drills where appropriate.

(2) Drills must test individual elements of the VSP, including response to security threats and incidents. Drills should take into account the types of operations of the vessel, vessel personnel changes, and other relevant circumstances. Examples of drills include unauthorized entry to a restricted area, response to alarms, and notification of law enforcement authorities.

(3) If the vessel is moored at a facility on the date the facility has planned to conduct any drills, the vessel may, but is not required to, participate in the facility's scheduled drill.

(4) Drills must be conducted within one week **from** whenever the percentage of vessel personnel with no prior participation in a vessel security drill on that vessel exceeds 25 percent.

(5) Not withstanding paragraph (b) (4) of this section, vessels not subject to SOLAS may conduct drills within 1 week from whenever the percentage of vessel personnel with no prior participation in a vessel security drill on a vessel of similar design and owned or operated by the same company exceeds 25 percent.

(c) *Exercises.* (1) Exercises must be conducted at least once each calendar year, with no more than 18 months between exercises.

(2) Exercises may be:

(i) Full scale or live;

(ii) Tabletop simulation or seminar;

(iii) Combined with other appropriate exercises; or

(iv) A combination of the elements in paragraphs (c)(2)(i) through (iii) of this section.

(3) Exercises may be vessel-specific or part of a cooperative exercise program to exercise applicable facility and Vessel Security Plans or comprehensive port exercises.

(4) Each exercise must test communication and notification procedures, and elements of co-ordination, resource availability, and response.

(5) Exercises are a full test of the security program and must include the substantial and active participation of relevant company and vessel security personnel, and may include facility security personnel and government authorities depending on the scope and the nature of the exercises.

[USCG-2003-14749, 68 FR 39302, July 1, 2003, as amended at 68 FR 60513, Oct. 22, 2003]

§ 104.235 Vessel recordkeeping requirements.

(a) Unless otherwise specified in this section, the Vessel Security Officer must keep records of the activities as set out in paragraph (b) of this section for at least 2 years and make them available to the Coast Guard upon request.

(b) Records required by this section may be kept in electronic format. If kept in an electronic format, they must be protected against unauthorized deletion, destruction, or amendment. The following records must be kept:

(1) *Training.* For **training under §** **104.225,** the date of each session, duration of session, a description of the training, and a list of attendees;

(2) *Drills and exercises.* For each drill or exercise, the date held, description of drill or exercise, list of participants; and any best practices or lessons learned which may improve the Vessel Security Plan (VSP);

(3) *Incidents and breaches of security.* Date and time of occurrence, location within the port, location within the vessel, description of incident or breaches, to whom it was reported, and description of the response;

(4) *Changes in Maritime Security (MARSEC) Levels.* Date and time of notification received, and time of compliance with additional requirements;

(5) *Maintenance, calibration, and testing of security equipment.* For each occurrence of main-tenance, calibration, and testing, the date and time, and the specific security equipment involved;

(6) *Security threats.* Date and time of occurrence, how the threat was communicated, who received or identified the threat, description of threat, to whom it was reported, and description of the response;

(7) *Declaration of Security (DoS).* Manned vessels must keep on board a copy of the last 10 DoSs and a copy of each continuing DoS for at least 90 days after the end of its effective period; and

(8) *Annual audit of the VSP.* For each annual audit, a letter certified by **the Company Security Officer or** the VSO stating the date the audit was completed.

(c) Any records required by this part must be protected from unauthorized access or disclosure.

[USCG-2003-14749, 68 FR 39302, July 1, 2003, as amended at 68 FR 60514, Oct. 22, 2003]

§ 104.240 Maritime Security (MARSEC) Level coordination and implementation.

(a) The vessel owner or operator must ensure that, prior to entering a port **or visiting an Outer Continental Shelf (OCS) facility,** all measures are taken that are specified in the Vessel Security Plan (VSP) for compliance with the MARSEC Level in effect for the port **or the OCS facility.**

(b) When notified of an increase in the MARSEC Level, the vessel owner or operator must ensure:

(1) If a higher MARSEC Level is set for the port in which the vessel is located or is about to enter, the vessel complies, without undue delay, with all measures specified in the VSP for compliance with that higher MARSEC Level;

(2) The COTP is notified as required by § 101.300(c) when compliance with the higher MARSEC Level has been implemented;

(3) For vessels in port, that compliance with the higher MARSEC Level has taken place within 12 hours of the notification; **and**

(4) If a higher MARSEC Level is set for the OCS facility with which the vessel is interfacing or is about to visit, the vessel complies, without undue delay,

with all measures specified in the VSP for compliance with that higher MARSEC Level.

(c) For MARSEC Levels 2 and 3, the Vessel Security Officer must brief all vessel personnel of identified threats, emphasize reporting procedures, and stress the need for increased vigilance.

(d) An owner or operator whose vessel is not in compliance with the requirements of this section must inform the COTP and obtain approval prior to entering any port, prior to interfacing with another vessel or with a facility or to continuing operations.

(e) For MARSEC Level 3, in addition to the requirements in this part, a vessel owner or operator may be required to implement additional measures, pursuant to 33 CFR part 6, 160 or 165, as appropriate, which may include but are not limited to:

(1) Arrangements to ensure that the vessel can be towed or moved if deemed necessary by the Coast Guard;

(2) Use of waterborne security patrol;

(3) Use of armed security personnel to control access to the vessel and to deter, to the maximum extent practical, a TSI; or

(4) Screening the vessel for the presence of dangerous substances and devices underwater or other threats.

[USCG-2003-14749, 68 FR 39302, July 1, 2003, as amended at 68 FR 60514, Oct. 22, 2003]

§ 104.245 Communications.

(a) The Vessel Security Officer must have a means to effectively notify vessel personnel of changes in security conditions on board the vessel.

(b) Communications systems and procedures must allow effective and continuous communication between the vessel security personnel, facilities interfacing with the vessel, vessels interfacing with the vessel, and national or local authorities with security responsibilities.

(c) Communication systems and procedures must enable vessel personnel to notify, in a timely manner, shore side authorities or other vessels of a security threat or incident on board.

§ 104.250 Procedures for interfacing with facilities and other vessels.

(a) The vessel owner or operator must ensure that there are measures for interfacing with facilities and other vessels at all MARSEC Levels.

(b) For each U.S. flag vessel that calls on foreign ports or facilities, the vessel owner or operator must ensure procedures for interfacing with those ports and facilities are established.

§ 104.255 Declaration of Security (DoS).

(a) Each vessel owner or operator must ensure procedures are established for requesting a DoS and for handling DoS requests from a facility or other vessel.

(b) At MARSEC Level 1, the Master or Vessel Security Officer (VSO), or their designated representative, of any cruise ship or manned vessel carrying Certain Dangerous Cargoes, in bulk, must complete and sign a DoS with the VSO or Facility Security Officer (FSO), or their designated representative, of any vessel or facility with which it interfaces.

(1) For a vessel-to-facility interface, prior to arrival of a vessel to a facility, the FSO and Master, VSO, or their designated representatives must coordinate security needs and procedures, and agree upon the contents of the DoS for the period of time the vessel is at the facility. Upon a vessel's arrival to a facility and prior to any passenger embarkation or disembarkation or cargo transfer operation, the FSO or Master, VSO, or designated representatives must sign the written DoS.

(2) For a vessel engaging in a vessel-to-vessel activity, prior to the activity, the respective Masters, VSOs, or their designated representatives must coordinate security needs and procedures, and agree upon the contents of the DoS for the period of the vessel-to-vessel activity. Upon the vessel-to-vessel activity and prior to any passenger embarkation or disembarkation or cargo transfer operation, the respective Masters, VSOs, or designated representatives must sign the written DoS.

(c) At MARSEC Levels 2 and 3, the Master, VSO, or designated representative of any manned vessel required to comply with this part must coordinate security needs and procedures, and agree upon the contents of the DoS for the period of the vessel-to-vessel activ-

ity. **Upon the vessel-to-vessel activity and prior to any passenger embarkation or disembarkation or cargo transfer operation, the respective Masters, VSOs, or designated representatives must sign the written DoS.**

(d) At MARSEC Levels 2 and 3, the Master, VSO, or designated representative of any manned vessel required to comply with this part must coordinate security needs and procedures, and agree upon the contents of the DoS for the period the vessel is at the facility. Upon the vessel's arrival to a facility and prior to any passenger embarkation or disembarkation or cargo transfer operation, the respective FSO and Master, VSO, or designated representatives must sign the written DoS.

(e) At MARSEC Levels 1 and 2, VSOs of vessels that frequently interface with the same facility may implement a continuing DoS for multiple visits, provided that:

(1) The DoS is valid for the specific MARSEC Level;

(2) The effective period at MARSEC Level 1 does not exceed 90 days; and

(3) The effective period at MARSEC Level 2 does not exceed 30 days.

(f) When the MARSEC Level increases beyond the level contained in the DoS, the continuing DoS becomes void and a new DoS must be signed and implemented in accordance with this section.

(g) The COTP may require at any time, at any MARSEC Level, any manned vessel subject to this part to implement a DoS with the VSO or FSO prior to any vessel-to-vessel **activity** or vessel-to-facility interface when he or she deems it necessary.

[USCG-2003-14749, 68 FR 39302, July 1, 2003, as amended at 68 FR 60514, Oct. 22, 2003]

§ 104.260 Security systems and equipment maintenance.

(a) Security systems and equipment must be in good working order and inspected, tested, calibrated and maintained according to the manufacturer's recommendation.

(b) The results of testing completed under paragraph (a) of this section shall be recorded in accordance with § 104.235. Any deficiencies shall be promptly corrected.

(c) The Vessel Security Plan (VSP) must include procedures for identifying and responding to security system and equipment failures or malfunctions.

§ 104.265 Security measures for access control.

(a) *General.* The vessel owner or operator must ensure the implementation of security measures to:

(1) Deter the unauthorized introduction of dangerous substances and devices, including any device intended to damage or destroy persons, vessels, facilities, or ports;

(2) Secure dangerous substances and devices that are authorized by the owner or operator to be on board; and

(3) Control access to the vessel.

(b) The vessel owner or operator must ensure that **the following are specified:**

(1) The locations providing means of access to the vessel where access restrictions or prohibitions are applied for each Maritime Security (MARSEC) Level. ``Means of access'' include, but are not limited, to all:

(i) Access ladders;

(ii) Access gangways;

(iii) Access ramps;

(iv) Access doors, side scuttles, windows, and ports;

(v) Mooring lines and anchor chains; and

(vi) Cranes and hoisting gear;

(2) The identification of the types of restriction or prohibition to be applied and the means of enforcing them; and

(3) The means of identification required to allow individuals to access the vessel and remain on the vessel without challenge.

(c) The vessel owner or operator must ensure that an identification system is established for checking the identification of vessel personnel or other persons seeking access to the vessel that:

(1) Allows identification of authorized and unauthorized persons at any MARSEC Level;

(2) Is coordinated, when practicable, with identification systems at facilities used by the vessel;

(3) Is updated regularly;

(4) Uses disciplinary measures to discourage abuse;

(5) Allows temporary or continuing access for vessel personnel and visitors, including **seafarers'** chaplains and union representatives, through the use of a badge or other system to verify their identity; and

(6) Allow certain long-term, frequent vendor representatives to be treated more as employees than as visitors.

(d) The vessel owner or operator must establish in the approved Vessel Security Plan (VSP) the frequency of application of any security measures for access control, particularly if these security measures are applied on a random or occasional basis.

(e) *MARSEC Level 1.* The vessel owner or operator must ensure security measures in this paragraph are implemented to:

(1) Screen persons, baggage (including carry-on items), personal effects, and vehicles for dangerous substances and devices at the rate specified in the approved Vessel Security Plan (VSP), **except for government-owned vehicles on official business when government personnel present identification credentials for entry;**

(2) Conspicuously post signs that describe security measures currently in effect and clearly state that:

(i) Boarding the vessel is deemed valid consent to screening or inspection; and

(ii) Failure to consent or submit to screening or inspection will result in denial or revocation of authorization to board;

(3) Check the identification of any person seeking to board the vessel, including vessel passengers and crew, facility employees, vendors, personnel duly authorized by the cognizant government authorities, and visitors. This check includes confirming the reason for boarding by examining at least one of the following:

(i) Joining instructions;

(ii) Passenger tickets;

(iii) Boarding passes;

(iv) Work orders, pilot orders, or surveyor orders;

(v) Government identification; or

(vi) Visitor badges issued in accordance with an identification system required in paragraph (c) of this section;

(4) Deny or revoke a person's authorization to be on board if the person is unable or unwilling, upon the request of vessel personnel, to establish his or her identity or to account for his or her presence on board. Any such incident must be reported in compliance with this part;

(5) Deter unauthorized access to the vessel;

(6) Identify access points that must be secured or attended to deter unauthorized access;

(7) Lock or otherwise prevent access to unattended spaces that adjoin areas to which passengers and visitors have access;

(8) Provide a designated secure area on board or in liaison with a facility, for conducting inspections and screening of people, baggage (including carry-on items), personal effects, vehicles and the vehicle's contents;

(9) Ensure vessel personnel are not subjected to screening, of the person or of personal effects, by other vessel personnel, unless security clearly requires it. Any such screening must be conducted in a way that takes into full account individual human rights and preserves the individual's basic human dignity;

(10) Ensure the screening of all unaccompanied baggage;

(11) Ensure checked persons and their personal effects are segregated from unchecked persons and their personal effects;

(12) Ensure embarking passengers are segregated from disembarking passengers;

(13) Ensure, in liaison with the facility, a defined percentage of vehicles to be loaded aboard passenger vessels are screened prior to loading at the rate specified in the approved VSP;

(14) Ensure, in liaison with the facility, all unaccompanied vehicles to be loaded on passenger vessels are screened prior to loading; and

(15) Respond to the presence of unauthorized persons on board, including repelling unauthorized boarders.

(f) MARSEC Level 2. In addition to the security measures required for MARSEC Level 1 in this section, at MARSEC Level 2, the vessel owner or operator must also ensure the implementation of additional security measures, as specified for MARSEC Level 2 in the approved VSP. These additional security measures may include:

(1) Increasing the frequency and detail of screening of people, personal effects, and vehi-

cles being embarked or loaded onto the vessel as specified for MARSEC Level 2 in the approved VSP, **except for government-owned vehicles on official business when government personnel present identification credentials for entry;**

(2) X-ray screening of all unaccompanied baggage;

(3) Assigning additional personnel to patrol deck areas during periods of reduced vessel operations to deter unauthorized access;

(4) Limiting the number of access points to the vessel by closing and securing some access points;

(5) Denying access to visitors who do not have a verified destination;

(6) Deterring waterside access to the vessel, which may include, in liaison with the facility, providing boat patrols; and

(7) Establishing a restricted area on the shoreside of the vessel, in close cooperation with the facility.

(g) MARSEC Level 3. In addition to the security measures required for MARSEC Level 1 and MARSEC Level 2, the vessel owner or operator must ensure the implementation of additional security measures, as specified for MARSEC Level 3 in the approved VSP. The additional security measures may include:

(1) Screening all persons, baggage, and personal effects for dangerous substances and devices;

(2) Performing one or more of the following on unaccompanied baggage:

(i) Screen unaccompanied baggage more extensively, for example, x-raying from two or more angles;

(ii) Prepare to restrict or suspend handling unaccompanied baggage; or

(iii) Refuse to accept unaccompanied baggage on board;

(3) Being prepared to cooperate with responders and facilities;

(4) Limiting access to the vessel to a single, controlled access point;

(5) Granting access to only those responding to the security incident or threat thereof;

(6) Suspending embarkation and/or disembarkation of personnel;

(7) Suspending cargo operations;

(8) Evacuating the vessel;

(9) Moving the vessel; and

(10) Preparing for a full or partial search of the vessel.

[USCG-2003-14749, 68 FR 39302, July 1, 2003, as amended at 68 FR 60514, Oct. 22, 2003]

§ 104.270 Security measures for restricted areas.

(a) *General.* The vessel owner or operator must ensure the designation of restricted areas in order to:

(1) Prevent or deter unauthorized access;

(2) Protect persons authorized to be on board;

(3) Protect the vessel;

(4) Protect sensitive security areas within the vessel;

(5) Protect security and surveillance equipment and systems; and

(6) Protect cargo and vessel stores from tampering.

(b) *Designation of Restricted Areas.* The vessel owner or operator must ensure restricted areas are designated on board the vessel, as specified in the approved plan. Restricted areas must include, as appropriate:

(1) Navigation bridge, machinery spaces and other control stations;

(2) Spaces containing security and surveillance equipment and systems and their controls and lighting system controls;

(3) Ventilation and air-conditioning systems and other similar spaces;

(4) Spaces with access to potable water tanks, pumps, or manifolds;

(5) Spaces containing dangerous goods or hazardous substances;

(6) Spaces containing cargo pumps and their controls;

(7) Cargo spaces and spaces containing vessel stores;

(8) Crew accommodations; and

(9) Any other spaces or areas vital to the security of the vessel.

(c) The vessel owner or operator must ensure that security measures and policies are established to:

(1) Identify which vessel personnel are authorized to have access;

(2) Determine which persons other than vessel personnel are authorized to have access;

(3) Determine the conditions under which that access may take place;

(4) Define the extent of any restricted area;

(5) Define the times when access restrictions apply; and

(6) Clearly mark all restricted areas and indicate that access to the area is restricted and that unauthorized presence within the area constitutes a breach of security.

(d) *Maritime Security (MARSEC) Level 1.* The vessel owner or operator must ensure the implementation of security measures to prevent unauthorized access or activities within the area. These security measures may include:

(1) Locking or securing access points;

(2) Monitoring and using surveillance equipment;

(3) Using guards or patrols; and

(4) Using automatic intrusion detection devices, which if used must activate an audible and/or visual alarm at a location that is continuously attended or monitored, to alert vessel personnel to unauthorized access.

(e) *MARSEC Level 2.* In addition to the security measures required for MARSEC Level 1 in this section, at MARSEC Level 2, the vessel owner or operator must also ensure the implementation of additional security measures, as specified for MARSEC Level 2 in the approved VSP. These additional security measures may include:

(1) Increasing the frequency and intensity of monitoring and access controls on existing restricted access areas;

(2) Restricting access to areas adjacent to access points;

(3) Providing continuous monitoring of each area, using surveillance equipment; and

(4) Dedicating additional personnel to guard or patrol each area.

(f) *MARSEC Level 3.* In addition to the security measures required for MARSEC Level 1 and MARSEC Level 2, at MARSEC Level 3, the vessel owner or operator must ensure the implementation of additional security measures, as specified for MARSEC Level 3 in the approved VSP. These additional security measures may include:

(1) Restricting access to additional areas; and

(2) Searching restricted areas as part of a security sweep of the vessel.

§ 104.275 Security measures for handling cargo.

(a) *General.* The vessel owner or operator must ensure that security measures relating to cargo handling, some of which may have to be applied in liaison with the facility **or another vessel,** are specified in order to:

(1) Deter tampering;

(2) Prevent cargo that is not meant for carriage from being accepted and stored on board the vessel;

(3) Identify cargo that is approved for loading onto the vessel;

(4) Include inventory control procedures at access points to the vessel; **and**

(5) **When there are regular or repeated cargo operations with the same shipper, coordinate** security measures with the shipper or other responsible party in accordance with an established agreement and procedures.

(b) *Maritime Security (MARSEC) Level 1.* At MARSEC Level 1, the vessel owner or operator must ensure the implementation of measures to:

(1) **Unless unsafe to do so, routinely** check cargo and cargo spaces prior to and during cargo handling **for evidence of tampering;**

(2) Check that cargo to be loaded matches the cargo documentation, or that cargo markings or container numbers match the information provided with shipping documents;

(3) Ensure, in liaison with the facility, that vehicles to be loaded on board car carriers, RO-RO, and passenger ships are subjected to screening prior to loading, in accordance with the frequency required in the VSP; and

(4) Check, in liaison with the facility, seals or other methods used to prevent tampering.

(c) *MARSEC Level 2.* In addition to the security measures required for MARSEC Level 1 in this section, at MARSEC Level 2, the vessel owner or operator must also ensure the implementation of additional security measures, as specified for MARSEC Level 2 in the approved Vessel Security Plan (VSP). These additional security measures may include:

(1) Increasing the frequency and detail of checking cargo and cargo spaces **for evidence of tampering;**

(2) Intensifying checks to ensure that only the intended cargo, container, or other cargo transport units are loaded;

(3) Intensifying screening of vehicles to be loaded on car-carriers, RO-RO, and passenger vessels;

(4) In liaison with the facility, increasing frequency and detail in checking seals or other methods used to prevent tampering;

(5) Increasing the frequency **and intensity of visual and physical inspections;** or

(6) Coordinating enhanced security measures with the shipper or other responsible party in accordance with an established agreement and procedures.

(d) *MARSEC Level 3.* In addition to the security measures for MARSEC Level 1 and MARSEC Level 2, at MARSEC Level 3, the vessel owner or operator must ensure the implementation of additional security measures, as specified for MARSEC Level 3 in the approved VSP. These additional security measures may include:

(1) Suspending loading or unloading of cargo;

(2) Being prepared to cooperate with responders, **facilities, and other vessels;** or

(3) Verifying the inventory and location of any hazardous materials carried on board.

[USCG-2003-14749, 68 FR 39302, July 1, 2003, as amended at 68 FR 60514, Oct. 22, 2003]

§ 104.280 Security measures for delivery of vessel stores and bunkers.

(a) *General.* The vessel owner or operator must ensure that security measures relating to the delivery of vessel stores and bunkers are implemented to:

(1) Check vessel stores for package integrity;

(2) Prevent vessel stores from being accepted without inspection;

(3) Deter tampering; and

(4) Prevent vessel stores and bunkers from being accepted unless ordered. For vessels that routinely use a facility, a vessel owner or operator may establish and implement standing arrangements between the vessel, its suppliers, and a facility regarding notification and the timing of deliveries and their documentation.

(b) *Maritime Security (MARSEC) Level 1.* At MARSEC Level 1, the vessel owner or op-

erator must ensure the implementation of measures to:

(1) Check vessel stores before being accepted;

(2) Check that vessel stores and bunkers match the order prior to being brought on board or being bunkered; and

(3) Ensure that vessel stores are controlled or immediately and securely stowed following delivery.

(c) *MARSEC Level 2.* In addition to the security measures required for MARSEC Level 1 in this section, at MARSEC Level 2, the vessel owner or operator must also ensure the implementation of additional security measures, as specified for MARSEC Level 2 in the approved Vessel Security Plan (VSP). These additional security measures may include:

(1) Intensifying inspection of the vessel stores during delivery; or

(2) Checking vessel stores prior to receiving them on board.

(d) *MARSEC Level 3.* In addition to the security measures for MARSEC Level 1 and MARSEC Level 2, at MARSEC Level 3, the vessel owner or operator must ensure the implementation of additional security measures, as specified for MARSEC Level 3 in the approved VSP. These additional security measures may include:

(1) Checking all vessel stores more extensively;

(2) Restricting or suspending delivery of vessel stores and bunkers; or

(3) Refusing to accept vessel stores on board.

§ 104.285 Security measures for monitoring.

(a) *General.* (1) The vessel owner or operator must ensure the implementation of security measures and have the capability to continuously monitor, through a combination of lighting, watchkeepers, security guards, deck watches, waterborne patrols, automatic intrusion-detection devices, or surveillance equipment, as specified in their approved Vessel Security Plan (VSP), the—

(i) Vessel;

(ii) Restricted areas on board the vessel; and

(iii) Area surrounding the vessel.

(2) The following must be considered when establishing the appropriate level and location of lighting:

(i) Vessel personnel should be able to detect activities on and around the vessel, on both the shore side and the waterside;

(ii) Coverage should facilitate personnel identification at access points;

(iii) Coverage may be provided through coordination with the port or facility; and

(iv) Lighting effects, such as glare, and its impact on safety, navigation, and other security activities.

(b) *Maritime Security (MARSEC) Level 1.* At MARSEC Level 1, the vessel owner or operator must ensure the implementation of security measures, which may be done in coordination with a facility, to:

(1) Monitor the vessel, particularly vessel access points and restricted areas;

(2) Be able to conduct emergency searches of the vessel;

(3) Ensure that equipment or system failures or malfunctions are identified and corrected;

(4) Ensure that any automatic intrusion detection device sets off an audible or visual alarm, or both, at a location that is **continuously** attended or monitored;

(5) Light deck and vessel access points during the period between sunset and sunrise and periods of limited visibility sufficiently to allow visual identification of persons seeking access to the vessel; and

(6) Use maximum available lighting while underway, during the period between sunset and sunrise, consistent with safety and international regulations.

(c) *MARSEC Level 2.* In addition to the security measures required for MARSEC Level 1 in this section, at MARSEC Level 2, the vessel owner or operator must also ensure the implementation of additional security measures, as specified for MARSEC Level 2 in the approved VSP. These additional security measures may include:

(1) Increasing the frequency and detail of security patrols;

(2) Increasing the coverage and intensity of lighting, alone or in coordination with the facility;

(3) Using or increasing the use of security and surveillance equipment;

(4) Assigning additional personnel as security lookouts;

(5) Coordinating with boat patrols, when provided; **and**

(6) Coordinating with shoreside foot or vehicle patrols, when provided.

(d) *MARSEC Level 3.* In addition to the security measures for MARSEC Level 1 and MARSEC Level 2, at MARSEC Level 3, the vessel owner or operator must ensure the implementation of additional security measures, as specified for MARSEC Level 3 in the approved VSP. These additional security measures may include:

(1) Cooperating with responders and facilities;

(2) Switching on all lights;

(3) Illuminating the vicinity of the vessel;

(4) Switching on all surveillance equipment capable of recording activities on, or in the vicinity of, the vessel;

(5) Maximizing the length of time such surveillance equipment can continue to record;

(6) Preparing for underwater inspection of the hull; and

(7) Initiating measures, including the slow revolution of the vessel's propellers, if practicable, to deter underwater access to the hull of the vessel.

[USCG-2003-14749, 68 FR 39302, July 1, 2003, as amended at 68 FR 60514, Oct. 22, 2003]

§ 104.290 Security incident procedures.

For each Maritime Security (MARSEC) Level, the vessel owner or operator must ensure the Vessel Security Officer (VSO) and vessel security personnel are able to:

(a) Respond to security threats or breaches of security and maintain critical vessel and vessel-to-facility interface operations, to include:

(1) Prohibiting entry into affected area;

(2) Denying access to the vessel, except to those responding to the emergency;

(3) Implementing MARSEC Level 3 security measures throughout the vessel;

(4) Stopping cargo-handling operations; and

(5) Notifying shoreside authorities or other vessels of the emergency;

(b) Evacuating the vessel in case of security threats or breaches of security;

(c) Reporting security incidents as required in § 101.305;

(d) Briefing all vessel personnel on possible threats and the need for vigilance, soliciting their assistance in reporting suspicious persons, objects, or activities; and

(e) Securing non-critical operations in order to focus response on critical operations.

§ 104.292 Additional requirements—passenger vessels and ferries.

(a) At all Maritime Security (MARSEC) Levels, the vessel owner or operator must ensure security sweeps are performed, prior to getting underway, after any period the vessel was unattended.

(b) As an alternative to the identification checks and passenger screening requirements in § 104.265 (e)(1), (e)(3), and (e)(8), the owner or operator of a passenger vessel or ferry may ensure security measures are implemented that include:

(1) Searching selected areas prior to embarking passengers and prior to sailing; and

(2) Implementing one or more of the following:

(i) Performing routine security patrols;

(ii) Providing additional closed-circuit television to monitor passenger areas; or

(iii) Securing all non-passenger areas.

(c) Passenger vessels certificated to carry more than 2000 passengers, working in coordination with the terminal, may be subject to additional vehicle screening requirements in accordance with a MARSEC Directive or other orders issued by the Coast Guard.

(d) Owners and operators of passenger vessels and ferries covered by this part that use public access facilities, as that term is defined in § 101.105 of this subchapter, must address security measures for the interface of the vessel and the public access facility, in accordance with the appropriate Area Maritime Security Plan.

(e) At MARSEC Level 2, a vessel owner or operator must ensure, in addition to MARSEC Level 1 measures, the implementation of the following:

(1) Search selected areas prior to embarking passengers and prior to sailing;

(2) Passenger vessels certificated to carry less than 2000 passengers, working in coordination with the terminal, may be subject to additional vehicle screening requirements in accordance with a MARSEC Directive or other orders issued by the Coast Guard; and

(3) As an alternative to the identification and screening requirements in § 104.265(e)(3) **and (f)(1)**, intensify patrols, security sweeps and monitoring identified in paragraph (b) of this section.

(f) At MARSEC Level 3, a vessel owner or operator may, in addition to MARSEC Levels 1 and 2 measures, as an alternative to the identification checks and passenger screening requirements in § 104.265(e)(3) **and § 104.265(g)(1),** ensure that random armed security patrols are conducted, which need not consist of vessel personnel.

[USCG-2003-14749, 68 FR 39302, July 1, 2003, as amended at 68 FR 60514, Oct. 22, 2003]

§ 104.295 Additional requirements— cruise ships.

(a) At all MARSEC Levels, the owner or operator of a cruise ship must ensure the following:

(1) Screen all persons, baggage, and personal effects for dangerous substances and devices;

(2) Check the identification of all persons seeking to board the vessel; this check includes confirming the reason for boarding by examining joining instructions, passenger tickets, boarding passes, government identification or visitor badges, or work orders;

(3) Perform security patrols; and

(4) Search selected areas prior to embarking passengers and prior to sailing.

(b) At MARSEC Level 3, the owner or operator of a cruise ship must ensure that security briefs to passengers about the specific threat are provided.

§ 104.297 Additional requirements—vessels on international voyages.

(a) An owner or operator of a U.S. flag vessel, which is subject to the International

Convention for Safety of Life at Sea, 1974, (SOLAS), must be in compliance with the applicable requirements of SOLAS Chapter XI-1, SOLAS Chapter XI-2 and the ISPS Code, part A (Incorporated by reference, see § 101.115 of this subchapter).

(b) Owners or operators of U.S. flag vessels that are required to comply with SOLAS, must ensure an International Ship Security Certificate (ISSC) as provided in 46 CFR § 2.01–25 is obtained for the vessel. This certificate must be issued by the Coast Guard.

(c) Owners or operators of vessels that require an ISSC in paragraph (b) of this section must request an inspection in writing, at least 30 days prior to the desired inspection date to the Officer in Charge, Marine Inspection for the Marine Inspection Office or Marine Safety Office of the port where the vessel will be inspected to verify compliance with this part and applicable SOLAS requirements. The inspection must be completed and the initial ISSC must be issued **on or before July 1, 2004.**

[USCG-2003-14749, 68 FR 39302, July 1, 2003, as amended at 68 FR 60515, Oct. 22, 2003]

Subpart C—Vessel Security Assessment (VSA)

§ 104.300 General.

(a) The Vessel Security Assessment (VSA) is a written document that is based on the collection of background information and the completion and analysis of an on-scene survey.

(b) A single VSA may be performed and applied to more than one vessel to the extent that they share physical characteristics and operations.

(c) Third parties may be used in any aspect of the VSA if they have the appropriate skills and if the Company Security Officer (CSO) reviews and accepts their work.

(d) Those involved in a VSA should be able to draw upon expert assistance in the following areas:

(1) Knowledge of current security threats and patterns;

(2) Recognition and detection of dangerous substances and devices;

(3) Recognition of characteristics and behavioral patterns of persons who are likely to threaten security;

(4) Techniques used to circumvent security measures;

(5) Methods used to cause a security incident;

(6) Effects of dangerous substances and devices on vessel structures and equipment;

(7) Vessel security requirements;

(8) Vessel-to-vessel **activity** and vessel-to-facility interface business practices;

(9) Contingency planning, emergency preparedness and response;

(10) Physical security requirements;

(11) Radio and telecommunications systems, including computer systems and networks;

(12) Marine engineering; and

(13) Vessel and port operations.

[USCG-2003-14749, 68 FR 39302, July 1, 2003, as amended at 68 FR 60515, Oct. 22, 2003]

§ 104.305 Vessel Security Assessment (VSA) requirements.

(a) *Background.* The vessel owner or operator must ensure that the following background information is provided to the person or persons who will conduct the on-scene survey and assessment:

(1) General layout of the vessel, including the location of:

(i) Each actual or potential point of access to the vessel and its function;

(ii) Spaces that should have restricted access;

(iii) Essential maintenance equipment;

(iv) Cargo spaces and storage;

(v) Storage of unaccompanied baggage; and

(vi) Vessel stores;

(2) Threat assessments, including the purpose and methodology of the assessment, for the area or areas in which the vessel operates or at which passengers embark or disembark;

(3) The previous VSA, if any;

(4) Emergency and stand-by equipment available to maintain essential services;

(5) Number of vessel personnel and any existing security duties to which they are assigned;

(6) Existing personnel training requirement practices of the vessel;

(7) Existing security and safety equipment for the protection of personnel, visitors, passengers, and vessels personnel;

(8) Escape and evacuation routes and assembly stations that have to be maintained to ensure the orderly and safe emergency evacuation of the vessel;

(9) Existing agreements with private security companies providing waterside or vessel security services; and

(10) Existing security measures and procedures, including:

(i) Inspection and control procedures;

(ii) Identification systems;

(iii) Surveillance and monitoring equipment;

(iv) Personnel identification documents;

(v) Communication systems;

(vi) Alarms;

(vii) Lighting;

(viii) Access control systems; and

(ix) Other security systems.

(b) *On-scene survey.* The vessel owner or operator must ensure that an on-scene survey of each vessel is conducted. The on-scene survey is to verify or collect information required in paragraph (a) of this section. It consists of an actual survey that examines and evaluates existing vessel protective measures, procedures, and operations for:

(1) Ensuring performance of all security duties;

(2) Controlling access to the vessel, through the use of identification systems or otherwise;

(3) Controlling the embarkation of vessel personnel and other persons and their effects, including personal effects and baggage whether accompanied or unaccompanied;

(4) Supervising the handling of cargo and the delivery of vessel stores;

(5) Monitoring restricted areas to ensure that only authorized persons have access;

(6) Monitoring deck areas and areas surrounding the vessel; and

(7) The ready availability of security communications, information, and equipment.

(c) *Analysis and recommendations.* In conducting the VSA, the Company Security Officer (CSO) must analyze the vessel background information and the on-scene survey, and while considering the requirements of this part, provide recommendations for the security measures the vessel should include in the Vessel

Security Plan (VSP). This includes but is not limited to the following:

(1) Restricted areas;

(2) Response procedures for fire or other emergency conditions;

(3) Security supervision of vessel personnel, passengers, visitors, vendors, repair technicians, dock workers, etc.;

(4) Frequency and effectiveness of security patrols;

(5) Access control systems, including identification systems;

(6) Security communication systems and procedures;

(7) Security doors, barriers, and lighting;

(8) Any security and surveillance equipment and systems;

(9) Possible security threats, including but not limited to:

(i) Damage to or destruction of the vessel or an interfacing facility or vessel by dangerous substances and devices, arson, sabotage, or vandalism;

(ii) Hijacking or seizure of the vessel or of persons on board;

(iii) Tampering with cargo, essential vessel equipment or systems, or vessel stores;

(iv) Unauthorized access or use, including presence of stowaways;

(v) Smuggling dangerous substances and devices;

(vi) Use of the vessel to carry those intending to cause a security incident and/or their equipment;

(vii) Use of the vessel itself as a weapon or as a means to cause damage or destruction;

(viii) Attacks from seaward while at berth or at anchor; and

(ix) Attacks while at sea; and

(10) Evaluating the potential of each identified point of access, including open weather decks, for use by individuals who might seek to breach security, whether or not those individuals legitimately have access to the vessel.

(d) *VSA report.* (1) The vessel owner or operator must ensure that a written VSA report is prepared and included as part of the VSP. The VSA report must contain:

(i) A summary of how the on-scene survey was conducted;

(ii) Existing security measures, procedures, and operations;

(iii) A description of each vulnerability found during the assessment;

(iv) A description of security countermeasures that could be used to address each vulnerability;

(v) A list of the key vessel operations that are important to protect;

(vi) The likelihood of possible threats to key vessel operations; and

(vii) A list of identified weaknesses, including human factors, in the infrastructure, policies, and procedures of the vessel.

(2) The VSA report must address the following elements on board or within the vessel:

(i) Physical security;

(ii) Structural integrity;

(iii) Personnel protection systems;

(iv) Procedural policies;

(v) Radio and telecommunication systems, including computer systems and networks; and

(vi) Other areas that may, if damaged or used illicitly, pose a risk to people, property, or operations on board the vessel or within a facility.

(3) The VSA **report** must list the persons, activities, services, and operations that are important to protect, in each of the following categories:

(i) Vessel personnel;

(ii) Passengers, visitors, vendors, repair technicians, facility personnel, etc.;

(iii) Capacity to maintain safe navigation and emergency response;

(iv) Cargo, particularly dangerous goods **and** hazardous substances;

(v) Vessel stores;

(vi) Any vessel security communication and surveillance systems; and

(vii) Any other vessel security systems, if any.

(4) The VSA **report** must account for any vulnerabilities in the following areas:

(i) Conflicts between safety and security measures;

(ii) Conflicts between vessel duties and security assignments;

(iii) The impact of watch-keeping duties and risk of fatigue on vessel personnel alertness and performance;

(iv) Security training deficiencies; and

(v) Security equipment and systems, including communication systems.

(5) The VSA **report** must discuss and evaluate key vessel measures and operations, including:

(i) Ensuring performance of all security duties;

(ii) Controlling access to the vessel, through the use of identification systems or otherwise;

(iii) Controlling the embarkation of vessel personnel and other persons and their effects (including personal effects and baggage whether accompanied or unaccompanied);

(iv) Supervising the handling of cargo and the delivery of vessel stores;

(v) Monitoring restricted areas to ensure that only authorized persons have access;

(vi) Monitoring deck areas and areas surrounding the vessel; and

(vii) The ready availability of security communications, information, and equipment.

(e) The VSA must be documented and the VSA report retained by the vessel owner or operator with the VSP. The VSA, **the VSA report,** and VSP must be protected from unauthorized access or disclosure.

[USCG-2003-14749, 68 FR 39302, July 1, 2003, as amended at 68 FR 60515, Oct. 22, 2003]

§ 104.310 Submission requirements.

(a) A completed Vessel Security Assessment (VSA) report must be submitted with the Vessel Security Plan (VSP) required in § 104.410 of this part.

(b) A vessel owner or operator may generate and submit a report that contains the VSA for more than one vessel subject to this part, to the extent that they share similarities in physical characteristics and operations.

(c) The VSA must be reviewed and revalidated, and the VSA report must be updated, each time the VSP is submitted for reapproval or revisions.

[USCG-2003-14749, 68 FR 39302, July 1, 2003, as amended at 68 FR 60515, Oct. 22, 2003]

Subpart D—Vessel Security Plan (VSP)

§ 104.400 General.

(a) The Company Security Officer (CSO) must ensure a Vessel Security Plan (VSP) is developed and implemented for each vessel. The VSP:

(1) Must identify the CSO and VSO by name or position and provide 24-hour contact information;

(2) Must be written in English, **although a translation of the VSP in the working language of vessel personnel may also be developed;**

(3) Must address each vulnerability identified in the Vessel Security Assessment (VSA);

(4) Must describe security measures for each MARSEC Level;

(5) Must state the Master's authority as described in § 104.205; and

(6) May cover more than one vessel to the extent that they share similarities in physical characteristics and operations, if authorized and approved by the Commanding Officer, Marine Safety Center.

(b) The VSP must be submitted to the Commanding Officer, Marine Safety Center (MSC) 400 Seventh Street, SW., Room 6302, Nassif Building, Washington, DC 20590-0001, in a written or electronic format. Information for submitting the VSP electronically can be found at http:// www.uscg.mil/HQ/MSC. Owners or operators of foreign flag vessels that are subject to SOLAS Chapter XI-1 or Chapter XI-2 must comply with this part by carrying on board a valid International Ship Security Certificate that certifies that the verifications required by Section 19.1 of part A of the ISPS Code (Incorporated by reference, see § 101.115 of this subchapter) have been completed. As stated in Section 9.4 of the ISPS Code, part A requires that, in order for the ISSC to be issued, the provisions of part B of the ISPS Code need to be taken into account.

(c) The VSP is sensitive security information and must be protected in accordance with 49 CFR part 1520.

(d) If the VSP is kept in an electronic format, procedures must be in place to prevent its unauthorized deletion, destruction, or amendment.

[USCG-2003-14749, 68 FR 39302, July 1, 2003, as amended at 68 FR 60515, Oct. 22, 2003; USCG-2004-18057, 69 FR 34925, June 23, 2004]

§ 104.405 Format of the Vessel Security Plan (VSP).

(a) A vessel owner or operator must ensure that the VSP consists of the individual sections listed in this paragraph (a). If the VSP does not follow the order as it appears in the list, the vessel owner or operator must ensure that the VSP contains an index identifying the location of each of the following sections:

(1) Security organization of the vessel;

(2) Personnel training;

(3) Drills and exercises;

(4) Records and documentation;

(5) Response to change in MARSEC Level;

(6) Procedures for interfacing with facilities and other vessels;

(7) Declarations of Security (DoS);

(8) Communications;

(9) Security systems and equipment maintenance;

(10) Security measures for access control;

(11) Security measures for restricted areas;

(12) Security measures for handling cargo;

(13) Security measures for delivery of vessel stores and bunkers;

(14) Security measures for monitoring;

(15) Security incident procedures;

(16) Audits and Vessel Security Plan (VSP) amendments; and

(17) Vessel Security Assessment (VSA) Report.

(b) The VSP must describe in detail how the requirements of subpart B of this part will be met.

§ 104.410 Submission and approval.

(a) In accordance with § 104.115, on or before December 31, 2003, each vessel owner or operator must either:

(1) Submit one copy of their Vessel Security Plan (VSP), **in English,** for review and approval to the Commanding Officer, Marine Safety Center (MSC) and a letter certifying that the VSP meets applicable requirements of this part; or

(2) If intending to operate under an Approved Security Program, a letter signed by the vessel owner or operator stating which approved Alternative Security Program the owner or operator intends to use.

(b) Owners or operators of vessels not in service on or before December 31, 2003, must comply with the requirements in paragraph (a) of this section 60 days prior to beginning operations or by December 31, 2003, whichever is later.

(c) The Commanding Officer, Marine Safety Center (MSC), will examine each submission for compliance with this part, and either:

(1) Approve it and specify any conditions of approval, returning to the submitter a letter stating its acceptance and any conditions;

(2) Return it for revision, returning a copy to the submitter with brief descriptions of the required revisions; or

(3) Disapprove it, returning a copy to the submitter with a brief statement of the reasons for disapproval.

(d) A VSP may be submitted and approved to cover more than one vessel where the vessel design and operations are similar.

(e) Each company or vessel, owner or operator, that submits one VSP to cover two or more vessels of similar design and operation must address vessel-specific information that includes the physical and operational characteristics of each vessel.

(f) A plan that is approved by the MSC is valid for 5 years from the date of its approval.

[USCG-2003-14749, 68 FR 39302, July 1, 2003, as amended at 68 FR 60515, Oct. 22, 2003]

§ 104.415 Amendment and audit.

(a) *Amendments.* (1) Amendments to a Vessel Security Plan that are approved by the **Marine Safety Center** (MSC) may be initiated by:

(i) The vessel owner or operator; or

(ii) The Coast Guard upon a determination that an amendment is needed to maintain the vessel's security. The Coast Guard will give the vessel owner or operator written notice and request that the vessel owner or operator propose amendments addressing any matters specified in the notice. The company owner or operator will have at least 60 days to submit its proposed amendments. Until amendments are approved, the company owner or operator shall ensure temporary security measures are implemented to the satisfaction of the Coast Guard.

(2) Proposed amendments must be sent to the **MSC** at the address shown in § 104.400(b) of this part. If initiated by the company or vessel, owner or operator, the proposed amendment must be submitted at least 30 days before the amendment is to take effect unless the **MSC** allows a shorter period. The MSC will approve or disapprove the proposed amendment in accordance with § 104.410 of this part.

(3) Nothing in this section should be construed as limiting the vessel owner or operator from the timely implementation of such additional security measures not enumerated in the approved VSP as necessary to address exigent security situations. In such cases, the owner or operator must notify the MSC by the most rapid means practicable as to the nature of the additional measures, the circumstances that prompted these additional measures, and the period of time these additional measures are expected to be in place.

(4) If the owner or operator has changed, the Vessel Security Officer (VSO) must amend the Vessel Security Plan (VSP) to include the name and contact information of the new vessel owner or operator and submit the affected portion of the VSP for review and approval in accordance with § 104.410 of this part.

(b) *Audits.* (1) The CSO or VSO must ensure an audit of the VSP is performed annually, beginning no later than one year from the initial date of approval and attach a letter to the VSP certifying that the VSP meets the applicable requirements of this part.

(2) The VSP must be audited if there is a change in the company's or vessel's ownership or operator, or if there have been modifications to the vessel, including but not limited to physical structure, emergency response procedures, security measures, or operations.

(3) Auditing the VSP as a result of modifications to the vessel may be limited to those sections of the VSP affected by the vessel modifications.

(4) Unless impracticable due to the size and nature of the company or the vessel, personnel conducting internal audits of the security measures specified in the VSP or evaluating its implementation must:

(i) Have knowledge of methods of conducting audits and inspections, and control and monitoring techniques;

(ii) Not have regularly assigned security duties; and

(iii) Be independent of any security measures being audited.

(5) If the results of an audit require amendment of either the VSA or VSP, the VSO or CSO must submit, in accordance with § 104.410 of this part, the amendments to the MSC for review and approval no later than 30 days after completion of the audit and a letter certifying that the amended VSP meets the applicable requirements of this part.

[USCG-2003-14749, 68 FR 39302, July 1, 2003; 68 FR 41915, July 16, 2003, as amended at 68 FR 60515, Oct. 22, 2003]

ONI Threat to World Shipping

28 Dec 05

OFFICE OF NAVAL INTELLIGENCE
CIVIL MARITIME ANALYSIS DEPARTMENT
WORLDWIDE THREAT TO SHIPPING
MARINER WARNING INFORMATION

POC: DAVID PEARL:
COMM (301) 669-4905
FAX (301) 669-3247
E-mail dpearl@nmic.navy.mil

CHARLES DRAGONETTE:
COMM (301) 669-3261
FAX (301) 669-3247
E-mail cdragonette@nmic.navy.mil

1. This message provides information on threat to and criminal action against merchant shipping worldwide.

   A. To aid in our reporting, please add the Office of Naval Intelligence (ONI) as an information addressee when possible to your normal corporate and organizational reporting requirements. The ONI message address is ONI WASHINGTON DC//11//, or the ONI Violence at Sea (VAS) desk may be contacted at commercial phone 301-669-3261 or via e-mail at cdragonette@nmic.navy.mil. Report may also be made to the National Response Center (U.S. Coast Guard) hotline: 800-424-0201 or the Maritime Administration Office of Ship Operations, MAR-613, 202-366-5735; FAX 202-366-3954, e-mail: opcentr1@marad.dot.gov.

   B. This Worldwide Threat to Shipping Report is available weekly to members of the Maritime Security Council via the MSCALERT. For information on corporate membership in the Maritime Security Council, contact Mr. Kim Petersen at mscalert@maritimesecurity. org or visit the MSC website at www.maritimesecurity.org. Message is also posted at the National Geospatial-Intelligence Agency site http://pollux.nss.nima.mil/onit/onit_j_main.html.

C. The International Maritime Bureau (IMB) also publishes a weekly piracy summary, based on reporting from the IMB Piracy Reporting Centre in Kuala Lumpur, Malaysia. Each week's report is published on Tuesday and may be accessed through their web page www.iccwbo.org.

D. Anti-piracy and crime current developments:

  1. No current incidents to report.

E. Source codes: Information contained in this report is derived through direct reporting and analysis of reports of other agencies and commercial sources. Source codes will be added to new reports to enable users requiring more detail to make contact.

Codes currently in use are:

  AFP, Agence France Presse

  AP, Associated Press

  BBC, BBC News

  BIMCO, Baltic and International Maritime
      Council, Denmark

  DHS, U. S. Department of Homeland Security

  DOJ, U. S. Department of Justice

  DOT, U. S. Department of Transportation

  FP, Fairplay, London

  GP, Greenpeace

  IMB, International Maritime Bureau, London and
      Kuala Lumpur

  IMO, International Maritime Organization, London

  INFO, Informa Group, formerly LLP, Llp Limited, London

  INTELL, Intellibridge

  LAT, Latitud38.com website

  LL, Lloyd's List, daily, London

  LM, local media

  MARAD, Maritime Administration, U.S.

  MSC, Maritime Security Council, U.S.

  NATO, North Atlantic Treaty Organization, Brussels

  NGA, National Geospatial-Intelligence Agency,
      Navigation Safety System

  ONI, Office of Naval Intelligence analysis and comment

  Operator, owner or operator of affected vessel

  OSAC, Overseas Security Advisory Council

  USCG, United States Coast Guard

  RAN, Royal Australian Navy

  REUTERS, Reuters

  RNZN, Royal New Zealand Navy

STATE, U.S. Department of State

TW, Tradewinds

2. Designation of a high threat area is based on an assessment of all source information relating to the existence of, or potential for piracy and other crime, terrorism, civil unrest or low intensity conflict. Every effort is made to ensure that incidents are not double-counted. In the event double counting is detected or an event is later learned not to be as initially reported, an explanation of the cancellation of the inaccurate report will be made in at least one message prior to dropping the erroneous report. Specific incidents will be reported for one month.

3. This week's highlights:

    A. Yacht boarded, robbed 16 Dec, Kingston harbor, Jamaica (Para 5.B.1.).

    B. Bulk carrier boarded, robbed 26 Dec, Bontang anchorage, Indonesia (Para 5.K.1.).

    C. Hijacked chemical tanker STEADFAST released with cargo intact, 24 Dec. (Para 5.K.2.).

    D. Greenpeace and Sea Shepherd vessels clash with Japanese whale research vessels 21–24 Dec, Eastern Indian-Antarctic (Para 5.N.1.).

4. Contents and summary of threat areas detailed in paragraph 5.

    A. NORTH AMERICA:

        1. No current incidents to report.

    B. CENTRAL AMERICA-CARIBBEAN:

        1. Yacht boarded, robbed 16 Dec, Kingston harbor, Jamaica.

    C. SOUTH AMERICA:

        1. Tanker boarded, robbed 3 Dec, Callao, Peru.

    D. ATLANTIC OCEAN AREA:

        1. No current incidents to report.

    E. NORTHERN EUROPE-BALTIC:

        1. No current incidents to report.

    F. MEDITERRANEAN-BLACK SEA:

        1. No current incidents to report.

    G. WEST AFRICA:

        1. Tug boarded, robbed 03 Sep, Total jetty, Douala, Cameroon (Per 29 Nov reporting).

    H. INDIAN OCEAN-EAST AFRICA:

        1. General cargo ship hijacked 07 Dec off Hobyo, Somalia.

        2. Container ship reported a suspicious craft 16 Dec, off east coast of Somalia.

        3. Cargo ship reports being chased; attempted boarding 11 Dec Gulf of Aden off Somalia.

        4. Cargo ship reports being chased 12 Dec off Somalia.

        5. Tanker chased, 16 Dec, NE coast Somalia.

6. Taiwanese fishing vessel hijacked, 30 Nov, Somalia.

7. Thai-flagged general cargo ship, hijacked 07 Nov off east coast of Somalia; released 4 Dec.

8. (TORGELOW) hijacked 10 Oct off the coast of Somalia while in route to El Maan, Somalia; arrived in El Maan 01 Dec, reported released.

9. Bulk carrier reported a suspicious approach 15 Dec, Gulf of Aden.

10. Containership boarded 15 Dec Dar Es Salaam outer anchorage, Tanzania.

11. Bulk carrier had an attempted boarding 15 Dec, Dar Es Salaam OPL anchorage.

   I. RED SEA:

1. No current incidents to report.

   J. PERSIAN GULF:

1. No current incidents to report.

   K. SOUTHEAST ASIA:

1. Bulk carrier boarded, robbed 26 Dec, Bontang anchorage, Indonesia.

2. Chemical tanker STEADFAST hijacked 18 Dec while in port Palembang, Indonesia. Released with cargo intact 24 Dec.

3. Suspicious approach to tanker 11 Dec Senipah, Indonesia.

4. Tug boarded, robbed 8 Dec Tanjung Geram Merak, Indonesia.

5. Bulk carrier boarded by armed man 8 Dec Merak, Indonesia.

6. Bulk carrier boarded, robbed under way 7 Dec near N. Sebuku Island, Indonesia.

7. Bulk carrier boarded, robbed 6 Dec, Bontang, Indonesia.

8. Bulk carrier boarded, robbed 01 Dec, Adang Bay anchorage, Indonesia.

9. LPG tanker reported attempted boarding, 02 Dec, off Vietnam.

   L. NORTH ASIA:

1. No current incidents to report.

   M. PACIFIC OCEAN AREA:

1. No current incidents to report.

   N. ENVIRONMENTAL AND ECONOMIC NON-STATE ACTIVIST GROUPS:

1. Greenpeace and Sea Shepherd vessels clash with Japanese whale research vessels 21–24 Dec, Eastern Indian-Antarctic.

2. Greenpeace activists boarded and briefly occupied decommissioned French aircraft carrier 12 Dec to protest asbestos and other hazards.

3. Greenpeace activists arrested 1 Dec at Le Havre attempting to stop loading of radioactive waste.

5. DETAILS: There is reported active violence against shipping, a credible threat to shipping, or the potential to develop into a direct threat to the safety of shipping in the following areas:

A. NORTH AMERICA: No current incidents to report.

B. CENTRAL AMERICA-CARIBBEAN:

1. JAMAICA: An unidentified Yacht was boarded 16 Dec at 0630 UTC while anchored off Kingston harbor. Five robbers, armed with assault rifles, boarded the yacht from a 25 ft canoe with an outboard motor. They took substantial equipment at gunpoint and escaped. Jamaican authorities informed. No injuries to crew (IMB).

C. SOUTH AMERICA: No current incidents to report.

1. PERU: An unidentified tanker was boarded 3 Dec Callao anchorage area no. 12 by an armed robber who threatened duty seaman with a gun and stole ship stores (IMB).

D. ATLANTIC OCEAN AREA: No current incidents to report.

E. NORTHERN EUROPE-BALTIC: No current incidents to report.

F. MEDITERRANEAN-BLACK SEA: No current incidents to report.

G. WEST AFRICA:

1. CAMEROON: An unidentified tug was boarded 03 Sep at 0400 local time while at Total jetty, Douala. Three robbers armed with knives and spears boarded the offshore tug. They confronted duty A/B and bosun and stole ships property and escaped (IMB).

H. INDIAN OCEAN-EAST AFRICA:

1. SOMALIA: An unidentified general cargo ship was hijacked 07 Dec off Hobyo, central east coast of Somalia. Hijackers have demanded ransom for release of 11 crewmembers and ship (IMB).

2. SOMALIA: An unidentified containership detected a suspicious craft 16 Dec at 2227 local time while under way in position 03:01.9N 051:17.7E, off the east coast of Somalia. Master notices the craft on radar and took evasive maneuvers to avoid collision. Craft changed course and continued to follow the ship. Master increased speed and the craft moved away (IMB).

3. GULF OF ADEN-SOMALIA: An unidentified general cargo ship reports being chased 11 Dec at 0810 local time while under way in position 13:07N 049:13E by persons in a small speedboat who attempted to board. Boarding was averted when Master increased speed and undertook evasive maneuvers (IMB).

4. SOMALIA: An unidentified general cargo ship reports being chased by an unidentified fishing trawler 12 Dec at 0200 UTC

while under way in position 04:50.5S 048:00.0E. Cargo ship undertook evasive maneuvers but trawler drew closer to 1.4 nm until abandoning the chase when cargo ship increased speed. Trawler, described as 50 to 60 mtrs long, white hull with single boom abandoned the chase when ship increased speed (IMB).

     5. SOMALIA: An unidentified tanker reported being chased 06 Dec while under way in position 12:01N, 050:35E. The vessel reported seeing individuals in speedboats armed with machine guns and other weapons. The Master contacted the owners and requested assistance from Coalition naval vessels in the area. The tanker was proceeding from Dubai to southern waters of Somalia to supply fuel to fishing vessels in the area (IMB).

     6. SOMALIA: Taiwanese fishing vessel (FENG JUNG No 16) reported hijacked 30 Nov. The longliner was reportedly fishing under the legal protection of the Somali fishery cooperation. The fishing vessel had three Taiwanese and 12 foreign crewmembers. The Somali government has been engaged to negotiate for the release of the vessel (INFO).

     7. SOMALIA: Thai-flagged general cargo ship (LAEMTHONG GLORY) was hijacked 07 Nov at 0600 UTC while under way off the east coast of Somalia. The captors forced the ship to anchor in 04:28N, 048.01E near the Somali coastline, Pirates demanded large ransom for the release of the ship, which was finally freed 4 Dec. ONI Comment: Anchorage location is not far from where recently released UN World Food Program M/V SEMLOW was reportedly held (near Haradheere) for over three months (see ONI World Wide Threat to Shipping report 28 Sep 05 Para 5.H.3) and are likely the same perpetrators of the attack on C/S SEABOURN SPIRIT on 05 Nov and the attack on the unidentified RORO on 06 Nov (LL, ONI).

     8. SOMALIA: Cargo ship (TORGELOW) reported hijacked as of 10 Oct while enroute El Maan. (TORGELOW) was reported to be carrying fuel and supplies to the recently released (SEMLOW), as well as a consignment of foodstuffs for a Somali businessman. The owner of the cargo on the hijacked M/V (TORGELOW), who was in negotiation with the hijackers, believed the gunmen would use (TORGELOW) to attract other ships. On 21 Nov local press reported a hefty ransom was demanded for release of the crew. Motaku Shipping representatives stated that negotiations were left to the cargo owner. Vessel was reported released and arrived in El Maan 01 Dec. All crew reported safe but expressed concern over being hijacked again, upon their return to Mombasa, Kenya (LL, REUTERS, LM).

     9. GULF OF ADEN: An unidentified bulk carrier reported a suspicious approach 15 Dec at 2040 local time while under way in position 12:12.8N 046:10.8E. An unlit white speedboat doing over

25kts came close to the vessel and persons inside asked the Master to stop. Master took evasive maneuvers and crew mustered. After 20 minutes, speedboat fled (IMB).

10. TANZANIA: An unidentified containership was boarded 15 Dec at 0100 local time while anchored at Dar Es Salaam outer anchorage. One robber boarded the vessel via grappling hook and removed the hawse pipe cover allowing three of his accomplices to board the vessel via the anchor chain. Duty A/B raised alarm and crew mustered. Robbers jumped overboard and escaped empty handed in a boat waiting with four additional accomplices (IMB).

11. TANZANIA: An unidentified bulk carrier had an attempted boarding 15 Dec at 0145 local time while anchored in position 06:44.7S 039:20.2E, Dar Es Salaam OPL anchorage. Seven persons in an unlit boat approached the vessel. Two persons attempted to board via anchor chain. Alert crew prevented boarding (IMB).

I.   RED SEA: No current incidents to report.

J.   PERSIAN GULF: No current incidents to report.

K.   SOUTHEAST ASIA:

1. INDONESIA: An unidentified bulk carrier was boarded 26 Dec at 0230 local time while anchored at Bontang anchorage. Eight robbers armed with long knives boarded the vessel at forecastle. Robbers stole ships stores and escaped (IMB).

2. INDONESIA: Chemical tanker (STEADFAST) hijacked 18 Dec while in port Palembang. An IMB special alert dated 20 Dec reports the owner lost contact with their vessel as of 19 Dec. The tanker departed Palembang, Indonesia for Singapore on 18 Dec laden with 16,585 MT of vegetable oil. Vessels last known location reported by the owner was 02:20N 106:41E at 0530 UTC on 19 Dec. Vessel arrived safely in Singapore 24 Dec with cargo intact. Pirates escaped. ONI Comment: In April of this year, pirates boarded a general cargo ship laden with tin ingot in Indonesian waters, forced the crew to take the vessel to a port in Malaysia and offload the cargo before returning to Indonesian waters and releasing the vessel and crew unharmed. The cargo was later found intact by Malaysian authorities in the same location it was offloaded. In July, pirates boarded a tug and barge while awaiting berth in a port in Malaysia and siphoned approximately 3,500 MT of crude palm oil into another product tanker. The Malaysian Marine Police found the product tanker and arrested the crew while the Indonesian Navy Pursuit Team arrested five individuals believed to have perpetrated the theft. In September, a general cargo vessel laden with 660 tons of tin ingot was boarded by pirates while under way off Indonesia. The 14 crewmembers were set adrift in a fishing boat and landed safely on

land. The vessel was later discovered sunk not far from where it was hijacked and salvage divers assessed the cargo to be intact. These incidents appear to represent a form of piracy not reported since China's crackdown on black-market activity starting in 1998, wherein a ship is targeted for seizure at its load port and the cargo is taken to some destination where arrangements for disposal have already been concluded. The complexity of the operation suggests transnational players at the ship selection and cargo-disposal ends of the operation. In these types of cases, crew and ship owner complicity must be considered, since they have no immediate financial interest in the cargo, per se. Since the crackdown on the illegal Chinese markets, hijackers have experienced difficulty disposing of their cargos. Since the STEADFAST was returned with its cargo intact, it is apparent criminal gangs have not solved their problem with disposal of stolen goods, which would indicate hijackings of these types will remain at lower levels compared to those prior to 1998 (IMB, ONI).

3. INDONESIA: An unidentified tanker reports approach 11 Dec at 2000 local time while anchored in position 01:55S 17:14E, Senipah, Indonesia. An unlit boat approached close to the stern. Crew alerted terminal via VHF, raised alarm and directed searchlights at the boat, which fled when a patrol boat arrived (IMB).

4. INDONESIA: An unidentified tug was boarded 8 Dec at 0430 local time while anchored in position 05:58.4S 105:58.6E. at Tanjung Gerem Merak. Eight persons armed with long knives escaped to a waiting speedboat when crew raised alarm (IMB).

5. INDONESIA: An unidentified bulk carrier was boarded 8 Dec at 0330 local time while anchored in position 05:54S 105:59E at Merak. One person armed with a long knife boarded but fled empty handed to a waiting boat with accomplices when crew raised alarm (IMB).

6. INDONESIA: An unidentified bulk carrier was boarded 7 Dec at 2010 local time while under way in heavy rain in position 03:17S 116:24E off Tanjung Mangkok, North Sebuku Island. Two persons armed with long knives stole forward life raft and were in the process of stealing stores when confronted by crew. They jumped overboard to an awaiting speedboat (IMB).

7. INDONESIA: An unidentified bulk carrier was boarded 6 Dec at 0520 local time in heavy rain while at Bontang anchorage. A single robber stole ships stores and escaped with accomplices in a waiting boat (IMB).

8. INDONESIA: An unidentified bulk carrier was boarded 01 Dec at 1745 local time while anchored in position 01:42.3S, 116:38.5E, Adang Bay anchorage. Five robbers, armed with guns and knives, boarded the vessel via poop deck and stole a life raft. D/O

raised alarm and crew mustered, but robbers threatened them with guns and escaped in their boat. Port control informed (IMB).

9. SOUTH CHINA SEA: An unidentified LPG tanker reported attempt to board 02 Dec while under way in position 10:19N, 108:50E, off Vietnam. Persons in a fishing boat attempted to board the vessel via grappling hook. Master altered course to prevent boarding. After a few attempts, the fishing boat gave up and fled (IMB).

L.   NORTH ASIA: No current incidents to report.

M.   PACIFIC-ANTARCTIC OCEAN: No current incidents to report.

N.   ENVIRONMENTAL AND ECONOMIC NON-STATE ACTIVIST GROUPS:

1. GREENPEACE - SEA SHEPHERD CONSERVATION SOCIETY - INSTITUTE OF CETACEAN RESEARCH - ANTARCTIC WHALING: According to the Japanese Institute of Cetacean Research, the Greenpeace vessels (ESPERANZA) and (ARCTIC SUNRISE) and the Sea Shepherd Conservation Society vessel (FARLEY MOWAT) follow and attempt to impede Japan's whale research efforts in the Antarctic as of 21 Dec. The Sea Shepherd Conservation Society's Web site describes a near collision between the (FARLEY MOWAT) and Japanese Research vessel (NISSHIN MARU) on 24 Dec in the vicinity of 62:55S 136:38E. Greenpeace rejects the claims made by Japan that its members are disregarding the laws of the sea as they trail the Japanese whalers, and denies claims they are working in conjunction with the Sea Shepherd Conservation Society. The Institute of Cetacean Research claims the fleet of six Japanese research vessels are operating under special permit in the Antarctic. ONI NOTE: Supporters of the Japanese projects are implying that Greenpeace and the Sea Shepherd Organization are acting in concert. ONI sees no evidence for this despite the fact that the current high-profile Japanese expedition has drawn the attention of both groups (GP, Institute of Cetacean Research, Sea Shepherd Conservation Society, ONI).

2. GREENPEACE-FRANCE-HAZARDOUS MATERIAL IN SCRAPPED SHIPS: Greenpeace activists boarded the decommissioned French aircraft carrier (CLEMENCEAU) 12 Dec at Toulon to protest plans to send the ship to scrap at Alang, India, despite the presence of residual asbestos. The ship had been partially cleared of asbestos and the decontamination firm claimed that the ships structure would be unacceptably weakened if further removal took place. The activists left the ship 14 Dec (LL).

3. GREENPEACE-FRANCE-RADIOACTIVE WASTE: French police arrested 20 Greenpeace activists 1 Dec at the port of Le Havre

after the activists occupied shoreside gantrys and two cranes aboard the Russian freighter (KAPITAN KUROPETEVWAS). The action, which began about 0100, was aimed at preventing loading of what Greenpeace claims is 47 containers with 450 tons of uranium waste for shipment to St Petersburg and thence overland to Siberia from a French reprocessing plant (LL).

6. Originator of this WWTTS report requests consumer feedback. Originator will incorporate all anti-shipping events and violence against the maritime industry into this weekly message where appropriate. The Office of Naval Intelligence (ONI) can be contacted via message traffic at ONI WASHINGTON DC//11// or, the ONI violence at sea (VAS) desk may be contacted at comm. phone (301) 669-3261 or via e-mail at cdragonette@nmic.navy.mil.

//

IMB Piracy Report

WEEKLY PIRACY REPORT
27 DECEMBER 2005–2 JANUARY 2006

The following is a summary of the daily reports broadcast by the IMB's Piracy Reporting Centre to ships in Atlantic, Indian and Pacific Ocean Regions on the SafetyNET service of Inmarsat-C from 27 December 2005 to 2 January 2006.

ALERT

SOMALIA—NE AND EASTERN COAST

Thirty-five incidents have been reported since 15.03.05. Heavily armed pirates are now attacking ships further away from the coast. Ships not making scheduled calls at Somali ports are advised to keep at least 200 nm from the Somali coast.

SUSPICIOUS CRAFTS

02.01.2006 at 0733 UTC in position 13:48N - 049:48E, Gulf of Aden.

Three speedboats with 3/4 persons onboard followed a tanker under way. Master altered course and boats moved away. Later at 0753 UTC in position 13:49N - 049:54E, another speedboat with three persons onboard followed for 30 minutes. Alarm was raised; boat stopped following.

RECENTLY REPORTED INCIDENTS

02.01.2006 at 0040 LT at Teluk Semangka anchorage, Indonesia.

Three robbers armed with long knives boarded a tanker at poop deck. Duty A/B raised alarm, crew mustered and robbers escaped empty handed in a waiting boat. Pertamina port control informed and a patrol boat arrived two hours later for investigation.

29.12.2005 at 1800 LT in position 21:40.3N - 088:00.9E, Sagar anchorage, India.

Two robbers boarded a containership awaiting berthing with pilot onboard. Duty A/B raised alarm and robbers escaped with ship's stores. Pilot station and port authority informed.

27.12.2005 at 0400 LT at Tg. Bara inner anchorage, East Kalimantan, Indonesia.

Robbers boarded a bulk carrier at forecastle. They tried to steal ship's stores but alert crew raised alarm and robbers escaped empty handed in a boat waiting with accomplices. Master suspects that stevedores may have collaborated with the robbers.

PIRACY PRONE AREAS AND WARNINGS

SE ASIA AND THE INDIAN SUBCONTINENT

- Bangladesh: Chittagong at berth and anchorage
- India: Chennai , Kandla
- Indonesia: Anambas/Natuna Island, Balikpapan, Belawan, Dumai, Gaspar/Bar/Leplia Str, Jakarta (Tg. Priok), Pulau Laut, Vicinity of Bintan Island
- Malacca straits: avoid anchoring along the Indonesian coast of the straits. Coast near Aceh is particularly risky for hijackings
- Singapore Straits

AFRICA AND RED SEA

- Gulf of Aden/Southern Red Sea
- Somalian waters—eastern and northeastern coasts are high-risk areas for hijackings. Ships not making scheduled calls to ports in these areas should stay away from the coast.
- West Africa: Abidjan, Conakry, Dakar, Douala, Freetown, Lagos, Tema, Warri

SOUTH AND CENTRAL AMERICA AND THE CARIBBEAN WATERS

- Brazil Rio Grande
- Haiti Port au Prince
- Dominican Republic - Rio Haina
- Jamaica - Kingston
- Peru Callao

INVENTUS UAV

The Inventus UAV (unmanned aerial vehicle) is a state-of-the-art reconnaissance system packaged in a highly efficient, highly stable flying wing form. Outfitted with cameras, the Inventus flies and covers a large ocean area and relays a real-time data link back to the ground station. This link provides real-time aerial surveillance and early warning of suspect or unauthorized craft movements to the coastal or law enforcement authority. Developed by Lew Aerospace, the Inventus is fully autonomous and can be launched and recovered even from a seagoing or patrol vessel. There are gas and electric formats and both fly in all weather conditions. Endorsed by the IMB the Inventus is yet another tool to aid in the maritime effort in its fight against piracy. For more information, please visit www.inventus. com.

SECURE-SHIP

Secure-Ship is the most recent and effective innovation in the fight against piracy. It is a non-lethal, electrifying fence surrounding the whole ship, which has been specially adapted for maritime use. The fence uses 9,000-volt pulse to deter boarding attempts. An intruder coming in contact with the fence will receive an unpleasant non-lethal shock that will result in the intruder abandoning the attempted boarding. At the same time an alarm will go off, activating floodlights and a very loud siren. The IMB strongly recommends ship owners to install this device onboard their ships. Further details can be obtained at www.secure-marine.com.

SHIPLOC

There are a number of reliable ship tracking devices available on the market today based upon Inmarsat and other satellite systems.

The IMB endorses ShipLoc, an inexpensive satellite tracking system that allows shipping companies, armed only with a personal computer with Internet access, to monitor the exact location of their vessels. In addition to anti-hijacking role, ShipLoc facilitates independent and precise location of ships at regular intervals. ShipLoc is fully compliant with the IMO Regulation SOLAS XI-2/6 adopted during the diplomatic conference in December 2002, concerning a Ship Security Alert System. The ship security alert system regulation that will be put into place as of July 2004 requires ships of over 500 GT to be equipped with an alarm system in order to reinforce ship security. The system allows the crew, in case of danger, to activate an alarm button that automatically sends a message to the shipowner and to competent authorities. The message is sent without being able to be detected by someone onboard or by other ships in the vicinity. ShipLoc is contained in a small, discrete waterproof unit, which includes: an Argos transmitter, a GPS receiver, a battery pack in case of main power failure, and a flat antenna. ShipLoc is one of the most reliable systems available today. For more information, please visit www.shiploc.com.

REPORTING OF INCIDENTS

Ships are advised to maintain anti-piracy watches and report all piratical attacks and suspicious movements of craft to the IMB Piracy Reporting Centre, Kuala Lumpur, Malaysia.
Tel + 60 3 2078 5763
Fax + 60 3 2078 5769
Telex MA34199 IMBPCI
E-mail IMBKL@icc-ccs.org
24 Hours Anti Piracy HELPLINE Tel: ++ 60 3 2031 0014

APPENDIX F
TDC Station Bill

1247
20050803

Maritime Services Possible Targets

PUBLIC ANNOUNCEMENT
U.S. DEPARTMENT OF STATE
Office of the Spokesman

This information is current as of today, Wed Aug 03 13:14:01 2005.

Worldwide Caution

August 02, 2005

This Public Announcement updates information on the continuing threat of terrorist actions and violence against Americans and interests overseas. This supersedes the Worldwide Caution dated March 8, 2005 and expires on February 2, 2006.

The Department of State remains concerned about the continued threat of terrorist attacks, demonstrations and other violent actions against U.S. citizens and interests overseas. Americans are reminded that demonstrations and rioting can occur with little or no warning. Ongoing events in Iraq have resulted in demonstrations and associated violence in several countries; such events are likely to continue for the foreseeable future. Nationwide elections in Afghanistan scheduled for mid-September may also trigger violent anti-American actions.

Current information suggests that Al Qaeda and affiliated organizations continue to plan terrorist attacks against U.S. interests in multiple regions, including Europe, Asia, Africa and the Middle East. These attacks may employ a wide variety of tactics to include assassinations, kidnappings, hijackings and bombings. Extremists may elect to use conventional or non-conventional weapons, and target both official and private interests. The latter may include facilities where U.S. citizens and other foreigners congregate or visit, including residential areas, business offices, clubs, restaurants, places of worship, schools, hotels and public areas.

In the wake of the July 2005 London bombings and the March 2004 train attacks in Madrid, Americans are reminded of the potential for terrorists to attack public transportation systems. In addition, extremists may also select aviation and maritime services as possible targets.

U.S. citizens are strongly encouraged to maintain a high level of vigilance, be aware of local events, and take the appropriate steps to bolster their personal security. For additional information, please refer to "A Safe Trip Abroad" found at http://travel.state.gov.

U.S. Government facilities worldwide remain at a heightened state of alert. These facilities may temporarily close or periodically suspend public services to assess their security posture. In those instances, U.S. embassies and consulates will make every effort to provide emergency services to U.S. citizens. Americans abroad are urged to monitor the local news and maintain contact with the nearest U.S. embassy or consulate.

As the Department continues to develop information on any potential security threats to U.S. citizens overseas, it shares credible threat information through its Consular Information Program documents, available on the Internet at http://travel.state.gov. In addition to information on the Internet, travelers may obtain up-to-date information on security conditions by calling 888-407-4747 toll-free in the U.S. or outside the U.S. and Canada on a regular toll line at 202-501-4444.

TDC ANALYSIS

CSOs/SSOs are reminded to provide this awareness information to ships and crews. Increased vigilance and reporting of suspicious activity is recommended. Crews are reminded to practice individual protective measures while traveling in Europe, Asia, Africa and the Middle East. Al Qaeda has a record of sea borne attacks in recent years including small boat attacks on the USS *Cole* and MV *Limburg;* thwarted attacks in Singapore and the Straits of Gibralter; and attacks on cruise ships in the Mediterranean, oil terminals in the Persian Gulf, and ferries in the Phillipines. Cruise liners, ferries, oil tankers and the infrastructure related to the petroleum industry should be especially vigilant. Increased surveillance is likely to precede an attack on an intended target and mariners are reminded to be on the lookout for signs of surveillance including persons with cameras, video equipment, persons in vehicles, suspicious boat approaches, or extensive questions concerning ships or ships movement or operations. Al Qaeda has included maritime attack tactics in their encyclopedia of Jihad. Mariners must be aware that attacks can be carried out at sea as well as in port with a variety of conventional and unconventional weapons. Attacks can take the form of a boarding, armed assault, small boat attack, underwater attack or by projected weapons such as mortars, rocket propelled grenades, rockets and aircraft. Small craft used in prior attacks include dingies, rubber raiding craft, dhows and small vessels. Crews should be well-trained on reporting procedures, while the security plan should include reporting procedures to port state control authorities, local naval and law enforcement authorities as well as MARAD for U.S. flag vessels.

—Compiled by the TDC Maritime Team

Acronyms and Abbreviations

AC Cyanide
ACPG Advanced Chemical Protective Garment
ACS Automated Commercial System
AIS Automatic Identification System
AMS Area Maritime Security
AMSC Area Maritime Security Committee
ANFO Ammonium Nitrate Fertilizer and Fuel Oil
ANOA Advanced Notice of Arrival
ASP Alternative Security Plan (Program)
ATO Advanced Technology Office
ATS Automated Targeting System
CANA Diazepam
CAPDS Chemical Agent Point Detection System
CBP Customs and Border Protection
CBR Chemical Biological and Radiological
CBR-D Chemical-Biological-Radiological
CBRNE Biological Warfare Agents
CCTV Closed Circuit Television (TV)
CFR Code of Federal Regulations
CG Phosgene
CK Cyanogen Cyanide
COP Code of Practice
COTP Captain of the Port
CPFC Chemical Protective Foot Covers
CPO Chemical Protective Overgarment
CSI Container Security Initiative
CSO Company Security Officer

CSR Continuous Synopsis Record
C-TPAT Customs-Trade Partnership Against Terrorism
CWDD Chemical Warfare Directional Detector
CX Phosgene Oxime
DECON Decontamination
DHS Department of Homeland Security
DoS Declaration of Security
DP Diphosgene
DRA Designated Restricted Area
DWO Deck Watch Officer
EMP Electromagnetic Pulse
EOD Explosive Ordnance Disposal
FARC Revolutionary Armed Forces of Colombia
FCC Federal Communications Commission
FMSC Federal Maritime Security Coordinator
FPSO Floating Production, Storage, and Offloading Facility
FSA Facility Security Assessment
FSO Facility Security Officer
FSP Facility Security Plan
GA Tabun
GAM Free Aceh Movement
GB Sarin
GD Soman
G-MSC Coast Guard-Maritime Security Compliance
GNOBFA Greater New Orleans Barge Fleeting Association
GRT Gross Register Tons
GSIS Global Shipping Information System
GT Gross Tonnage
HD Distilled Mustard
HL Mustard Lewisite
HN Nitrogen Mustards
HSAS Homeland Security Advisory System
IBADS Interim Biological Agent Detection System
ICE Immigration and Customs Enforcement
IED Improvised Explosive Device

ILO International Labor Organization
IMB International Maritime Bureau
IMO International Maritime Organization
INS Immigration and Naturalization Service
IPSLO International Port Security Liaison Officer
IPSP International Port Security Program
ISPS International Ship and Port Facility Security Code
ISSC International Ship Security Certificate
JI Jemaah Islamiyah
L Lewsite
LRIT Long Range Identification and Tracking
LTTE Liberation Tigers of Tamal Ealam
MARSEC Maritime Security
MODU Mobil Offshore Drilling Unit
MOU Memorandum of Understanding
MSC Marine Safety Center
MTSA Maritime Transportation Security Act
NAPP Nerve Agent Pyridostigmine Pretreatment
NBC Nuclear-Biological-Chemical
NII Nonintrusive Inspection (Technology)
NMCC National Military Command Center
NOA Notice of Arrival
NOAA National Oceanographic Atmospheric Administration
NMSAC National Maritime Security Advisory Committee
NSC National Security Council
NTC National Targeting Center
NVIC Navigation and Vessel Inspection Curricular
NVMC National Vessel Movement Center
NVOCC Nonvessel Operating Common Carrier
OCS Outer Continental Shelf
ONI Office of Naval Intelligence
PAF Public Access Facility
PF Port Facility Engaged in International Trade
PFSO Port Facility Security Officer
PFSP Port Facility Security Plan

PSA Port Security Assessment
PSAC Port Security Advisory Committee
PSC Port State Control
PSO Port Security Officer
PSP Port Security Plan
PT Potential Target
RCA Riot Control Agents
RDD Radiological Dispersal Device
RSO Recognized Security Organization
SA Arsine
SAA Security Assessment Audit
SOLAS Safety of Life at Sea Convention
SSA Ship Security Assessment
SSAS Ship Security Alert Systems
SSO Ship Security Officer
SSP Ship Security Plan
SUA Supression of Unlawful Acts
TNT Trinitrotoluene
TRAM Threat and Risk Analysis Matrix
TSA Transportation Security Administration
TSI Transportation Security Incident
TWIC Transportation Worker Identification Credential
USCG United States Coast Guard
VACIS Vehicle and Cargo Inspection System
VBIED Vehicle Borne Improvised Explosive Device
VDR Voyage Data Recorder
VHF Very High Frequency
VSA Vessel Security Assessment
VSO Vessel Security Officer
VSP Vessel Security Plan
VTS Vessel Traffic System
WCO World Customs Organization
WMD Weapons of Mass Destruction

Glossary

Alternative Security Program (ASP) A third-party or industry organization standard that the Commandant has determined provides an equivalent level of security to that established by the Maritime Security regulations (33 CFR Subchapter H).

Area Commander The U.S. Coast Guard officer designated by the Commandant to command a Coast Guard Area.

Area Maritime Security (AMS) Assessment An analysis that examines and evaluates the infrastructure and operations of a port taking into account possible threats, vulnerabilities, and existing protective measures, procedures, and operations.

Area Maritime Security (AMS) Plan Developed by the Area Maritime Security Committee (AMS), based upon the Area Maritime Security Assessment. This plan may be the port security plan developed pursuant to NVIC 09-02 provided it meets the requirements of part 103 of this subchapter.

Area Maritime Security (AMSC) Committee The committee established pursuant to 46 U.S.C. 70112(a) (2) (A). This committee can be the Port Security Committee established pursuant to Navigation and Vessel Inspection Circular (NVIC) 09-02.

Area of Responsibility (AOR) A Coast Guard area, district, marine inspection zone or COTP zone described in 33 CFR part 3.

Audit An evaluation of a security assessment or security plan performed by an owner or operator, the owner or operator's designee, or an approved third party, intended to identify deficiencies, nonconformities and/or inadequacies that would render the assessment or plan insufficient.

Barge A nonself-propelled vessel (46 CFR 24.10-1).

Barge fleeting facility A commercial area, subject to permitting by the Army Corps of Engineers, as provided in 33 CFR part 322, part 330, or pursuant to a regional general permit the purpose of which is for the making up, breaking down, or staging of barge tows.

Bulk or in bulk A commodity that is loaded or carried onboard a vessel without containers or labels, and that is received and handled without mark or count.

Captain of the Port (COTP) The local Coast Guard officer exercising authority within an assigned area of responsibility (zone). These COTP zones are described in 33 CFR part 3. The COTP is the Federal Maritime Security Coordinator and also the Port Facility Security Officer as described in the ISPS Code, part A.

Cargo Any goods, wares, or merchandise carried, or to be carried, for consideration, whether directly or indirectly flowing to the owner, charterer, operator, agent, or any other person interested in the vessel, facility, or outer continental shelf facility, except dredge spoils.

Cargo ship SOLAS defines a cargo ship as any ship that is not a passenger ship.

Cargo vessel A vessel that carries, or intends to carry, cargo as defined in this glossary.

Certain Dangerous Cargo (CDC) Defined in 33 CFR 160.204.

Company Any person or entity that owns any facility, vessel, or OCS facility subject to the requirements of this subchapter, or has assumed the responsibility for operation of any facility, vessel, or OCS facility subject to the requirements of this subchapter, including the duties and responsibilities imposed by this subchapter.

Company Security Officer (CSO) The person designated by the company as responsible for the security of the vessel or OCS facility, including implementation and maintenance of the vessel or OCS facility security plan, and for liaison with their respective vessel or Facility Security Officer and the Coast Guard.

Company Security Officer (CSO-ISPS) The person ashore designated by the company to develop and revise the Ship Security Plan and for liaison with the Port Facility Security Officer and the SSO.

Contracting Government The authority under which a ship or facility is operating. For instance, a ship that is registered by the State of Liberia is operating under the guidelines of Liberia as its contracting government.

Cruise ship Any vessel over 100 gross register tons, carrying more than 12 passengers for hire that makes voyages lasting more than 24 hours, of which any part is on the high seas. Passengers from cruise ships are embarked or disembarked in the U.S. or its territories. Cruise ships do not include ferries that hold Coast Guard Certificates of Inspection endorsed for "Lakes, Bays, and Sounds," which transit international waters for only short periods of time on frequent schedules.

Dangerous goods and/or hazardous substances Cargoes regulated by 33 CFR parts 126 (Handling of Dangerous Cargo at Waterfront Facilities), 127 (Waterfront Facilities Handling Liquefied Natural Gas and Liquefied Hazardous Gas), or 154 (Facilities Transferring Oil or Hazardous Material in Bulk).

Dangerous substances or devices Any material, substance, or item that reasonably has the potential to cause a transportation security incident.

Declaration of Security (DoS) 33 CFR 104.255 and 105.245 An agreement executed between the responsible Vessel and Facility Security Officer, or between Vessel Security Officers in the case of a vessel-to-vessel activity, that provides a means for ensuring that all shared security concerns are properly addressed and security will remain in place throughout the time a vessel is moored to the facility or for the duration of the vessel-to-vessel activity, respectively.

Exercise A comprehensive training event that involves several of the functional elements of the AMS, vessel, or facility security plan and tests communications, coordination, resource availability, and response.

Facility Any structure or facility of any kind located in, on, under, or adjacent to any waters subject to the jurisdiction of the U.S. and used, operated, or maintained by a public or private entity, including any contiguous or adjoining property under common ownership or operation.

Facility Security Assessment (FSA) An analysis that examines and evaluates the infrastructure and operations of the facility taking into account possible threats, vulnerabilities, consequences, and existing protective measures, procedures, and operations. (33 CFR 105 Subpart C)

Facility Security Officer (FSO) The person designated as responsible for the development, implementation, revision, and maintenance of the facility security plan and for liaison with the COTP and Company and Vessel Security Officers.

Facility Security Plan (FSP) The plan developed to ensure the application of security measures designed to protect the facility and its servicing vessels or those vessels interfacing with the facility, their cargoes, and persons onboard at the respective MARSEC levels.

Federal Maritime Security Coordinator (FMSC) The COTP who is tasked with the following: (1) establish, convene, and direct the Area Maritime Security (AMS); (2) appoint members to the AMS committee; (3) develop and maintain, in coordination with the AMS committee, the

AMS plan; (4) implement and exercise the AMS plan; and (5) maintain the records required by 33 CFR 103.520.

Flag State Country where the ship is registered

Floating Production, Storage, and Offloading (FPSO) Facility A floating facility for production, storage, and offloading of oil. Oil in the submarine oil field is drawn from the sea bottom oil well through riser pipes to the FPSO facility and is stored in the tanks provided in its hull after making primary process in oil treatment facility on deck. The produced crude oil is offloaded onto shuttle tankers periodically.

Foreign vessel A vessel of foreign registry or a vessel operated under the authority of a country, except the U.S., that is engaged in commerce.

Gross register tons (GRT) The gross ton measurement of the vessel under 46 U.S.C. chapter 145, Regulatory Measurement. For a vessel measured under only 46 U.S.C. chapter 143, Convention Measurement, the vessel's gross tonnage, ITC is used to apply all thresholds expressed in terms of gross register tons.

Gross tonnage, ITC (GT ITC) The gross tonnage measurement of the vessel under 46 U.S.C. chapter 143, Convention Measurement. Under international conventions, this parameter may be referred to as "gross tonnage (GT)."

Hazardous materials Hazardous materials subject to regulation under 46 CFR parts 148, 150, 151, 153, or 154, or 49 CFR parts 171 through 180.

Infrastructure Facilities, structures, systems, assets, or services so vital to the port and its economy that their disruption, incapacity, or destruction would have a debilitating impact on defense, security, the environment, long-term economic prosperity, public health, or safety of the port.

International Ship Security Certificate (ISSC) An International Ship Security Certificate is issued after the initial or renewal verification. This certificate is valid for a maximum of five years.

International voyage A voyage between a country to which SOLAS applies and a port outside that country. A country, as used in this definition, includes every territory for the internal relations of which a contracting government to the convention is responsible or for which the United Nations is the administering authority. For the United States, the term "territory" includes the Commonwealth of Puerto Rico, all possessions of the United States, and all lands held by the United States under a protectorate or mandate. For the purposes of this subchapter, vessels solely navigating the Great Lakes and the St. Lawrence River as far east as a straight line drawn from Cap des Rosiers to West Point, Anticosti Island and, on the north side of Anticosti Island, the 63rd meridian, are considered on an "international voyage" when on a voyage between a U.S. port and a Canadian port.

International Voyage A voyage from a port in one state to a port within another state.

ISPS Code The International Ship and Port Facility Security Code, as incorporated into SOLAS.

Maritime Security (MARSEC) Directive An instruction issued by the Commandant or his/her delegate, mandating specific security measures for vessels and facilities that may be involved in a transportation security incident.

Maritime Security (MARSEC) Level The level set to reflect the prevailing threat environment to the marine elements of the national transportation system, including ports, vessels, facilities, and critical assets and infrastructure located on or adjacent to waters subject to the jurisdiction of the U.S.

MARSEC Security Level 1 Level for which minimum appropriate protective security measures shall be maintained at all times. HSAC threat level Green, Blue, or Yellow.

MARSEC Security Level 2 Level for which appropriate additional protective security measures shall be maintained for a period of time as a result of heightened risk of a security incident. HSAC threat level Orange.

MARSEC Security Level 3 Level for which further specific protective security measures shall be maintained for a limited period of time when a security incident is probable or imminent, although it may not be possible to identify the specific target. HSAC threat level Red.

Master The holder of a valid license that authorizes the individual to serve as a Master, operator, or person in charge of the rated vessel. For the purposes of this subchapter, Master also includes the person in charge of a MODU, and the operator of an uninspected towing vessel.

Mobile offshore drilling unit (MODU) A vessel capable of engaging in drilling operations for the exploration or exploitation of subsea resources.

OCMI Officer in Charge, Marine Inspection—OCMI is responsible for the following functions: Inspection of vessels in order to determine that they comply with the applicable laws, rules, and regulations relating to safe construction, equipment, manning, and operation and that they are in a seaworthy condition for the services in which they are operated; shipyard and factory inspections; the investigation of marine casualties and accidents; the licensing, certificating, shipment, and discharge of seamen; the investigating and initiating of action in cases of misconduct, negligence, or incompetence of merchant marine officers or seamen; and the enforcement of vessel inspection, navigation, and seamen's laws in general.

OCS Facility Security Assessment (OCS FSA) An analysis that examines and evaluates the infrastructure and operations of the facility taking into account possible threats, vulnerabilities, consequences, and existing protective measures, procedures, and operations.

OCS Facility Security Officer (OCS FSO) The person designated as responsible for the development, implementation, revision, and maintenance of the OCS facility security plan and for liaison with the COTP and Company and Vessel Security Officers.

OCS Facility Security Plan (OCS FSP) The plan developed to ensure the application of security measures designed to protect the facility and its servicing vessels or those vessels interfacing with the facility, their cargoes, and persons onboard at the respective MARSEC levels.

Offshore supply vessel A motor vessel of more than 15 gross tons but less than 500 gross tons as measured under section 14502 of this title, or an alternate tonnage measured under section 14302 of this title as prescribed by the Secretary under section 14104 of this title that regularly carries goods, supplies, individuals in addition to the crew, or equipment in support of exploration, exploitation, or production of offshore mineral or energy resources.

Outer Continental Shelf (OCS) Facility Any artificial island, installation, or other complex of one or more structures permanently or temporarily attached to the subsoil or seabed of the OCS, erected for the purpose of exploring for, developing, or producing oil, natural gas or mineral resources. This definition includes all mobile offshore drilling units (MODUs) not covered under 33 CFR part 104, when attached to the subsoil or seabed of offshore locations, but does not include deepwater ports or pipelines.

Owner or operator Any person or entity that owns or maintains operational control over any facility, vessel, or OCS facility subject to this subchapter. This includes a towing vessel that has operational control of an unmanned vessel when the unmanned vessel is attached to the towing vessel and a facility that has operational control of an unmanned vessel when the unmanned vessel is not attached to a towing vessel and is moored to the facility; attachment begins with the securing of the first mooring line and ends with the casting off of the last mooring line.

Passenger Ship (ISPS) Any ship that carries more than 12 passengers. It is common that a cargo vessel, for instance, one that is primarily used for carrying containers, will also carry passengers. A passenger is anyone other than the Master or members of the crew, or otherwise employed on the vessel in the business of the ship.

Passenger vessel (1) On an international voyage, a vessel carrying more than 12 passengers, including at least one passenger-for-hire; and
(2) On other than an international voyage:
  (i) A vessel of at least 100 gross register tons carrying more than 12 passengers, including at least one passenger-for-hire;
  (ii) A vessel of less than 100 gross register tons carrying more than 6 passengers, including at least one passenger-for-hire;
  (iii) A vessel that is chartered and carrying more than 12 passengers;
  (iv) A submersible vessel that is carrying at least one passenger-for-hire; or
  (v) A wing-in-ground craft, regardless of tonnage, that is carrying at least one passenger-for-hire.

Passenger-for-hire A passenger for whom consideration is contributed as a condition of carriage on the vessel, whether directly or indirectly flowing to the owner, charterer, operator, agent, or any other person having an interest in the vessel.

Port Facility A location, as determined by the contracting government or by the designated authority, where the ship/port interface takes place. This includes areas such as anchorages, waiting berths, and approaches from seaward, as appropriate.

Port Facility Security A port facility is required to act upon the security level set by contracting government.

Port Facility Security Assessment (PFSA) An essential and integral part of the process of developing and updating the port facility security plan. The assessment will be periodically reviewed and updated, taking into account changing threats and/or minor changes in the port facility and will always be reviewed and updated when major changes to the port facility take place.

Port Facility Security Officer (PFSO) The person designated as responsible for the development, implementation, revision, and maintenance of the port facility security plan and for the liaison with ship and Company Security Officers.

Port Facility Security Plan (PFSP) A port facility security plan will be developed and maintained for each port facility, on the basis of a port facility security assessment.

Port State Country where ships call.

Records Records of security activities addressed in the Ship Security Plan.

Registered length The registered length as defined in 46 CFR part 69.

Restricted areas The infrastructures or locations identified in an area, vessel, or facility security assessment or by the operator that require limited access and a higher degree of security protection. The entire facility may be designated the restricted area, as long as the entire facility is provided the appropriate level of security.

Screening A reasonable examination of persons, cargo, vehicles, or baggage for the protection of the vessel, its passengers, and crew. The purpose of the screening is to secure the vital government interest of protecting vessels, harbors, and waterfront facilities from destruction, loss, or injury from sabotage or other causes of similar nature. Such screening is intended to ensure that dangerous substances and devices, or other items that pose a real danger of violence or a threat to security are not present.

Security Incident Any suspicious act or circumstance threatening the security of a ship, including a mobile offshore drilling unit and a high-speed craft, or of a port facility or of any ship/port interface or any ship-to-ship activity.

Security Levels (ISPS)

> **Security Level 1** The level for which minimum appropriate protective security measures shall be maintained at all times.

> **Security Level 2** For each activity detailed above, additional protective security measures shall be maintained for a period of time as a result of heightened risk of a security incident.

> **Security Level 3** Further specific protective security measures shall be maintained for a period of time when a security incident is probable or imminent, (although it may not be possible to identify the specific target).

Ship Includes mobile offshore drilling units and high-speed craft.

Ship Security A ship is required to act upon the security level set by contracting government.

> **Security Level 1** The level for which minimum appropriate protective security measures shall be maintained at all times.

Security Level 2 For each activity detailed above, additional protective security measures shall be maintained for a period of time as a result of heightened risk of a security incident.

Security Level 3 Further specific protective security measures shall be maintained for a period of time when a security incident is probable or imminent (although it may not be possible to identify the specific target).

Ship Security Assessment (SSA) The identification of the possible threats to key shipboard operations, existing security measures and weaknesses in the infrastructure, policies, and procedures.

Ship Security Officer (SSO) The person onboard the ship, accountable to the Master, designated by the Company as responsible for the security of the ship, including implementation and maintenance of the Ship Security Plan and for the liaison with the CSO and the Port Facility Security Officer.

Ship Security Plan (SSP) A plan developed to ensure the application of measures onboard the ship designed to protect persons onboard, the cargo, cargo transport units, ship's stores, or the ship from the risks of a security incident.

Ship/port interface The interactions that occur when a ship is directly and immediately affected by actions involving the movement of person, goods, or the provisions of port services to or from the ship.

Ship-to-Ship activity Any activity not related to a port facility that involves the transfer of goods or persons from one ship to another.

SOLAS A product of the International Maritime Organization (IMO), an agency of the United Nations. SOLAS applies to all mechanically propelled cargo and tank vessels of 500 or more gross tons (GT), and to all mechanically propelled passenger vessels that engage in international voyages carrying more than 12 passengers.

SPAR A vertical floating cylinder attached, by means of cables, to anchors placed on the sea floor more than a kilometer away

Tanker A self-propelled tank vessel constructed or adapted primarily to carry oil or hazardous material in bulk in the cargo spaces.

Tankship A self-propelled vessel constructed or adapted primarily to carry oil or hazardous material in bulk in the cargo spaces.

Tension Leg Platforms Used in water depths greater than 300 meters. They consist of a floating deck structure anchored to pile heads on the sea floor by means of long pipes that are always kept in tension, and thus can be flexible without risk of a column buckling collapse failure due to very high Kl/r ratios.

Training, Drills, and Exercises (Facilities) Ensure the effective implementation of the facility security plan, drills shall be carried out at appropriate intervals taking into account the facility type, facility personnel changes, the type of ships visiting the port facility and other relevant circumstances. The PFSO shall ensure the effective coordination and implementation of facility security plans by participating in exercises at appropriate intervals.

Training, Drills, and Exercises (Ships) Ensure the effective implementation of the Ship Security Plan, drills shall be carried out at appropriate intervals taking into account the ship type, ship personnel changes, port facilities to be visited, and other relevant circumstances. The CSO shall ensure the effective coordination and implementation of Ship Security Plans by participating in exercises at appropriate intervals.

Transportation security incident (TSI) A security incident resulting in a significant loss of life, environmental damage, transportation system disruption, or economic disruption in a particular area.

Uninspected vessel A vessel not subject to inspection under section 3301 of this title that is not a recreational vessel.

Verification and Certification Each ship to which ISPS Code applies is subject to certain verifications such as the International Ship Security Certificate.

Vessel Security Assessment (VSA) An analysis that examines and evaluates the vessel and its operations taking into account possible threats, vulnerabilities, consequences, and existing protective measures, procedures, and operations.

Vessel Security Officer (VSO) The person onboard the vessel, accountable to the Master, designated by the Company as responsible for security of the vessel, including implementation and maintenance of the Vessel Security Plan, and for liaison with the Facility Security Officer and the vessel's Company Security Officer.

Vessel Security Plan (VSP) The plan developed to ensure the application of security measures designed to protect the vessel and the facility that the vessel is servicing or interacting with, the vessel's cargoes, and persons onboard at the respective MARSEC levels.

Vessel-to-facility interface The interaction that occurs when a vessel is directly and immediately affected by actions involving the movement of persons, cargo, vessel stores, or the provisions of facility services to or from the vessel.

Vessel-to-port interface The interaction that occurs when a vessel is directly and immediately affected by actions involving the movement of persons, cargo, vessel stores, or the provisions of port services to or from the vessel.

Waters subject to the jurisdiction of the U.S. Includes all waters described in section 2.36(a) of 33 CFR Part 104; the Exclusive Economic Zone, in respect to the living and nonliving resources therein; and, in respect to facilities located on the Outer Continental Shelf of the United States, the waters superjacent thereto.

About the Author

Captain Joseph Ahlstrom is a graduate of SUNY Maritime with a bachelor's degree in marine transportation. He completed his master's degree in transportation management with honors also from State University New York Maritime College. Captain Ahlstrom has commanded six merchant ships including a tanker, containership, break bulk carrier, and research and training ship. He sailed for 15 years in the U.S. and Foreign Merchant Marine. In January 1996 Captain Ahlstrom started teaching at SUNY Maritime College.

During his time at SUNY Maritime he was Captain of the Training Ship *Empire State* from 1998–2000. He was also chairman of the Marine Transportation Department from 2003 until May 2005. He is currently an Associate Professor focusing on Maritime Security and Maritime Communications. In addition to being an unlimited Master Mariner, Captain Ahlstrom is a Captain (0–6) in the United States Navy Reserve. He lives on Staten Island and is married to Carolyn and has two children, Emma and Brendan.

More Titles from Cornell Maritime Press

American Merchant Seaman's Manual
William B. Hayler, Editor in Chief
ISBN 10: 0-87033-549-9, ISBN 13: 978-0-87033-549-5

Applied Naval Architecture
Robert B. Zubaly, ISBN 10: 0-87033-475-1, ISBN 13:
978-0-87033-475-7

Behavior and Handling of Ships
Henry H. Hooyer, ISBN 0-87033-306-2, ISBN 13: 978-0-87033-306-4

Business of Shipping
Lane C. Kendall and James J. Buckley
ISBN 0-87033-526-X, ISBN 13: 978-0-87033-526-6

Cornell Manual, The
John M. Keever, ISBN10: 0-87033-559-6, ISBN 13:
978-0-87033-559-4

Diesel Engines
Leo Block, P.E., ISBN 10: 0-87033-418-2, ISBN 13:
978-0-87033-418-4

Formulae for the Mariner
Richard M. Plant, ISBN10: 0-87033-361-5, ISBN 10: 13: 0-87033-361-3

Handbook of Rights and Concerns for Mariners
Roberto Tiangco and Russ Jackson
ISBN 0-87033-530-8, ISBN 13: 978-0-87033-530-3

Marine Cargo Operations
Robert J. Meurn and Charles L. Sauerbier
ISBN 10: 0-87033-550-2, ISBN 13: 978-0-87033-550-1

Marine Radionavigation and Communications
Jeffrey W. Monroe and Thomas L. Bushy
ISBN 10: 0-87033-510-3, ISBN 13: 978-0-87033-510-5

Marine Refrigeration and Air-Conditioning
James A. Harbach
ISBN 10: 0-87033-565-0, ISBN 13: 978-0-87033-565-5

Master's Handbook on Ship's Business
Tuuli Anna Messer
ISBN 10: 0-87033-531-6, ISBN 13: 978-0-87033-531-0

Modern Marine Engineer's Manual, Volume I
Everett C. Hunt, Editor in Chief
ISBN 10: 0-87033-496-4, ISBN 13: 978-0-87033-496-2

Modern Marine Engineer's Manual, Volume II
Everett C. Hunt, Editor in Chief
ISBN 10: 0-87033-537-5, ISBN 13: 978-0-87033-537-2

Modern Towing
John S. Blank, 3rd, ISBN 10: 0-87033-372-0, ISBN 13:
978-0-87033-372-9

Nautical Rules of the Road
B. A. Farnsworth and Larry C. Young
ISBN 10: 0-87033-408-5, ISBN 13: 978-0-87033-408-5

Primer of Towing
George H. Reid, ISBN 10: 0-87033-563-4, ISBN 13:
978-0-87033-563-1

Real Time Method of Radar Plotting
Max H. Carpenter and Wayne M. Waldo
ISBN 10: 0-87033-204-X, ISBN 13: 978-0-87033-204-3

Shiphandling for the Mariner
Daniel H. MacElrevey and Daniel E. MacElrevey
ISBN 10: 0-87033-558-8, ISBN 13: 978-0-87033-558-7

Shiphandling with Tugs
George G. Reid, ISBN 10: 0-87033-354-2, ISBN 13:
978-0-87033-354-5

Stability and Trim for the Ship's Officer
William E. George, ISBN 10: 0-87033-564-2, ISBN 13:
978-0-87033-564-8

Survival Guide for the Mariner, Second Edition
Robert J. Meurn, ISBN 10: 0-87033-573-1, ISBN 13: 978-0-87033-573-0

Tanker Operations
Mark Huber, ISBN 10: 0-87033-528-6, ISBN 13: 978-0-87033-528-0

Vessel Traffic Systems
Charles W. Koburger, Jr.
ISBN 10: 0-87033-360-7, ISBN 13: 978-0-87033-360-6

Watchstanding Guide for the Merchant Officer
Robert J. Meurn, ISBN 10: 0-87033-409-3, ISBN 13:
978-0-87033-409-2

ISBN 10: 0-87033-570-7
ISBN 13: 978-0-87033-570-9